Just a
Shot Away

Just a
Shot Away

PEACE, LOVE, AND
TRAGEDY WITH

the Rolling Stones
at Altamont

Saul Austerlitz

Thomas Dunne Books
St. Martin's Press ≈ New York

THOMAS DUNNE BOOKS.

An imprint of St. Martin's Press.

JUST A SHOT AWAY. Copyright © 2018 by Saul Austerlitz. All rights reserved. Printed in the United States of America. For information, address St. Martin's Press, 175 Fifth Avenue, New York, NY 10010.

www.thomasdunnebooks.com
www.stmartins.com

Book design by Michelle McMillian

Photograph on p. ii courtesy of Robert Altman

Library of Congress Cataloging-in-Publication Data

Names: Austerlitz, Saul, author.
Title: Just a shot away: peace, love, and tragedy with the Rolling Stones at Altamont /
  Saul Austerlitz.
Description: First edition. | New York: Thomas Dunne Books, 2018. | Includes index.
Identifiers: LCCN 2018001404 | ISBN 9781250083197 (hardcover) | ISBN
  9781250083203 (ebook)
Subjects: LCSH: Altamont Festival (1969: Tracy, Calif.) | Rock concerts—California—
  Tracy. | Rolling Stones. | Hell's Angels. | Homicide—California. | Rock music—
  California—Tracy—1961–1970—History and criticism. | Counterculture—United
  States—History—20th century.
Classification: LCC ML28.A29 A474 2018 | DDC 781.66078/79455—dc23
LC record available at https://lccn.loc.gov/2018001404

Our books may be purchased in bulk for promotional, educational, or business use. Please contact your local bookseller or the Macmillan Corporate and Premium Sales Department at 1-800-221-7945, extension 5442, or by email at MacmillanSpecialMarkets@macmillan.com.

First Edition: July 2018

10   9   8   7   6   5   4   3   2   1

To Annie and Ali,
and the enduring love of sisters

No failure in America, whether of love or money, is ever simple; it is always a kind of betrayal, of a mass of shadowy, shared hopes.

—GREIL MARCUS, *MYSTERY TRAIN*

Contents

Introduction

There had been a fire. The walls were scorched, and scrub as they might, they could not quite get the stain out. The day I was scheduled to first interview Dixie Ward, after six months of planning and discussion, I received an email from Ward's daughter Taammi Parker. Her mother had had a small kitchen fire the night before, and the interview would have to be postponed until later in the day. When I arrived at Ward's home in Oakland, just off Telegraph Avenue, on a rainy Sunday afternoon in December, her nephew Larry, who is blind, was precariously perched on a stepstool in the kitchen, scrubbing at the white walls with a fistful of paper towels and a bottle of Fantastik.

I waited in the living room while Dixie oversaw the work in the kitchen, looking out at the colorful murals visible just outside the window on her quiet, leafy street, and studying the objets d'art on display: an oversized pocket watch, framed prints of leaves, wooden bookends carved to resemble African tribal masks, and a marble statue of a pearl-clad mother cradling two children. Glass cabinets flanked a mirrored fireplace, with a series of figures pinned to the glass. The figures, on closer inspection, appeared to be running.

That day, Ward and I wound up talking for more than five hours, beginning with my prepared list of questions and proceeding to a more freewheeling conversation. At the end of our interview, I gingerly mentioned that I had gone earlier in the week to visit the grave of her brother, Meredith Hunter. In response to one of my questions, Ward had mentioned that over the years, she had not made a habit of going there: "I don't go to cemeteries, because I have to go too often. I'm the only one left standing." I was concerned she might see it as my chiding her for her oversight. But I had wanted her to know that someone had been there, that her brother, dead these forty-six years, was not forgotten.

I took out my iPhone and offered to show Ward some photographs I had taken at the gravesite. She studied them intently, looking at the place only a few miles from her home where her brother was interred, and where she could not bring herself to go. She had had to attend too many funerals, had to face the bleak future too many times from the windswept plateau of an unfilled grave. Each time had been like the end of a world, and the pain of each loss accrued, one piling atop the other in an endless pyramid of grief: her first husband, her mother, her siblings, and above all, her brother, snatched away violently at the age of eighteen. He would never become a man, never raise children, never make a life for himself. And Dixie would have to carry on without him.

Eric Garner. Michael Brown. Tamir Rice. Trayvon Martin. Jordan Davis. The news had been full of the stories of young black men (and black boys) who had been killed, each of them targeted for death by overzealous police officers or crusading self-appointed vigilantes. There was a renewed debate rocketing around the country, impassioned and tragically necessary once more, over the value of young African-American lives. Visiting Meredith Hunter's grave, speaking to his sister, watching the video footage of the last moments of his life furnished to me by the Alameda County Sheriff's Office, I was reminded that this was hardly a new story. We had come so far as a country, and yet we still acted out these miniature dramas of racial discord and violent backlash.

The week prior had been the forty-sixth anniversary of Altamont, and of Hunter's death, stabbed by a Hells Angel at a free Rolling Stones concert intended to be the West Coast Woodstock. Altamont's story had often been told as a musical tragedy, or a cultural one, but its epicenter was not to be found at the speedway, now a derelict ruin, or the Haight-Ashbury, but here in this living room. Here was where the catastrophe of Altamont had taken root. Here was where the story of Meredith Hunter's all-too-brief life and horrific death had lived for nearly half a century, untold and unrecognized.

Talking to Dixie Ward, feeling her still-raw anguish, reminded me of Lucia McBath. McBath was the mother of Jordan Davis, shot and killed by a middle-aged white man after an argument over loud music in a Florida gas station. The man, Michael Dunn, had been sentenced to life in prison without the possibility of parole (a notably different outcome from many of these other cases), and Mc-Bath had addressed her son's murderer in court at the sentencing hearing: "For me, there will be no college graduation. For me, there will be no daughter-in-law. For me, there will be no grandchildren. For me, there will be no future generation to carry on the heritage of mine. For me, there is only the hope I cling to that I will walk hand-in-hand with Jordan again when I come home to heaven to rest." Here was another African-American woman left to live her life wrestling with an absence. She was haunted by the life unlived. There were so many things her brother had never had the chance to do.

For decades, Altamont had served as a shorthand version of the story of the counterculture formed in the Bay Area in the 1960s, or of the violence endemic to American life during that decade. It was a symbol, a totem that could serve as a free-floating indictment of the hippies, or the Hells Angels, or the Rolling Stones. What it almost never was was a story about an African-American family whose son and brother and uncle was snatched away from them by violent men who had been pledged to protect him. The story of Altamont was, as so many American stories were, about the fundamental trauma of race. A black man had gone somewhere white men did not want him to be, and had never come home.

Meredith Hunter was a familiar name to students of the 1960s, or those who had lived through the turbulent decade, but his was a name with no face, no body. He was just another forgotten black man, killed in part for his presumption to equality in an American republic that often sought to deny him that right. Jordan Davis or Michael Brown could have been Meredith Hunter's grandsons, had he been granted the chance to live. They were reminders, on this rainy December afternoon, that the promise of America had not yet been fulfilled for everyone, that some were protected while others were at the mercy of the elements.

When I had driven up from Los Angeles, earlier that week, and pulled through the gate of Skyview Memorial Lawn in Vallejo, twenty-five miles north of Oakland, I had swiftly realized that the information I had in hand for the grave's location—Lot 63, Grave C—was not enough to find Meredith Hunter's final resting place. After a helpful cemetery employee pointed me in the right direction, I walked down a sloping hill in the mostly bare cemetery— no burbling fountains, no benches, no crypts, no real décor to speak of—and wound up standing under the shade of a willow tree whose drooping branches shaded the grave from the afternoon sun. I had been told that Hunter's grave was unmarked, and was given the name of Madeleine De Vos to steer by. When I came to De Vos's gravestone, I would know that Hunter's would be the next one above it.

As it turned out, Hunter's grave, which had once been unmarked, now did have a stone. Still, finding De Vos was the easiest mode of navigation, and my eye settled on the small pot of purple-and-white flowers resting on her grave. "1904–2005," her gravestone read, a reminder of the span of a full life.

I knew nothing of Madeleine De Vos, but her 101 years were a tangible aide-mémoire. I was surrounded by people who had lived full lives, spanning the twentieth century and the early years of the twenty-first, but I was here to visit someone who would be, tragically, forever young. Flower petals dripped onto the ground, and the only sound came from the cawing of crows and the distant hush of cars on Interstate 780. I stood there silently for a number of minutes, taking in the final resting place of a man who had been dead nearly three times as long as he had lived. For an exceedingly brief moment, the name of Meredith Hunter had been on the lips of practically every young person in America. Now, he was just the answer to a trivia question, a dimly remembered name from the past.

There was something especially melancholy about an unvisited grave, a place intended for memory that no one remembered. I knew Hunter's family still kept Meredith's memory alive, but this place stood as an erasure of an erasure, a forgotten place for a forgotten man. I decided to find a stone to leave on Hunter's grave. In Jewish tradition, cemetery visitors leave behind stones as a marker of memory. The stone is an indication that the dead are not forgotten. We would go on remembering for as long as the stone itself would go on existing.

I placed my Mets cap atop my head and recited the words of the kaddish—the ritual prayer for the dead. The recitation of the kaddish ended with two fervent wishes that were all the more poignant for being so rarely fulfilled: "Y'hei shlama raba min-sh'maya

The Rolling Stones at Altamont. (Courtesy of Robert Altman)

v'chayim aleinu v'al-kol-yisrael, v'im'ru: amen. Oseh shalom bim-
romav, hu ya'aseh shalom aleinu v'al kol-yisrael, v'imru: amen."
("May there be abundant peace from heaven, and life, for us and for
all Israel; and say, amen. He who creates peace in His celestial heights,
may He create peace for us and for all Israel; and say, amen.") The
words, repeated so regularly they had become rote, took on special
significance for me. I fervently wished that Meredith Hunter, whose
life had ended so abruptly, and with such violence, had found some
measure of peace in death. More than that, I hoped that his family
might, too.

. . .

Dixie handed back my phone and quietly asked if it would be possible for her to have a copy of the photos. Dixie did not have a smartphone or an email account, so I offered to plug my phone into her computer and upload them there. I sat at a small desk in the kitchen while Larry bustled behind me, scouring the scorch marks. I sought unsuccessfully to get Dixie's computer to find my iPhone, and eventually just emailed the photos to myself, opened them in my Gmail account on her computer, and saved them to the hard drive in a new folder I labeled "Meredith's gravesite." While I was at work, Dixie glanced over my shoulder, directing my attention to a folder on her desktop. In it were JPEGs of family snapshots that had been lovingly scanned and collected.

The folder only held twenty or so pictures, but they spanned generations, taking in the sweep of a family's journey from Texas to California, and the story of a life foreshortened. There was Meredith and Dixie's mother, Altha Anderson, as a child, and, later, as a woman, staring at the camera with bloodshot eyes from the seat of a barstool; there was Meredith as a baby, Meredith in a cap and gown. The folder of photos felt empty, lacking all the pictures that should have been: Meredith as a young man, Meredith in middle age, Meredith in recent years. They were a reminder that there were no pictures of Meredith's children, or of his grandchildren. He had been denied the chance to pass a part of himself on to the next generation.

Dixie's house was a repository of memory, a place where the family's past lingered on. Sometimes this was metaphorical; mostly, it was quite literal. Dixie led me into the dining room, where a glass cabinet was stuffed with elegant dishware and silver. It was all, she told me, unwanted. Her mother had collected these things, all these markers of elegance that might prove life was not quite so brutal as it might otherwise seem. Altha had saved them, and now she was gone. Dixie was stuck with her mother's treasures, stuck with the unusable past. They were her inheritance, constant reminders of how tiring the journey had been. Now more than seventy years old, she was worn down by a life of unending crisis. Being asked about Meredith—his death, and his life—was a reminder of what she had lived through, and each repetition was another descent into the depths of the past. But it would have to be endured. Her brother had died, and it was important that someone remember.

Dixie returned to the figures near the fireplace, which she mentioned she had found to decorate the living room cabinets. Only after having them for some years did she realize they were running—running just as her brother had. Every time Dixie looked at her reflection in her living room, she also saw this mute runner gazing back at her, a tiny apparition reminding her of all she had lost.

She had never watched the footage of her brother's last moments, the footage that was all anyone outside her family had seen of Meredith Hunter's life. But in her head, she could see him there, could feel his terror and shock, could see him running for his life. Some stains, Dixie Ward knew, could not be scrubbed away.

The story of the Altamont festival would become forever intertwined with that of Meredith Hunter, the eighteen-year-old who attended the concert and never came home. Hunter's fate would come to stand in for a nearly endless array of dashed hopes, foiled dreams, and crushed expectations. The late 1960s offered the promise of inevitable social and cultural change, and music was at the white-hot center of that promise. Music was to be the linchpin of progress, and everyone involved in Altamont, from the musicians to the organizers to the attendees, knew it.

Instead, Altamont became an easy symbol of the failings of that hopeful time. Hunter's fate would represent the idealism and naïveté of a lost moment in American history, one that summoned three hundred thousand young men and women to a racetrack fifty miles east of San Francisco for their encounter with destiny. That the encounter would prove to be nothing like what they had imagined would be Meredith Hunter's tragedy above all, but it would also form the untold stories of so many others who turned up to hear the Rolling Stones perform on December 6, 1969.

Part One

PREPARATIONS

1. Woodstock West

They arrived in cars and repurposed school buses and with thumbs lifted heavenward in hopes of hitching a ride for the once-in-a-lifetime occasion. They came with friends and boyfriends and girl-friends and children, and with babies yet to be born still in their bellies. They yanked down fences and ignored so many requests for tickets that the show was eventually declared free. They came for the music. They came for the drugs and for the sunshine that arrived only in patches. But more than anything, they came to be together, to feel the power of an enormous mass of human beings gathered in the same place, at the same time, pooling their collective strength and love.

The weather did not cooperate. The site was a last-minute replace-ment, selected when two prior locations had fallen through. There were not nearly enough restroom facilities, and those that were avail-able mostly flooded or malfunctioned over the course of the week-end. Security was minimal. Abandoned cars littered the roads for miles. Gate-crashing was omnipresent. There was so little food that a local Jewish community center sent along forty pounds of meat, two hundred pounds of bread, and two gallons of pickles to feed hungry concertgoers.

The acid was bad. "If you feel like experimenting," a voice announced over the public-address system, "only take half a tab. Thank you." Children were everywhere, naked, playing in the dirt, carried on their fathers' backs, banging on drum kits.

A doctor was called to the stage midshow and requested to bring full suturing gear to help deliver a baby. Nervous announcements went out over the PA system requesting that fans climb down from the rickety lighting towers, out of the unstated fear that they might topple over onto the crowd. During a freak thunderstorm, the stage equipment was hastily disassembled or covered with tarps. Nine women suffered miscarriages. Three people died. One man's appendix burst. An eighteen-year-old Vietnam veteran overdosed on heroin. A tractor ran over a sleeping teenage boy. The governor eventually declared the entire site a disaster area.

A young woman wearing dark sunglasses stood in line, talking to some documentary filmmakers while waiting to use a payphone to call her parents. "They think this is going to be another Chicago," she said, making reference to the massive unrest at the previous year's Democratic Party convention. "Like I'm going to get my head beaten in. They're terrified," she said. "So I'm going to call and tell them, 'Ha ha, fooled you! I'm alive.'"

Michael Lang and the promoters of Woodstock had hastily set up the phones on the grounds of Max Yasgur's farm in Bethel, New York, as part of the preparations for an influx of four hundred thousand young people who would gather on the weekend of August 15 through 18, 1969. The woman waited her turn to crow to her concerned parents about Woodstock's success, but failure had been avoided only by the narrowest of margins.

Competing philosophies—one passive and happy-go-lucky, the other conspiratorially minded—surged through the crowd. Jerry

Garcia of the Grateful Dead gushed about the "Biblical, epical, unbelievable scene," and a shirtless man with a ponytail encouraged a group trying out kundalini yoga that "all you gotta score is some clean air." Others muttered darkly about the helicopters hovering overhead at the start of the concert and insisted that airplanes had been seeding the clouds so the concert would be rained out. Why didn't the media report *that*?

The concert was a catastrophe, but mostly a well-natured one. Attendees treated the setbacks as badges of honor, and mellow good cheer was the rule, on display everywhere. People let their toddlers run free in giant crowds, or took copious amounts of drugs procured from strangers, or arrived nine months pregnant and simply trusted in the goodwill of others. The fields were trampled, the second-cut hay all vanished by the end of the weekend, but even the locals were placid about the interruption to their lives. Residents who had not been able to buy food for days praised "the kids" for their enthusiasm and spirit. Woodstock was an act of learned naïveté, celebrated in part because so much went wrong, and so much more could have.

Everyone was taken aback by the sheer number of people gathering in relative peace. One concertgoer declared Woodstock to temporarily be the second-biggest city in the state of New York. Another, her grasp of math less assured, called it the third-largest city in the world. And the sheer numbers granted a collective force to the hopes and ambitions of the people in the crowd. Woodstock was more than just a concert for the musicians and attendees; it was a mass effort to change the world and reverse the course of a disastrous war in Vietnam. The U.S. Army sent in medical teams to assist the overworked doctors and nurses on site. As camouflage-colored helicopters hovered overhead, symbolically bringing the war home to upstate New York, an ebullient announcement came from the stage: "They're with us, man. They're not against us!" There was power in a crowd, a force and cohesion beyond words or demonstrations of intent.

There was joy, too, in sharing a space with so many others, content in the knowledge that shared purpose had been transformed into physical contact.

The crowd had magical powers. "If you think really hard," someone told the audience during the freak thunderstorm, "maybe we can stop this rain!" Even the hated war in Vietnam could be ended if only people wanted it enough. "Listen, people, I don't know how you expect to ever stop the war if you can't sing any better than that," Country Joe McDonald chastised the crowd during his rendition of "I-Feel-Like-I'm-Fixin'-to-Die-Rag." "There's about three hundred thousand of you fuckers out there. I want you to start singin'." Woodstock sought to start a dialogue about the future of the country and open a space for American youth to have their say. These gatherings were a kind of secular ritual, a mass whose officiants donned guitars and held microphones and drumsticks instead of censers and holy water.

The musical performances themselves displayed a hodgepodge of styles, from Sha Na Na's matching astronaut-leisure-suit outfits and coordinated dance moves to the Who's rock-god heroics to Arlo Guthrie's drug-mule blues. Joe Cocker's sweaty, ecstatic, head-thrown-back rendition of the Beatles' "With a Little Help from My Friends," a paean to comradeship, moved the crowd, as did Jimi Hendrix, wielding his white-on-white guitar like a feedback-drenched angel, looming over the audience as he wailed out the piercing opening notes of "The Star-Spangled Banner."

Meanwhile, Jerry Garcia came off the stage at Woodstock, convinced he had blown the opportunity to impress the largest crowd he had ever faced. He was only mildly frustrated that his band, the Grateful Dead, had bungled their chances at a defining moment in their careers. This had been their opportunity, and they had not made the most of it. Perhaps it was the overwhelming infinitude of the crowd, stretching for what seemed like miles in upstate New

York, or perhaps it was the inevitable nerves that arose from knowing so many eyes were on you. "We fucked up all the big ones," Garcia would later note, with Woodstock joining Monterey, where the Dead had been sandwiched between the Who and Jimi Hendrix, in the pantheon of the band's missed opportunities.

By the time the concert neared its end, the mishaps had mostly been forgotten, overwhelmed by the sheer relief of Woodstock having gone off without any major calamities—or so they believed. "It's looking like there ain't gonna be no fuckups," singer John Sebastian shouted to the crowd, as surprised as he was pleased. "This is gonna work!" Sebastian suggested that everyone "just love everybody all around you, and clean up a little garbage on your way out, and everything gonna be all right!"

Woodstock had been close to a disaster, though: poorly planned, poorly executed, with little foresight and less on-the-ground leadership. The festival had been saved by the desire of its audience for a collective triumph, in which an overcrowded, drug-infested, occasionally unruly mass gathering became an instant cultural high point for a decade, and for an entire generation of American youth. A frosty *New York Times* editorial compared the pull Woodstock had on young men and women to "the impulses that drive the lemmings to march to their deaths in the sea." But other, hipper publications immediately understood the near-biblical import of Woodstock on youth culture. "They came to hear the music, and they stayed to dig the scene and the people and countryside," critic Greil Marcus wrote in *Rolling Stone*, raving about the sheer firepower of the musical lineup. "It's like watching God perform the Creation. 'And for my next number.'"

Earlier that same summer, the Rolling Stones had been preparing for a massive outdoor concert of their own. It would be the first live appearance for the wildly successful British rock group in more than two years, after being sidetracked by numerous arrests and drug problems. Much had changed for the Rolling Stones and the world of popular music in the time between the Stones' last show and the one set to take place in London's Hyde Park in July 1969. While "Like a Rolling Stone" and *Sgt. Pepper's Lonely Hearts Club Band* and "Purple Haze" had each remade the landscape of rock, the Stones had matured from youthful blues enthusiasts armed with an impressive arsenal of Keith Richards's killer riffs and Brian Jones's ear for pop melodies to craftsmen capable of such sustained bursts of musical innovation as their most recent album, *Beggars Banquet*, which featured the indelible hits "Sympathy for the Devil" and "Street Fighting Man."

Mick Jagger had been a middle-class teenager in Dartford, Kent, with the disposable income to buy blues albums directly from the United States. He had sent in his orders to the Chess label in Chicago, home to Etta James, Howlin' Wolf, and Muddy Waters. He began with Waters's epochal *Live at Newport*, then branched out to more esoteric fare. Jagger would carry three or four discs at a time under his arm around the school playground.

He met Brian Jones, another middle-class kid with a startling rebellious streak that scandalized the polite Jagger. Jones was a father at the age of sixteen, having impregnated a fourteen-year-old; by twenty, he had three children with three different women. He was, an onlooker from the era once noted, "a beautiful mixture of politeness and rudeness." Jagger and Jones shared an abiding love for the Chicago blues, and when they decided to form a band, Jones named it after their mutual hero Waters's song "Rollin' Stone." Jagger, still carrying his records under his arm, met his former childhood schoolmate Keith Richards on a train platform; they bonded over their mutual love for Waters and Chuck Berry, and formed a lifelong attachment. He, too, would join the band.

The Rolling Stones were, at first, Jones's band; he was the front man, the preeminent figure, and the mastermind of the group. He was also, by a substantial measure, the most skilled musician in the group, which besides Jagger now also included Richards on guitar and pianist Ian Stewart. They played their first gig in July 1962, and bassist Bill Wyman and drummer Charlie Watts joined soon after.

Then the Beatles broke, and the Stones found a new manager named Andrew Loog Oldham. Oldham promoted the Rolling Stones as the anti-Beatles, unkempt and quasi-criminal where their putative rivals were polite and fun-loving. It was ironic for a group primarily composed of art-school students, and doubly so given that the polished Beatles were the actual working-class heroes. Oldham placed deliberately inflammatory stories about the band in the London press, like the one in the *Daily Express* that wondered "Would You Let Your Daughter Marry a Rolling Stone?" Oldham also booted Stewart from the band (he looked "too normal") and shifted the focus of attention from Jones to Jagger.

The British Invasion revitalized rock in the early 1960s, its paragon acts catapulting to fame on the strength of deceptively simple two-minute numbers. The music was the expression of an attitude. The Rolling Stones were ritualistically contrasted with the Beatles, the London bad boys pitted against the genial, charming Liverpudlians. The Stones were thought of as crude, sex-obsessed, thuggish, their music dense and pitted where the Beatles' was airy and harmonic. It was odd that so much intellectual energy was invested into defining, and contrasting, the two signature groups of the British Invasion when what united them both was a restless experimentalism and a desire to expand outward, from the simple to the complex.

The caricature did not match the Stones' music, which grew increasingly subtle and varied over the course of the decade. Mick Jagger and Keith Richards were guitar-slinging British rockers who had co-opted the blues, created and nurtured by African-Americans, and made it safe for screaming teenage girls. Over the course of six years, the Stones had grown from blues enthusiasts emulating their musical heroes to the creators of a sound all their own, mingling sex and politics, blues and country, Richards's tossed-off electricity and Jagger's erotic swagger.

Oldham locked Jagger and Richards in an apartment and refused to let them out until they had written a song together. The Stones' early hits were mostly blues covers, thrilling in 1964 and mostly unexceptional thereafter, but Jagger and Richards soon discovered that they could write their own songs, indebted to the blues but possessed of their own rude, brutal force. Beyond the driving numbers like "Get Off of My Cloud" and the timeless "Satisfaction," the Stones became, to their own surprise, masters of the blues ballad, penning songs like "Time Is on My Side" and "As Tears Go By" (originally written for Jagger's girlfriend Marianne Faithfull).

Jones was now a decidedly second-tier band member, but his musical daring gave the Rolling Stones the sonic filigree that would dot superb midperiod albums like 1966's *Aftermath*: the sitar on "Paint It Black" and "Mother's Little Helper," the marimba on "Under My Thumb."

Jones began taking acid and beating his girlfriend Anita Pallenberg, and slipping out of the orbit of the band, which increasingly belonged to Jagger and Richards. Richards looked like a recently exhumed Cro-Magnon and had a drug habit that would fell five NFL offensive linemen, but he proved himself a surprisingly limber songwriter with a gift for melody that even Jones could not match. And Jagger? Mick Jagger was simply a star. Andrew Oldham had known, even before the singer himself had, that this young man was born to stand in the heat of the spotlight. Here was the rare figure who would flourish there.

. . .

A band devoted to cranking out singles for a rabid audience of in-
fatuated teenagers had grown into artists entering the most fruitful
phase of their careers. Savvy lead singer Mick Jagger, on the cusp
of turning twenty-six, had the brilliant idea of coming up with the
money for the Hyde Park show by offering British television net-
work Granada Television the opportunity to make a documentary
film of the concert.

Hyde Park came at a hinge point in the Rolling Stones' story: the
band's past tragically shucked off, and its future still unknowable.
Brian Jones, the band's cofounder, had died only three days prior to
the show, drowned in his own swimming pool at the age of twenty-
seven. Erratic personal behavior, drug addiction, alcoholism, and
persistent run-ins with the law had led to Jones departing the band
just a few weeks earlier, and now, shockingly and yet not at all surprisingly, he was dead.

The Hyde Park show's organizer, Sam Cutler, took to the mic before the Stones started their set to tell the crowd they should feel
proud. There were three hundred thousand people present, three
times as many attendees as at a recent sold-out Wembley Stadium
British Cup final, and "there's not yet been one incident reported to
the organizers. We managed to assure everyone that crowds that attend pop concerts attend because they want to listen to music."

Jagger asked Cutler to prepare the audience for a somber moment
midconcert, calming the deafening roar of the crowd so he could
deliver his planned tribute to his former bandmate and comrade.
Having quieted the crowd to his satisfaction, Jagger went on to read
a portion of Percy Bysshe Shelley's "Adonais," an elegy written for
Shelley's friend and fellow Romantic poet John Keats, dead at the age of
twenty-five. "'Tis *we*, who lost in stormy visions keep with phantoms

an unprofitable strife. And in mad trance, strike with our spirit's knife," Jagger read. "Fear and grief convulse us, and consume us day by day . . ."

After some polite applause, Jagger shouted "All right!" as if to call a halt to the depressing lesson. The Rolling Stones, young men in love with not just the sound of rock 'n' roll but its embrace of youth and vigor, could face the idea of death for only so long before itching to return to life, and to music. Stones crew members released a horde of butterflies—many of them already dying or dead—from boxes poised at the edges of the stage.

Following the show, volunteers stuck around and cleaned up the park in exchange for the promise of a free Stones album. "On the whole they were a pretty well-behaved crowd," a police officer told *The Boston Globe*. "They don't give us the trouble soccer fans do." A security force composed of self-declared Hells Angels—including a number of pensioners and, it seemed, at least one "Angel" who was a teenage boy with a stenciled-on leather jacket—had helped to protect the peace.

Cutler, the adopted son of working-class socialists who had discovered rock concert production through working with local jazz acts, was proud that such a large show, the biggest ever put on in Britain, had generated so few problems. He was exceptionally pleased, also, to be asked by the Rolling Stones to accompany them on their American tour. He would be their tour manager, in charge of seeing to the band's day-to-day needs like an older brother looking after his scatterbrained siblings. If Richards needed a ride to the guitar shop, Cutler would find a car and drive him. If Jagger needed new clothes, Cutler would buy or borrow some for the next show. If the band wanted to visit a friend, Cutler would get them there.

The tour would be crucial for the band for two reasons. First, it would reintroduce the Rolling Stones to America, after—by the rock standards of the time—an uncommonly lengthy hiatus. Second, it would hopefully bring in some much-needed revenue. Reestablishing their prowess as a touring group, after the interruptions of the past three years, would be crucial to the long-term health of the band. The band was in the process of divorcing itself from its longtime manager Allen Klein, and its finances were wildly disorganized. In the months before the American tour, they had been reduced to begging Klein for money simply to pay the rent on their London office.

Hyde Park was a triumph of English politesse and sheer good fortune. Its success, along with that of the yet-larger Woodstock, encouraged the Rolling Stones to consider headlining a free show at the end of their upcoming American tour—an idea that San Francisco counterculture heroes the Grateful Dead had been contemplating for some time.

Dead manager Rock Scully had been invited to London by Sam Cutler to discuss the idea of a free show featuring the Grateful Dead and Jefferson Airplane in Hyde Park. Cutler said the Rolling Stones would pay for the costs of the show. Scully later met with Keith Richards, trading talk of glittering potential concert locales: Golden Gate Park, Stonehenge, the Taj Mahal.

Between tugs from Keith Richards's joint and snorts of Nembutal, Scully suggested that the band come to San Francisco at the end of their tour and join the Grateful Dead for a free concert in Golden Gate Park. The idea of a free San Francisco show in the vein of past impromptu Dead and Airplane gigs intrigued Cutler. He noted that the Stones had used the Hells Angels for their Hyde Park show, and Richards, enthusiastic about the experience, remarked that it had been "beautiful."

The Dead were longtime fans of the Rolling Stones and were hoping to bring them to California as a treat for their local fans. Having the Stones headline the Golden Gate Park show would transform a local festival into another Hyde Park, a Woodstock West. It would be legendary. The Stones expressed their tentative interest; details would follow later.

The Grateful Dead had always been masters at surprising a crowd. On their first East Coast trip, back in 1967, the New York City parks commissioner had unexpectedly approached them. Sure they were about to be busted for smoking joints in Central Park, or some other misdemeanor, the band were wary. But the commissioner had a request: there had been a protracted squabble over the band shell at Tompkins Square Park in Manhattan's East Village, with African-Americans and Puerto Ricans from the neighborhood battling over its use. Would the Grateful Dead be willing to play a free show at the band shell?

Why the commissioner believed the arrival of an LSD-inhaling band of San Francisco hippies would still this particular dispute is lost to the mists of time, but the Dead dutifully played for the bickering Tompkins Square parkgoers, to the eternal appreciation of the New York City Parks Department, and the likely confusion of the crowd.

The truth was, the Dead liked an audience best of all. While groups like the Beatles discovered the glories of the recording studio, the Dead were at best reluctant to record their own music. "God," guitarist Jerry Garcia once muttered, "we make shitty records." The true magic was found up on a stage, surrounded by an audience willing to be moved: by the drugs, by the music, by the spectacle, by the moment. The band played the Human Be-In in Golden Gate Park, and were delighted to discover an audience that resembled a mirror. There were, as Scully later described it, "thirty thousand pot-smoking, headband-wearing acid-heads—an entire medium-sized town composed entirely of freaks!"

They played at Monterey for the International Pop Festival, surrounded by amateur guitar pickers and ebullient children and

Sioux-style tepees, and all the hassle of fending off scheming L.A. wheeler-dealers was instantly justified. Woodstock had not been the first major gig the Dead had blown. They had always bombed these shows, but the kids who increasingly flocked to their shows never truly minded. Everyone knew the Grateful Dead were not like other bands. They were not to be judged solely on the basis of their musicianship, or even their ability to remain sober for long enough to play their instruments, but on the entirety of the spectacle that inevitably accompanied them everywhere they set up the elaborate gear that had been purchased for them by friend and LSD wizard Owsley Stanley. This was a traveling carnival, and the Grateful Dead were merely the ebullient impresarios.

And the freaks were suddenly everywhere. Many of the fans who had traveled to Monterey for the festival wound up in San Francisco after the show, homeless and hungry, their thirst for the hippie scene trumping all other needs. The radical activists of the Diggers, local anarchists with a theatrical flair, were rummaging the city for day-old bread and wilting lettuce to serve cheese sandwiches and lettuce soup to the hippies-to-be. The Dead sought to chip in, too. They ran extension cords into fans' apartments in order to play impromptu shows in Panhandle Park. They showed up unexpectedly on Haight Street, setting up their amplifiers, rocking the crowd that showed up, and then inviting them to walk over to Golden Gate Park and enjoy the setting sun. The Grateful Dead trusted their audiences to appreciate the delicate, ephemeral pleasures on offer, and the audience trusted the Dead to provide a warm, intimate, and safe environment.

Scully had first met the band in 1965 while promoting another band's concert. Owsley Stanley had invited him to the Fillmore to check out a show, and after meeting them, Stanley prodded him into taking a job as the Grateful Dead's manager. The Dead saw themselves as "lysergic storm troopers," exuberantly promoting a new life of psychedelic-drug experimentation that they viewed as far more radical than anything being peddled by the soapbox preachers in nearby Berkeley. Musically, the Dead were a bevy of mismatched parts: Jerry Garcia, product of the folkie coffeehouse scene in Palo Alto; electronic-music student Phil Lesh; impassioned blues fan Ron "Pigpen" McKernan, whose father had been a DJ for an African-American R&B station; and Bob Weir, who had once been Garcia's guitar student. They were a blues group whose players pulled in mutually exclusive directions, crafting a sound not entirely formed. They were the promise of a future utopia whose present had not yet fully congealed.

The American tour would be the Rolling Stones' own show. The band would book the venues, hire the opening acts, and (they hoped) collect the revenue. Part of the attraction of working without Klein, in addition to the surer stream of money, was the ability to book their own opening acts, bringing in some of the African-American performers who were their idols and inspirations.

Integration was a matter of musical and ethical principle for the Rolling Stones, who understood the depth of their debt to the blues and sought to repay it in whatever fashion they could. This meant bringing along Jagger and Richards's teenage idol Chuck Berry to school youthful audiences blissfully unaware that rock 'n' roll hadn't been invented in Liverpool, or the Haight. It would even mean insisting that the students at Auburn University, only integrated five years prior, watch a dazzling African-American performer like Berry open for the band.

The Rolling Stones decamped for Los Angeles in the summer of 1969 with the vague plans for the free San Francisco show still hovering in the distance, a capstone to what they hoped would be a successful American tour. Jagger, Richards, Cutler, and the newest Stone, guitarist Mick Taylor, lived together at the Laurel Canyon home they rented from Stephen Stills of Crosby, Stills, Nash & Young, in an atmosphere of casual chaos, rampant drug use, and unexpected guest visitors. Walking into the house, visitors might find Little Richard had dropped by, playing the keyboards for a hushed audience of rock stars and hangers-on. Unsatisfied with the studio at Stills's house, the band practiced on the Warner Bros. soundstage in Burbank, on a set being used for Sydney Pollack's Depression-era dance-marathon drama *They Shoot Horses, Don't They?* A large sign hung ominously over the band's heads: "HOW LONG WILL THEY LAST?"

Scully and Emmett Grogan of the Diggers trekked south from the Bay Area to Los Angeles to discuss the details of the free show. The Diggers were perambulatory dramatists, the sidewalks of San Francisco their stages for such provocations as passing out free marijuana in the Haight-Ashbury, burning dollar bills, and holding a funeral ceremony for "the death of money and the birth of free." They opened free stores and medical clinics, seeking, in the description of Digger Peter Coyote, to imagine a world they would like to live in.

The Diggers were, as Todd Gitlin would later call them, "anarchists of the deed," and they hoped to channel that spirit for the concert. They had been approached to help put on a party for the Stones, and said they would be happy to have a blowout bash as long as a bunch of British rock stars were not the cause of the celebration. Instead, they suggested erecting a half dozen or so stages and passing out redwood seeds and bolts of silk. It would be a local party with an ecologically minded, planetary frame of reference.

When Scully and Grogan arrived, Gram Parsons of the country-rock group Flying Burrito Brothers, who were opening for the Stones on a number of dates during the American tour, was tearing up the house in search of a misplaced baggie of hashish. Keith Richards, Parsons's druggie pal, instantly accused Scully and Grogan of having pilfered Parsons's stash. The meeting was postponed.

Being relative newcomers to the ways of the Bay, the Rolling Stones turned to the Grateful Dead for guidance about planning the show. The idea being batted around was to ape the vibe of the Dead's free shows, with everything from its location to its security staff matching the already established tradition of free shows in Golden Gate Park.

The Grateful Dead were to be cohosts and guiding spirits for the free show. They believed that this free concert would work best as a surprise for fans. No advance warning, no tickets—just the rumor mill and the drift of Keith Richards's guitar over the rooftops of the Haight. The Dead had always employed the Hells Angels as their security force. They recommend hiring the Angels for this free show, and the Stones, having worked with what they believed was a British offshoot of the motorcycle club at Hyde Park, gladly assented.

The Golden Gate Park event would be a relatively intimate affair, with fifty thousand to seventy-five thousand people in attendance, and the music bookended by theatrical performers and other acts. The show presented an opportunity to bring San Francisco's then-warring clans—bikers, Black Panthers, Brown Berets, and others—together. The Stones would help to pay for the beer and concessions, and headline the show. Music would help to heal a fractured community. Initial reports singled out The Band and Ali Akbar Khan as potential acts, and mentioned that the radical San Francisco Mime Troupe were asked to perform. The Mime Troupe, affiliated with Grogan's Diggers, agreed to appear, on condition that the concert's proceeds be directed toward the defense fund for the violent political activists the Weathermen.

Jagger would later acquire a reputation as a micromanager, but at this early stage in the life of the Rolling Stones, he was inclined to leave the details to others. Chip Monck, a former Connecticut prep school boy who had run away with the circus as a teenager and discovered the magic of dramatic lighting, had just finished staging the triumphant show at Woodstock when he was summoned to meet the Rolling Stones in Los Angeles. Monck visited the band at Stills's house, taking in the wall of mirrors reflecting the view of the city below, and invited Jagger to join him in the backyard to escape the ceaseless musical, alcoholic, and narcotic racket indoors. He had set out his carefully drawn-up staging and lighting plans for the tour poolside for Jagger's perusal, but after fifteen minutes or so, Jagger's eyes began to glaze over. "Oh, fuck it. Just do it, will you?" Jagger said, and marched back inside. The details of the Stones' tour—and, more important, of the free concert to come—were too grubby to be of much concern to the band.

The San Francisco show stayed a secret—and mostly on the back burner during the tour, which passed in a blur of interchangeable locations, double shows, late-night food crawls in shuttered towns, and charter flights, booked when the forever-tardy band failed to arrive on time for yet another commercial flight.

The Rolling Stones were a circus, and they attracted other performers, some legends in their own right and some merely in their own minds. Governor Claude Kirk of Florida crashed their Palm Beach show, set to take place in front of forty thousand exuberant fans, and threatened the Stones: "You can't play anywhere in this state or Palm Beach County." He eventually skulked away, and the concert went on as scheduled. Abbie Hoffman, founder of the leftist-anarchist japesters the Yippies, caught the band in Chicago and saw affinities between his work and that of the Stones: "Your thing is sex, mine's violence."

Encountering the band's new manager (and their former manager Allen Klein's nephew) Ronnie Schneider, Hoffman asked him for some money for his upcoming trial, to no avail. Jimi Hendrix stopped by the dressing room and borrowed Mick Taylor's guitar, turning it upside down to accommodate his left-handedness. Cutler had to offer a recalcitrant Janis Joplin a bump of cocaine to get her to clear the dressing room before one show. Groupies were omnipresent, and persistent. One, nicknamed the Butter Queen, poured hot butter on a roadie's penis and then licked it off as the Stones' crew watched.

The Rolling Stones' return to America was a successful reunion with the fans who had waited impatiently for years to see their idols in the flesh, but it also prompted accusations of price gouging. Rock journalists like the *San Francisco Chronicle*'s Ralph J. Gleason claimed that the Stones were ripping off their dedicated followers with inflated ticket prices for their tour dates. Gleason called for the band to give back to their loyal Bay Area audience with a free show, not knowing that they were already in talks to host one. The planned concert at Golden Gate Park would be an ideal opportunity to demonstrate their hippie-culture bona fides and undercut the growing criticism in the press.

A late November cover story in *Rolling Stone* proclaimed "IT'S GOING TO HAPPEN!" even though Jagger himself was notably more circumspect. "It depends on whether we can get a place," he told the counterculture's newspaper of record. "There are so many obstacles put in front of us. It's gotten so fucking complicated." Jagger's longtime assistant Jo Bergman remained confident, her spine stiffened by the Stones' traditional modus operandi: "It's going to happen. We've always done everything at the end, at the last minute, and it works." Chip Monck, still anxiously awaiting final word on a site, said that he could set up anywhere, as long as he had three days, with a full crew pulling triple shifts, to get organized.

The Rolling Stones' plans to participate attracted local stars interested in sharing the spotlight. The Mime Troupe and The Band had fallen out of consideration, but David Crosby heard about the show and suggested Crosby, Stills, Nash & Young for the bill. Local groups like Santana and Jefferson Airplane wanted in, also.

In the fall of 1969, the Rolling Stones reached out to acclaimed cinematographer Haskell Wexler with a job offer. They were about to tour the United States, and were looking for a battle-tested filmmaker to shoot some footage at their concerts at Madison Square Garden in New York. There was no larger project yet; the band merely looked to preserve their New York performances for potential future use. Wexler mulled taking the job, but couldn't free himself up. Instead, he called Albert and David Maysles from San Francisco and said that the band would be at the Plaza Hotel the next day. Would they be interested in meeting Mick Jagger?

The Maysles brothers were the acclaimed filmmakers (along with codirector Charlotte Zwerin) behind 1968's critically acclaimed documentary *Salesman*, which tagged along with a quartet of itinerant Bible salesmen on a jaunt down to Florida. The film gave viewers the privileged sense of lurking unobserved as ordinary American men went about their daily business.

Work was work, and both men were intrigued by the Rolling Stones, so they dutifully made their way to the Plaza, and agreed to take the job. The band gave the Maysles brothers $14,000 to cover the expenses of the shoot. They rushed to Baltimore to take in that night's show, and were both impressed with the band's star power and musical skill. The filmmakers recorded the Stones' show at Madison Square Garden, which went off without a hitch. The diminutive Al perched on sound recordist Stan Goldstein's shoulders to shoot much of the concert.

The Maysles brothers were taken with the band, with David in particular enamored of Mick Jagger's panache and raw magnetism, and they asked for permission to follow the band to Muscle Shoals studios in Alabama, where they were recording their new album *Sticky Fingers*. They also made plans to be in California in early December for the proposed free concert, now only a few weeks away. The Stones advanced them a further $120,000 for the concert shoot, which granted the band a 50 percent share of any profits that might accrue if a film were made.

There was no deal yet between the filmmakers and the band, nor had they officially agreed to allow their images to be used, but the Stones were already thinking of re-creating the Hyde Park arrangement. While free concerts might be free for the audience, they cost money for the promoters putting it on. Hyde Park, which had been amply covered by the payment from Granada Television, had given the band an idea for how to pay for the San Francisco show: hire a film crew to record the proceedings and sell the film rights.

The Rolling Stones were the furthest thing imaginable from Bible salesmen—even the film's wisecracking, sardonic variety of Bible salesmen—but they had summoned the Maysles brothers in the hopes of similarly capturing lightning in a bottle. For all the millions of fans, in the United States and overseas, who could not be present in San Francisco, a documentary could serve as the next best thing, a virtual front-row-center seat to the *other* concert of the year.

The San Francisco show was to be a capstone to a successful return American engagement, and a generous gift for fans. The peacefulness and good cheer of Hyde Park, and the enormous success of Woodstock, encouraged the Stones, the Grateful Dead, and the other bands involved to believe that a shared desire for the success of such mass gatherings would prevent any and all outbursts of bad behavior. Planners no longer had to worry about worst-case scenarios, because outdoor festivals like Woodstock were more than just concerts. They were gatherings of like-minded young men and women intent on changing the world, and who would come to such an event to disrupt the good vibes?

A substantial and noticeable police and security presence was simply unnecessary in the new order. There would be no uniformed officers near the stage when the Rolling Stones played on their American tour, leading one usher at the Forum, in Los Angeles, to wonder, "What happens when twenty thousand kids rush the stage?" Practical realities like bathrooms and medical personnel could be addressed at a later stage, if at all. Mass concerts would turn out well because they always had in the past. There was a new paradigm now, one that required none of the careful attention that might be expected for any gathering of hundreds of thousands of people. Blind optimism was the new faith of the counterculture, but belief sometimes ran headlong into a wall of uncompromising reality.

While the Stones were on tour, the Grateful Dead were camped at Alembic Sound in Marin County, where the Dead's rehearsal space and offices were located. The band and its staff had been placed in charge of the planning for the concert by default, and the mood was spiky, nettled. The Grateful Dead and their advisers were simultaneously the servants of another, more famous band, and the default organizers of a concert whose most important details they did not actually control. Emmett Grogan placed a tongue-in-cheek notice on the bulletin board at Alembic advertising the "First Annual Charlie Manson Death Festival." Grogan was joshing, but there was already a sense that this concert would not be the magical-mystical union of souls that others imagined.

"Curiously," *Rolling Stone* later observed, "while the Stones concert was the only topic of conversation (among *our* people) for days beforehand, there was precious little about it in the news media." While local newspapers and magazines remained mostly mum about the Stones show, local radio stations (*our* media, in *Rolling Stone*'s description) were abuzz during the month of November with talk of a giant concert. FM stations competed to offer the most up-to-the-moment rumors about the show. The free concert became *the* topic of conversation in the Bay Area, with talk of where it might take place and who would be there butting up against the fervently held hopes that San Francisco would get to host its own Woodstock.

The location of the Rolling Stones' free concert, according to an agreement with the city's parks department, would be kept secret until twenty-four hours before the show to prevent any chaotic scenes caused by early arrivals. And the announcement of the headlining act was also to be kept under wraps. But word of the Rolling Stones as headliners, smuggled into the press by unknown sources, helped to scuttle the deal.

Ronnie Schneider had ceased all communications with his uncle Allen Klein after going to work full time for the Rolling Stones in August, but Klein may still have been leaking information about the proposed Golden Gate Park show to the media. And the inconsistent, hot-and-cold Jagger was mostly uninterested in the details of the San Francisco concert, content to leave the planning to underlings like Cutler. As word of the location spread, the informal arrangement between the concert planners and the city of San Francisco crumbled in the light of day. The concert was scheduled to take place in less than one week.

Jerry Garcia believed that as soon as Golden Gate Park was out of the equation, the concert should have been called off. The whole point was to have a Haight-Ashbury-style free show. If that couldn't happen, what was the point of putting on this concert at all? But the Rolling Stones were traveling the country in their armored bubble, impervious to criticism and deaf to all suggestions. They were unreachable.

A scramble was on for a replacement site. That Wednesday, three days before the concert, a man named Craig Murray called with an incredible offer: he had a huge, well-located site that he wanted to donate for the concert, free of charge. Sears Point Raceway in Sonoma, some thirty miles from Golden Gate Park, had room for one hundred thousand cars to park—more than the total number of expected attendees. All the band would have to do was acquire health and safety permits, hire additional security, and pay for any damages. The Stones and Murray also agreed that the band would donate any profits from the show's film and recording rights to a fund for Vietnamese orphans. Jo Bergman, who had gone out to California together with Sam Cutler to organize the show, recommended Sears Point to the Stones as ideal for their needs.

The word had gone out via the media that the Sears Point show was on, but with only a few days until the first set would be played, little had been done to prepare the site for the influx of concertgoers— now estimated to be in the hundreds of thousands. Chip Monck began moving equipment there, and teams of volunteers deployed to assist in the task of creating a concert site out of nothingness.

Then Craig Murray's backers added a last-minute, poison-pill rider to the agreement: they wanted sole control of the rights to distribute the documentary film the band planned to release, or an upfront payment of $100,000. They also wanted $100,000 held in escrow to cover any potential damages to the site. The real Sears Point owners turned out to be a company called Filmways. The Stones had stiffed a Filmways subsidiary out of a lucrative second show at the Forum in Los Angeles in November. A Sears Point show, and the attendant film rights, could reimburse Filmways for the loss.

Schneider bluntly told the Filmways representatives to go fuck themselves, and the unexpected saviors of the Bay Area free show departed as suddenly as they had appeared. A concert being promoted in the press and hyped on local radio for that Saturday now had nowhere to go. Unexpected good fortune had already provided a new last-minute concert location. The odds of it happening again? Cutler expected that the concert would be canceled; Schneider, fearful of the haphazard planning, hoped it would be.

Maysles associate Stan Goldstein, prompted by Schneider, called and pleaded with local legal celebrity Melvin Belli (whose number had been passed along to Jagger by *Rolling Stone* founder Jann Wenner) to save the day for the Stones. "All you have to do is help us find a venue," Maysles producer Porter Bibb told Belli, "and you will be the hero of San Francisco and rock 'n' roll." The Stones advanced some money to cover Belli's fees, and he agreed to pitch in. As providence would have it, another phone call came in, this time from a local racetrack executive named Dick Carter. In search of publicity for his struggling business, Carter invited the Stones to hold the concert at his site in eastern Alameda County.

Cutler, sitting in the Grateful Dead's Marin County offices, chartered a helicopter to look at the potential third site. He sent Monck, who had already scouted Sears Point, together with Rock Scully and Woodstock producer Michael Lang. After a quick flyover of the site, they all agreed: a concert would be challenging, but ultimately feasible. Monck reluctantly agreed, but the first impressions he noted were hardly encouraging. It was a bit trashy, he thought. A mildly inclined bowl with a three-foot stage at the bottom of it, and no barrier, would mean that all the audience pressure would be pointed at the stage, with nothing in the way of protection. There would be no time to build a new stage, or do much at all in the way of advance preparation. The name of the new site was the Altamont Speedway.

2. Burning Crosses

Years later, Dixie Ward would remember the bags of food her family lugged onto the train that brought her to California. It was 1944, and black soldiers were invading Normandy and fighting the Germans at the Battle of the Bulge, but in San Angelo, Texas, to be black was to be second-class. African-Americans had been freed from slavery more than eighty years prior, but were still enshrined in Southern law as less than full citizens, kept in a permanent twilight of cruel and capricious treatment. To live under Jim Crow was to never know when you crossed an invisible line separating the deferential from the potentially catastrophic.

Jim Crow said Dixie's family could not vote or attend white schools, and also said that restaurants and shops could refuse to serve them. African-American families like Dixie's rode in segregated train cars if they rode at all, assured only of lesser service and not guaranteed any of the comforts promised to other passengers. And so the bags of food ensured that two-year-old Dixie, her older brother Donald, and their mother Altha Anderson would be able to eat on the journey to California. Easily procured food was a luxury only promised to those whose skin was the right color.

San Angelo was waves of heat shimmering on the hot summer tar, and red ants crawling through shotgun shacks. It was a community of shared struggle, of the kindness engendered by the cruelty of others, but the lure of the westward-bound train offered the promise of an escape from Jim Crow. There were parts of the country where black men and women could prosper, could stand upright, no longer forced to cower before the men who called themselves masters. There was a place called California where all things were possible.

California beckoned for Altha in the form of her sisters Tommie and Claudia, both already living in the Bay Area. Tommie owned a tumbledown restaurant in Oakland. When black performers like Sarah Vaughan came to town, they often stayed at Tommie's, barred as they were from white hotels. Claudia had a hair salon in San Francisco that welcomed celebrities like Billie Holiday who were looking to have their hair fixed by an experienced hand.

Altha, Donald, and Dixie came to town while the war still raged, and rented an apartment in Berkeley, at the corner of Ashby and Harper Streets. They sought to remake themselves as Californians— as Americans, no longer subject to the violent injustices of Jim Crow. But not all of life's problems could be erased by a change of location.

Altha, like her sisters, was a beautiful woman. In one photograph from the era, she is sitting on a bar stool, half-turned to face the camera, her luxurious curls tumbling over her ears and onto her forehead, dressed in a striking off-the-shoulder dress, earrings sparkling in her ears. She holds a sweating glass in her left hand, and her eyes have swiveled to their corners to take in the photographer. She is alluring, but the set of her mouth speaks to struggles that no smile could offset.

By the time Dixie was old enough to attend school, she would sometimes come home in the afternoon and find her mother catatonic, lying immobile on her bed. Altha's body was an empty vessel, temporarily bereft of a host. And when Altha would return to herself, it would sometimes be worse. She would hear voices, see presences no one else could make out. Her words would come out in a tangle of disjointed phrases, jumbled together into a lexically indistinguishable morass.

By the late nineteenth century, psychiatrists already knew to call what Altha was suffering from schizophrenia, but if you were black and schizophrenic, there was little hope of fruitful treatment. White doctors had little interest in helping African-Americans struggling with mental illness, and many blacks, perhaps preemptively anticipating the shame of being denied treatment, preferred to avoid all encounters with mental health professionals. Altha self-medicated, drinking herself into oblivion in the hopes of drowning out the terrifying voices that plagued her.

Schizophrenics were treated like outcasts, doomed to an existence on the margins of an already marginalized group. Few people with steady jobs and stable families wanted to socialize with the likes of Altha, so Altha found companionship among those who would accept her. Physical beauty and mental illness were a toxic combination, attracting the interest of men who did not have Altha's best interests at heart. A steady string of boyfriends came into Altha's life, taking all that they could.

Altha's struggles with her health made it difficult for her to hold down a job, and the family would regularly move from one apartment to another, dragging their few possessions with them on another short jaunt to their next temporary home. They would live in four different apartments on the 2900 block of Ellis Street alone, but 2942 Ellis would stick out most prominently in Dixie's mind. The back apartment was no bigger than twelve feet by fifteen feet. It had no electricity, and a tiny refrigerator was crammed into the undersized kitchen. Rats crawled out of the walls with impunity, no longer fearful of human contact after so many encounters. There was no

Meredith Hunter as a child, early 1950s. (Courtesy of Dixie Ward)

heat at 2942 Ellis, just a gas-burning kerosene stove, and Altha and the rest of the family would crowd around it, sitting in a semicircle around its mouth while trying to summon warmth from its belly.

Altha came home one night with a man named Curley Hunter, a full-blooded Cherokee Indian. He wound up moving in to the family's apartment. Curley, Dixie believed, was a bad omen for the family, for reasons she could not yet articulate. When Dixie was eight years old, in 1951, Altha gave birth to her son with Hunter. She named him Meredith. Ellis Street was a harsh and unforgiving home, and Altha was besieged by her own demons, but Meredith Hunter was loved from the moment he was born. Curley left soon after the birth of Meredith's sister Gwen in 1952. Meredith would never know much else about his father.

The family custom was to avoid the evil eye by not acquiring clothing or furniture for the new baby until he was safely at home. When Meredith arrived, neighbors came by with piles of clothes for the newborn, and Tommie and Claudia brought the blankets they had sewn for him. Altha took a banana box, painted it yellow and placed colorful decals all around its exterior to form a bassinet for the baby. She lined the new makeshift crib with sheets and her sisters' new blankets before placing the baby to sleep inside.

In her more lucid moments, Altha was an amateur poet and an enthusiastic believer in education. Her children would surpass and exceed her, she hoped, and their schooling would lift them to places far beyond San Angelo, far beyond the Berkeley streets. But children needed stability, and the chance to dream of the future, and Altha could not provide that.

Altha had given birth to Meredith, but the work of caring for him fell mostly to Dixie. By the time she was eleven, Dixie understood that it would be her responsibility to look after her younger siblings, three-year-old Meredith and two-year-old Gwen. She was her mother's mother, and she never questioned it. It was her job, and she did it ably and diligently, even though Altha would regularly lash out, taking out her frustration over her own failures on the daughter who took her place. And the community was always there, too, helping in ways acknowledged and unacknowledged. If she needed to be somewhere, there would always be another woman who would take the children in for a few hours. And even when Dixie and her siblings broke the rules, the community looked on forgivingly. They would steal into their neighbors' yards and make off with apples from their fruit trees, amazed by their own daring. Only years later did Dixie realize the neighbors had left bags out by the trees, silently endorsing and encouraging their raids.

The children often went hungry. Altha was rarely around, and Dixie could only do so much with little money and two younger siblings to watch. A Safeway supermarket nearby regularly threw away perfectly good fruit and vegetables and bread. When the hunger pangs grew strong enough, Dixie and Meredith would walk over to the store and dumpster dive. Dixie would have to crawl in, surrounded by moldering lettuce and rotting eggs, and carefully pick through the detritus for salvageable food. Poverty was a constant humiliation, stripping you of your pride and your dignity, and then doing it over and over, each time your stomach grumbled.

Around this time, Altha got involved with a man named Ray. Schizophrenia was an unforgiving master, one that encouraged its sufferers to seek relief from anything that promised a temporary respite from its hammerlock on the mind. Ray was a savior, at first, offering an escape from the terrors of the ordinary. Altha took the drugs Ray brought her to ease her pain, finding solace in the temporary balms he offered.

Ray soon turned the still-striking Altha out on the streets, forcing her to turn tricks. He would beat her when she got out of line, or refused to cooperate, or when the drugs and the drinking were not enough to keep her battered brain from balking at an unmanageable reality. Instead of being treated with medication, or cared for in a clinic, Altha was out on the streets, day after day and night after night, selling her body to strangers for money. None of the men knew of her illness, or cared much so long as it did not interfere with their hasty pleasure. Her problems were her own, and none of their affair. The men in Altha's life abused her—both the ones who professed to care for her, and the ones who came in search of their own gratification. A life lived at the mercy of others had its horrors imprinted on her body. Her ear was torn off, and one of her fingers rendered forever unusable.

How does a child grow when surrounded by terrors he can hardly understand? Dixie, a surrogate mother while still herself a child, tried to give Meredith a routine, a comforting presence in the midst of so much uncertainty. She would make sure his meals were prepared, his clothes clean, his bed made. She would make sure he got to school on time each day. School was a comfort, an escape as certain as Altha's and far less injurious. Like his mother, Meredith liked to create. He would write and paint, picking up the tools that would lead him to the words and the images that expressed his truth. At school he could be himself, but the school day always ended, and then he had to return home.

The family's new home on Sixty-third Street, with four people crammed into a one-bedroom apartment with a tiny kitchen facing the back, was too small to allow Meredith much room to play, or to dream. The outdoors offered an escape. Meredith would take the bike his aunt Tommie had given him and pedal it into the Berkeley hills, or to Tilden Park, nestled between the hills and the San Pablo Ridge. Dixie was a city girl, who once mistook a sheep for a particularly overgrown and hirsute dog, but her younger brother loved animals and insects of all kinds, likely seeing in their frailty and helplessness an analogue to his own. He would come home laden with specimens, seeking to rescue them, over Altha's objections about an already full house.

One day, Meredith brought home a stray dog he had fallen in love with on one of his bike rides. Altha flat-out refused to let it in the house, concerned that her furniture would be ruined by a dog intent on marking his territory, and Meredith fetched a stick, ready to neuter it with whatever was close to hand. It was less an act of cruelty than an ill-formed attempt at kindness toward a creature in need. Meredith, so helpless, wanted to find, like Dixie, a sense of strength through caring for others. There was always someone more in need of help than you, someone who could benefit from being looked after.

Perhaps even then Meredith similarly dreamed of being rescued, of being swept away from this house of unnatural quiet and unpredictable menace to somewhere where childhood was protected, cared for like a butterfly collector cradling a prized specimen. Dixie did all she could for him, more of a mother to him than his own mother ever was or could be, but there were limits to how much protection a teenage girl could offer. There was school for Dixie, too, and a life of her own to live.

When Altha wasn't in Ray's grip, walking the streets, she attended the Holiness church across the street from Dixie and Meredith's school. Holiness churches strictly banned drinking and card-playing, but they also held out the possibility of Jesus's perfect love, in which the reborn Christian could purify herself of all past transgressions, and scrub away original sin itself. Even while away at school, her mother's pain, her desperate desire for healing, made itself audible. Dixie could sometimes hear the congregation's prayers drift across the street while she sat in her classroom. The church must have called to Altha as a suggestion of solace in a life so drastically short of it. Suffering from a disease she did not understand, and beset by lovers who loved nothing about her, the church might have been seen as God offering his outstretched hand, telling her that all the sins prompted by a life of privation and pain could be scoured away.

Dixie and Meredith would occasionally pick up their mother's Bible and read through it, intrigued without ever being remotely as moved as Altha was. They would unpack and unravel the stories, and wonder whether this cruel world could really be capable of such all-encompassing salvation. They would quiz Altha intently about her newfound faith, and she would look hard at them, unblinking. "I'll pray for you," she would tell them firmly, sensing their partially stifled skepticism. Perhaps Altha did not want to engage with her children's biblical critique because some part of her knew their cynicism was well founded.

The Holiness church ultimately provided her little comfort, little balm for her suppurating wounds. It was another all-encompassing hard sell, another demonstration of wares that could not reach her most hidden places. The church was near to a cult, a physically and emotionally demanding congregation that required regular attendance at evening and weekend services. Altha may have been saving her soul, but for her children, the results were much the same. Whenever she was not absent and out on the streets, she was absent and in church, calling to God instead of Ray.

Soon Ray was coming around at home, too, a steady fixture at their apartment. He would look at the teenage Dixie a glance too long, stealing glimpses out of the corner of his eye. By Dixie's own estimation, she was not half as beautiful as her mother or aunts, but she could feel Ray getting too friendly with her. Ray kept watching Dixie with the same calculating eye he had cast on her mother. Dixie worried that she would find him sneaking into her bed one night. She could see herself easily sliding into the same morass of prostitution and violence that her mother had, and it terrified her. Would Ray put her out on the streets, too? Altha, no longer able or willing to protect herself, still looked out for Dixie. She gave Dixie a gun, and told her that if Ray ever approached her, she should kill him. Dixie was sixteen years old.

Tommie did not want the family staying where they were, endangered by the rough neighborhood as well as the threats closer to home. She helped them move to Aileen Street in Oakland, into a slightly less downtrodden apartment. Her aunt invited Dixie to stay with her to keep her away from Ray's perverse designs, but what would that mean for her siblings, essentially growing up without parents? It was suggested that Gwen, then seven, be placed in foster care, at least temporarily, while the family found its footing. The sentiment was well meant, but terrifying. All the siblings had was each other, and Dixie, as the elder and caretaker, made it her mission to offer her younger siblings the illusion of normalcy. No one would break her family up.

Of all her siblings, Dixie felt the most affinity with Meredith. They saw the world the same way, talked about it with the same words, comforted themselves with the same jokes. You put one foot in front of the other, sticking to the path you had already laid out for yourself, without questioning its purpose or value. If there was school the next day, you laid out your clothes and packed your bag. And when the morning came, you got dressed and walked to school, in the hope that whatever took place inside its walls could save you.

Life was an unending barrage of catastrophes, until chaos began to feel like the fabric from which daily life was constructed. This was Meredith's childhood: sick, absent mother, parasitical father figures, struggling siblings, and creeping poverty. One day, Ray disappeared, with no warning, and no explanation forthcoming from Altha. A new boyfriend, Troy, soon replaced Ray, but little else changed for Altha and her children. Altha's mood swings and her boyfriends' criminal malevolence made their apartment anything but a home for the children, who sought escape in any form they could find it.

Meredith was eleven years old when he had his first run-in with the authorities in 1962. He was booked as a ward of the juvenile court, accused of being "beyond the control" of his parents, guardian, or custodian, and sent to Alameda Juvenile Court. (Although what did it mean to be in violation of that law when your own mother was herself beyond her own control?) Meredith spent eight months in a juvenile facility, then was arrested again just one month after being released and spent five more months in juvie.

The truth was, though, that Meredith was more than a little relieved to be arrested. He had chosen to act up in the hope of being taken away from his home, and found a sliver of normalcy in the regimentation of a juvenile detention center—a school with high walls, from which there was no dismissal at the end of each day.

Meredith's teenage years were a closed circuit: home, the streets, and juvie. He was away for most of the years between the ages of eleven and eighteen, never home for longer than a year at a time. His family would send him packages when they could, and he would write them funny letters about the mundane details of life in juvie.

In all, Meredith was free for little more than two years in total during that span. Things changed at home—Troy was gone now, replaced by Charles Talbot, whom Altha now lived with—but most everything else remained the same.

Each time Meredith was released, he was soon back under the authority of the state of California. Three counts of burglary in October 1964, at age thirteen; two counts of burglary in January 1966; another burglary charge in April 1967; a parole violation a year later. Home life would be a short respite before another arrest, another incarceration. Or was it the other way around, and being locked up the respite from what seemed to be a life sentence at home?

He was only Meredith at home. Everywhere else, he went by Murdock—a name that divested him of any traces of femininity, any genteel airs. Murdock sounded like a revolutionary or a warrior, the kind of person who might break into another's home and make off with what they needed. Along with his cousin Richard Baker, he ran with a gang called the East Bay Executors, who were petty criminals and recreational drug users. Meredith liked to smoke weed, and occasionally injected crystal meth.

When Meredith was home, he was on the hustle. Anything that brought in some money was welcome, whether legal or otherwise. Stealing was welcome, but so was a job that might provide a modicum of financial stability. He applied for work at the post office. A cousin lined up a job for Meredith at a restaurant, and for a time, that helped make ends meet. But adulthood was a strange land, one rarely visited and rarely discussed. Meredith had been forced to grow up too quickly, in ways few of the middle-class flower children in nearby Berkeley could even imagine. It was hard to know what it meant to be an adult, though, when so few role models were around to demonstrate maturity in action.

He was terrified by Altha's example, scared of her illness, her weakness, and the ways she had been abused by an uncaring world. And yet, Meredith was more like her than he would have wanted to know, or acknowledge. Here he was, too, out in the streets, seeking whatever companionship he could find. Anyone who accepted him was a friend, just like Altha. He hungered for acceptance, hungered to be part of a crew. And while some of the friends Meredith made were loyal, and decent, others did not have his best interests at heart. Were those friends egging him on to criminal mischief? His family never knew, but he was a teenage boy, and teenage boys regularly made mistakes and disappointed those who cared about them. It was part and parcel of the passage to manhood.

Dixie left home in those years, having met the man who would become her husband. Jesse Parker was in the trucking business, and his work often took him to the less visited rural corners of northern California. He and Dixie had driven around remote Yuba County, north of Sacramento, looking for scrap steel to haul away, and more than once encountered burning crosses on the hills. Even when he found suitable scrap, Parker would have to perform for these white men, playing the role they expected of him: that of the deferential black worker, only able to make his living because of the generosity of his superiors. So it was "yes, Mr. Smith" and "no, Mr. Jones" until they would finally deign to let him take away their scrap. He would have to beg to remove their trash, and Dixie found it distasteful that her husband, a proud man, was reduced to such abject pleading. He was, she later thought, playing the "good nigger," and it made her stomach hurt to see him like that. But those were the times they lived in. Even in the era of LBJ and MLK, the Voting Rights Act and the Civil Rights Act, news of the advances made for African-Americans was only halting and irregular here in the rural corners of northern California.

The Bay Area, and the East Bay cities of Oakland and Berkeley in particular, was a promised land for blacks fleeing the South, but as with so many other moments in America's warped, traumatic racial history, unspoken rules governed where and how African-Americans could be themselves. Blacks knew where, when, and how they were not welcome. The rules of their world were written and enforced by whites, and became so intertwined with their daily lives that they might as well have been law.

Meredith and his siblings knew the boundaries of their world: from Dwight Way to Shattuck, from Alcatraz to Ashby, with Oakland's black downtown their central hub. Meredith and Dixie did not believe there were all that many white people in the Bay Area, because they so rarely saw them. Their world was so enclosed by unofficial segregation that it came to seem the natural order of the world. Oakland, and to a lesser extent Berkeley, were safe spaces for African-Americans, nestled in a more unforgiving metropolitan area where they did not always feel at home.

When he was home, Meredith mostly stayed at Dixie's, about six blocks away from their mother's apartment. He and Dixie would take the 15 bus to Washington, near the old courthouse, where they would window-shop, and dream. There was the Hale Brothers department store at Washington and Tenth, with men's dresswear on the second floor, and Cannon Shoes just on the next block. Meredith was always a sharp dresser, always interested in clothes, and his eye was naturally drawn to the boldly colored, well-cut suits on display.

When you had nothing, your clothing served as your armor. What would it mean to be someone who would draw the attention of passersby on the street?

The burgeoning white counterculture leaned toward casual dress as an expression of disdain toward the gray-flannel world of their elders. Jeans and T-shirts were the new uniform of youth, but Meredith did not want to blend in, did not want to be another drably dressed cog in the youth-culture machine. He preferred dapper clothing: brightly colored suits, and wide-brimmed hats. The clothes he wore told the strangers he passed by something about himself, something about his story. And he bought his siblings new clothes as a tangible way of showing them how much he cared about them. They could wear his love.

Segregation and redlining and a grossly unfair justice system kept blacks incarcerated in vast open-air prisons, taunting them with the promise of better lives ahead while delivering any such advances with aggravating slowness. The counterculture offered a reed of hope. Here were young people who planned to change the world: end the war in Vietnam, overturn the poisonous legacy of racism, and transform America in their image. It was intoxicating. Their Berkeley and Meredith's were separated by mere steps and light-years. Over here, poverty and uncertainty; over there, the possibility of a more just society. Meredith had always liked concerts and dances, and the white counterculture's celebration of music was thrilling, its belief that music itself could be transformative. Music allowed you to lose yourself, to meld with a crowd, to become a small part of an incredibly powerful, unified whole, not just a lonely cog.

Meredith was invigorated by the Haight-Ashbury psychedelic scene, and all it offered. He liked the local rock bands (although he mostly preferred to listen to soul and jazz), but he loved the atmosphere of their shows, their implicit promise of the community bound together in mutual kindness and forbearance. There was free love, he told his sister after a few initial forays into the other Berkeley, impressed and titillated. "Nothing's free, Meredith," she responded.

That was just how they spoke to each other: joking, taunting, piercing the assaults of the exterior world with a well-placed verbal barrage. Life had given both Meredith and Dixie a dark sense of humor. It was what they had always done: take the bleakest moments of a life, the darkest feelings that bubbled up, and transmute them into black humor. That was what oppressed, beaten-down people everywhere did. It was how they survived.

Whatever ate away at them, whether Altha's illness or the constant threat posed by their mother's string of terrifying, abusive boyfriends, they joked about it, and it would feel ever so slightly less oppressive. Laughter brought them together, perhaps in part because Altha, oppressed by her own demons, had so little sense of humor left.

The psychedelic scene offered more than music; it also offered the possibility of temporary obliteration of the self. Drugs tempted Meredith for the same reasons the counterculture's rhetoric attracted him: it promised the undoing of a seemingly inflexible order. Meredith was young and energetic and silver-tongued, but there was a reason he spoke so rarely, except in the vaguest possible terms, about the future. What could the future have to offer him, a black teenager with a lengthy record, no hope for a college degree, few professional prospects, and a family that was as much an albatross as an anchor? White flower children took drugs to find themselves. Meredith, like his mother, took drugs to lose himself, if only for a few hours. The weight of being himself—in this body, in this skin, in this family, in this crumbling neighborhood—was crushing, and drugs would temporarily lift that burden off his shoulders, allowing him to float free, if only for a moment.

In June 1969, Dixie got a call at her home from Yuba County. They asked her to come to the county morgue to identify a body, and that was how she learned that her husband Jesse was dead. While out on a job, a piece of machinery had accidentally snipped a power line, and he had been instantly electrocuted. Dixie was left alone with three small children to care for, and siblings still requiring her assistance, with no one to turn to for relief. Her oldest son Tim was six years old, and her younger daughter, Taammi, was just two at the time of Jesse's death, too young to even remember her father. Dixie had escaped the gnarled, airless atmosphere of her mother's house and painstakingly built her own family life, only to have it unexpectedly implode in the flash of an eye. Life could be so fleeting, and so cruel.

Meredith came to stay at the house on Julia Street in Berkeley after Jesse's death, there to comfort the bewildered Tim, Tanya, and Taammi, and soothe the grieving Dixie. Meredith was loving and kind with the children, always playing with them, always hugging them, and giving freely of himself. They drank in his attention, needing a father figure in the sudden, disorienting absence of their own father. He always let them know he was proud of them, devoting his time to reading to them and talking with them. "This is my guy," he would say to his nieces and nephew, reminding them that there were still people in the world to whom they belonged.

When home from juvie, Meredith would often hang out in the park across the street from Berkeley High School, shooting the shit with the guys and flirting with the girls. During free periods, students would wander out the school doors and find their way to the park, and Meredith would already be there, ready to listen to all the latest installments in the perpetually unfurling emotional sagas of adolescence. He fell in with a group of African-American boys and white girls who would spend time together, often at the home of one girl whose liberally minded mother didn't mind interracial fraternizing.

Meredith was very tall, already six-foot-two by the time he was eighteen, with his father's naturally straight hair. He would use Tide detergent and vinegar to reverse-engineer his hair into a natural do, fluffing it out into a small Afro. A seventeen-year-old sophomore named Patti Bredehoft, part of the Berkeley High clique at the park, took notice of Meredith, quietly observing that girls flocked to him, anxious to have his ear. He wore big-brimmed hats and colorful jackets, sometimes with matching nail polish on his fingers, and there was a certain swagger to his walk, as if he were more comfortable in his skin than all the other teenage boys and girls still adjusting to their adult bodies.

He prided himself on his conversational skills, letting his charm and his fundamental sweetness win others over. Meredith was not a player so much as someone who often preferred the company of women. One time, he and Patti were in a car together, playing a game of the dozens. The game was usually an excuse for comic cruelty, a series of knives flung at your friends and confidants, but it struck Patti how fundamentally kind Meredith was, even when he was supposed to be filleting you.

Patti would run into Meredith in the park across from school, and at their friend's house, and by the fall, the two teenagers were spending much of their time together, sharing delightful adventures like going in to San Francisco to see the Temptations. Others would confide in Meredith, but he rarely spoke of his private life to others, even to Patti. He never talked to her about his family, his criminal record, or his burgeoning interest in drug culture. Instead, he preferred to share those private feelings that were too strong, too messy for public consumption.

Meredith had an eye for white girls in particular, which Dixie believed reflected the damage Altha had wrought on her children. He might not even be fully aware of it, she thought, but Dixie believed Meredith saw black women as susceptible to the same pitfalls that had ensnared his mother. His mother was weak, and his family was fractured and atomized. Meredith saw this as the curse of blackness, dooming him to an eternal repetition of the same tragic story.

White girls were a less risky bet. He invited Patti over to the house once, the first girl he had ever brought home to meet his family, but there was no spark, no warmth there. Dixie thought her lacking in friendliness, and Patti felt that Meredith's family was skeptical about her presence. What did this white girl want with their Meredith, anyway?

Meredith and Patti continued to spend time together, his family's skepticism notwithstanding. Meredith had read Eric Berne's pop-psychology bestseller *Games People Play*, and he enjoyed directing Patti's attention, when they were out, to others' conversations. "What are they doing?" he would ask. "They're talking," Patti would duti-fully answer, and then Meredith would analyze their body language, the silent details of their interaction to demonstrate his awareness of all that went unspoken in human affairs.

Word spread, in late November and early December 1969, about a huge free concert set to come to the Bay Area, and Meredith told his sister he was thinking of attending. He had been to the Monterey Jazz Festival and enjoyed himself, and hoped for another glorious day of sunshine and good vibes and music. He did not much care about the Rolling Stones, but the idea of soaking in the love and warmth and companionship that came from hundreds of thousands of well-meaning young people gathered together was too tempting to pass up. Perhaps, too, the idea of another Woodstock reminded Meredith of his own childhood excursions to the Berkeley hills, communing with the frogs and the strays. Nature offered him calm where nothing else could, and Meredith, practically a grown man now, still took pleasure from the natural world. Being out in the countryside for the day with his girlfriend and his friends, listening to music, interacting with thousands of like-minded souls—what could be better?

Dixie, reminded of her rides on her husband's truck and the burning crosses she had seen out the passenger window, told him it wasn't safe in the outer fringes of Alameda County. Violent racism was still alive and well in America, and Meredith was too naïve— too trusting—to see it. "You *do not* need to be out there," she told him firmly. Their family had long known that as African-Americans, you were treated differently, wherever you went. You were held to a mysterious standard, one whose rules you often would not know until you had been accused of breaking them.

But Meredith was too excited to listen to Dixie's concerns, perhaps seeing them as the pent-up worries of a woman still in the earliest stages of recovering from the trauma of her husband's death. And besides, Berkeley was not Mississippi. Meredith and Patti had been dating for two months, and would regularly walk down the street without anyone batting an eye. Why should this concert be any different?

Meredith was receptive enough to his sister's concerns that he decided he was going to protect himself at the concert at the Altamont Speedway. "You know what happens to people who look like us," he told her. Dixie responded with a chuckle. It was just like her brother to act tough but not even be capable of following through. "I see you got a gun," she laughed, looking at his .22 Smith & Wesson pistol. "I bet you don't have any bullets for it." It would just be there to scare off any hoodlums who decided to pick on a black teenager at a rock 'n' roll show. He told Dixie not to worry. He would not have to deal with any of that, anyway.

He called Patti and told her he was planning a trip to the free Stones show, and that his friend Ronnie Brown, whom everyone called Blood, would be joining them with his girlfriend Judy. He would have the use of Charles Talbot's champagne-beige '65 Mustang, and the show would be a blast. "Come on out," he inveigled, and she readily agreed. Meredith got himself fully kitted out in his favorite lime-green suit, with a black silk button-down shirt underneath the jacket, and a broad-brimmed black hat atop his head. Patti was decked out, too, in more traditional flower-child garb, with a short suede skirt and a cream-colored blouse, covered by a white cable-knit top knit by her mother.

It was early December, still some weeks before the end of the year, and the decade, but that morning, when Meredith prepared to get on the road, Altha already had a Christmas tree up in the living room. Altha had always loved Christmas, and the tree seemed to promise all the things she had never received in her own life: revival, redemption, new life. After the winter, new green shoots would come with the spring. Meredith pulled away from the house and began heading east, toward the Altamont Speedway.

3. Staging the Show

The last-minute shift from Sears Point to Altamont meant a scramble to provide the necessary accommodations at a venue that had never before hosted an event of this size. Public transit was nonexistent, food mostly unavailable, bathroom facilities scarce, and the question of security remained unresolved. Each element of the concert—the staging, the transportation, the parking, the security, and the music—was in flux, with little in the way of leadership or oversight to ensure a successful show. With so little time in which to execute the myriad tasks necessary to put on a concert of this size, much was left to chance, or to wishful thinking and misplaced hopefulness.

Rock Scully, working out of the Grateful Dead's office, placed a frantic phone call to Michael Lang, who had overseen the triumphant Woodstock festival in August. Lang agreed to fly out from New York to coordinate the last-minute planning, and arrived on Thursday—just two days before the concert. The show was in such disarray that a kind of festival triage had to be implemented. Potential pitfalls hid in plain sight everywhere. There were too few toilets. The speedway's neighbors had not been informed of the concert. There were too few trees to provide adequate shade for the crowd. The stage would likely be entirely surrounded by fans and their cars.

There simply was no time, Lang realized, to bring food and water out to Altamont, or to plan for the parking nightmare that would undoubtedly ensue. But in his public pronouncements, Lang betrayed no evidence of concern: "I think we can hold as many people as want to come."

Melvin Belli had originally been brought in by the festival's organizers to help them find the new venue, but once Altamont had been secured, he was charged with smoothing the transition from Sears Point to the speedway. The scene in Belli's office on Montgomery Street in San Francisco was chaotic, with Belli, who had once represented Jack Ruby, holding court before an audience of supplicants and band hangers-on.

Belli, his face framed by his omnipresent owlish black glasses, was an acerbic local fixer, best known for firing off a cannon and raising a pirate flag above his offices after winning a case. Belli was tasked with coordinating efforts with speedway owner Dick Carter, the Alameda County sheriff, and other stakeholders in the concert, but some basic questions remained unanswered. "Sheriff wants to know who's gonna go to the bathroom and where," Belli told the assembled crowd in his office. "They know practically when every john is flushed, and the orderly habits of the bathroom of all of their voters." Belli, too, was a performer, his role that of the caustic magus paternalistically aiding the idealistic young kids. "You take the publicity," he told Carter, "and the Rolling Stones don't want any money, it's for charity, so I'll take the money."

The discussion in Belli's office betrayed a mounting panic about the sheer size of the concert. "There's not enough room for it," one onlooker told Belli, and rumors spread that as many as twenty thousand fans were on their way from across the country. "It's like the lemmings of the sea," said one onlooker, perhaps unconsciously echoing the *New York Times*' description of the Woodstock crowd. The speedway, Dick Carter told the Alameda County sheriff over the telephone, had room for approximately 150 cars per acre. By that calculation, the eighty-acre property could hold 12,000 cars, while the concert planners expected as many as 80,000 automobiles. "If there's fifty thousand cars Mr. Carter can't park," the sheriff argued, "we're in trouble." On hearing the news, Belli briefly glanced up at the Maysles brothers' cameras before looking back down, hesitant to meet the camera's gaze.

Michael Lang had been hired by the Grateful Dead's representatives, but it was not entirely clear to him precisely who was in charge of the concert. Were the Dead taking responsibility for the show, or was it now in the hands of the Rolling Stones? Arrangements were all disconcertingly loose, predicated on the assumption that if everything had worked out at Hyde Park, and at Woodstock, then they undoubtedly would here, as well. The stark differences between Altamont and its predecessors—the lack of adequate medical and bathroom facilities, the shortages of food—were glossed over, too insignificant to matter.

Lang knew he would not have time to put out all the smoldering fires, and chose to concentrate his efforts on what he saw as the most pressing need: the construction of the stage and the build-out of the lighting and sound systems. Lang and the Stones' tour manager, Sam Cutler, ushered all the crews to Altamont and oversaw their efforts. All of Friday, local radio stations like KSAN and KFRC had been regularly issuing calls for volunteers to head out to Altamont early and help Chip Monck and his crew.

Rolling Stones stage manager Monck, who had overseen the

Stones' tour that fall, was already at the speedway on Friday morning, scrambling to get the concert stage in place. The stage had been designed for the Sears Point site, where it was intended to be nestled in a niche set atop a small plateau. The crowd was to look up at the bands, guitar-slinging prophets bearing a new set of tablets for the people of the LP. But now, the same stage had to be employed in a space for which it was dramatically unsuited. Monck's equipment did not even arrive until Friday afternoon, less than twenty-four hours before the concert was to begin. Altamont had little in the way of usable infrastructure, and the speedway's only décor were the hulks of thirty or forty junked cars that had been wrecked during demolition derbies.

Monck did not have time to worry about the stage as he frantically searched through mislabeled boxes of gear. Why hadn't these boxes been properly packed and sorted? And why was the planner of the biggest rock concert to ever grace the Bay Area required to make do with a skeleton crew of fifty, composed of the bands' roadies, union crews, and unpaid volunteers, during the single day of preparation granted to its coordinator?

Over the course of the Stones' grueling tour, Monck had grown accustomed to the process of loading and unloading the band's own sound and lighting equipment at each venue—a heretofore unprecedented idea in rock concert production. The Rolling Stones did not want to depend on the vagaries of equipment quality at less-than-professional concert venues. In a matter of hours, Monck would not only set up an entire sound system, he would teach the latest batch of green workers assigned to him how to man a lighting system. The frenzy was nothing new for the band, but the scope of the concert—and of the disorganization—were unprecedented.

At Altamont, the precarious stage design demanded its own unique lighting technique. The stage could not be raised higher than three and a half feet. There were not even any parallels—the small, unfolding, drum-riser-like platforms that might have elevated the stage—to be found anywhere in the Bay Area. There were no follow spots—none had arrived—and so the only illumination was twenty-four thousand watts of backlighting. Monck made do with the limited resources he had, but he was also looking out for the musicians. With only backlighting, there would be no lights in the Stones' eyes, blinding them. If someone—heaven forbid—chose to launch a beer bottle at the band, they would be able to see it coming.

The situation was so disorganized and frenzied that crew members with other responsibilities were pressed into service. A small army of roadies and techs worked through the night in the bitter thirty-degree cold, unloading boxes and assembling equipment with hardly a complaint. They were energized by the copious amounts of high-grade cocaine floating around the Stones' camp, which kept them working through the night.

The lighting towers went up with the assistance of oversized derricks that lifted them into the air, the sound systems were assembled, and the stage that had been originally designed for Sears Point went in. Approximately one hundred portable toilets were delivered by truck during the night—welcome, but hardly enough for the enormous crowd scheduled to arrive the next morning.

The stage was in place by nine o'clock that night, and Monck's crew wrapped up their work just before midnight. The rough, unsanded bones of Altamont's infrastructure were together, if little else. It would now be possible for a concert to take place at the speedway, but with so little time to organize, a great many necessities would have to be done without. There would be no higher stage, no fencing, and no crew of experienced technicians to hammer out any difficulties as they arose. This hectic dash would be all that would protect the temporary residents of Altamont from chaos.

The audience, too, would be fed into the maw of the disorganized situation. There would be no aisles, and no barriers to separate the fans from the stage, or from each other. The inherent flaws of the concert space were exacerbated by the setup, in which fans' natural urge to get closer to the bands encouraged them to push downhill, and create a potentially calamitous crunch near the stage. Monck imagined creating pens for the fans, segregating them in smaller spaces from which they could not exert any force. They would be treated like cattle, and would undoubtedly complain, but the threat of a stampede or a crushing incident would be neutralized. But there was not enough time to organize the pens, or a clear chain of command. Who, exactly, was in charge here?

Pulling the plug on the concert might have been preferable, but it was simply too late to even contemplate it. Fans were already trickling in to the speedway, and many others were on their way as his crew frantically rushed to complete their work. Even for those who had not yet left their homes, how would the word be spread? Not everyone would turn on the radio to confirm that the concert was still on before they got in their cars. The risk of hundreds of thousands of fans gathering at the Altamont Speedway, with no infrastructure in place, and no music to placate them, was simply too great to take.

Security, too, would be nothing like it had been at Woodstock. Lang had originally hired five hundred off-duty New York Police Department officers to provide security at Woodstock. Even after the NYPD revoked its approval of the arrangement, many of the cops had worked the festival anyway, under false names like Mickey Mouse and Donald Duck. Lang was only too happy to have experienced law-enforcement representatives keeping order at Woodstock. He'd only asked that they undergo an initial interview in which they were quizzed about potential antipathy to the counterculture, and that they arrive unarmed and out of uniform.

The arrangement had been, by all accounts, a rousing success.

Altamont, by contrast, was to have a minimal police presence, with the bulk of the security staff provided by the Hells Angels.

Everyone in the Bay Area rock scene knew the deal. When the Grateful Dead or Jefferson Airplane played an impromptu free show at Speedway Meadows in Golden Gate Park, or some other local venue, the Hells Angels would show up, invited to occupy prime real estate. The Angels would position themselves next to the generators and look fierce to keep any potential jokers or saboteurs from damaging the band's equipment and spoiling the show. By the fearsomeness of their mere presence, the bikers maintained the peace, and allowed the hundreds or thousands of fans gathered for the outdoor concerts to enjoy the music without interruption.

But those earlier shows had been relatively self-contained. They had been in San Francisco itself, in a park whose size naturally limited the number of attendees. They were often relatively spur of the moment, designed as surprise appearances for diehard fans. And the Angels were present as glorified teamsters, there to look menacing and keep anyone from ripping off the bands. As long as no one took a swipe at the Dead's amplifiers, attendees were unlikely to have any interaction with the Angels. And so a constrained set of encounters without much opportunity for contact came to appear as a long history of peaceable interaction. Many in the Bay Area scene believed that if the Grateful Dead had blessed the Hells Angels, nothing could possibly go wrong.

Back when the free concert had been scheduled for Golden Gate Park, the Grateful Dead had suggested hiring the Hells Angels for security. Rock Scully had dispatched Stones tour manager Sam Cutler to meet with a San Francisco Angel and longtime friend of the Dead named Pete Knell, and the two men hashed out the rough details of a deal. The primary task would be to guard the band's generators, protecting them from overzealous fans who might be inclined to damage the Stones' power source. The fee would be five hundred dollars, paid out in six-packs of beer. Cutler likely received the money from Melvin Belli, planning to eventually collect one hundred dollars from each of the other bands, evenly splitting the security costs between the five acts scheduled to play.

When the venue shifted, first to Sears Point, and then to Altamont, the Angels were kept on as security staff, even when the nature of the gig changed from standing guard around a generator to protecting an entire stage of musicians. The promoters were asking the Hells Angels to take on responsibilities they were ill-equipped to handle.

Moreover, even if the Hells Angels acquitted themselves honorably, the nature of their remit was wildly inadequate for the scope of the event being planned. Who would ensure the safety and security of the attendees? No plans had been made to protect the crowd. And to make matters worse, the Hells Angels were not milquetoast security guards, but thin-skinned bikers with a history of violent militancy. The wolf had been invited into the henhouse, a product of twinned, fateful misunderstandings of the nature of the event they were planning, and of the Angels themselves.

John Jaymes, the shadowy businessman who had cozied up to the Stones on their tour by falsely claiming to represent Chrysler and providing them with free cars, had told Sam Cutler he would provide fifteen off-duty police officers. But the Hells Angels would be positioned directly in front of the stage, without the benefit of a barrier or moat that would protect them from the crowd. With the stage at the bottom of a natural bowl, a surge in the crowd, perched precariously on the hills above the stage, could push those concertgoers standing closest to the performers into direct contact with the Hells Angels. And how would the bikers react?

The Rolling Stones were equally misinformed about the Hells Angels. They had employed a group that referred to itself as Hells

Angels to provide security at their Hyde Park show in London earlier in the summer, but the hodgepodge of leather-clad poseurs and clueless teenagers bore little resemblance to the genuine made-in-America product. Now, they were headlining another enormous concert, in an unfamiliar place, and agreeing to turn security over to a group of men whose most fundamental belief was in the righteousness of violence as an act of manhood. Both the Grateful Dead and the Rolling Stones ignored the potential pitfalls of employing the Hells Angels, wanting to link themselves, and their music, to the outlaw allure of the biker gang. What could be cooler than rolling onto the stage in the presence of a posse of badass bikers in leather, Harleys roaring?

For the performers scheduled to play at Altamont, a purposeful ignorance regarding the nagging details of the show paved the way for untrammeled optimism about its effects. This would be another triumph, another celebration of the counterculture in which artist and audience would share the limelight, each basking in the glow of a youthful nation's approval. Jefferson Airplane guitarist Paul Kantner had played many of the already legendary shows at the Fillmore, and in Golden Gate Park, and come away deeply impressed with the air of carnival that pervaded these goings-on. A carnival, as Kantner would know, was participatory. There was no such thing as to be a mere spectator; to watch was to take part. Distinctions of class and race and gender, of social status and fame, were wiped away.

The poor had temporarily become rich, the lowly had become great, and the outcasts of society found a place that was theirs alone. This was to be more than a concert. It would be the fulcrum from which another triumphant moment in youth culture would be broadcast to a grateful American public.

For the musicians, the concerns about the preparation for the show were mere details, distractions from the sheer magnitude of the celebration to come. Even the music was secondary to the simple fact of another, even grander gathering of the tribes. "I think the concert's an excuse," Mick Jagger told the press the night before the concert. "The thing is, it's just like everyone coming and having a good time. The concert's not actually like the proscenium of the theater. It's an excuse for everyone to get together and talk to each other . . . ball each other, get very stoned, and just have a nice night out, and a good day." The goodwill of the community was essential. The stars counted on their audience to paper over any gaps in the preparations with their enthusiasm and benevolence. Both sides were guilty of misplaced confidence in the good intentions of all involved parties.

Mick Jagger had flown to the site via helicopter during the evening to check on its progress, accompanied by Keith Richards, bodyguard Tony Funches, manager Ronnie Schneider, journalist Stanley Booth, with the action all filmed by Albert and David Maysles. Jagger briefly pressed the flesh with fans, accepting one young woman's offer of a yellow scarf to protect his neck. Funches was dispatched to find them a joint. A young woman came by, offering to blow smoke into Jagger's and Richards's mouths. Jagger asked for some mescaline to take the next day after his performance so he could luxuriate in the glow of the crowd. Grateful Dead manager Rock Scully gave the band some advice: they should go on at about five o'clock, with sunset the next day set for 4:50 p.m. All seemed well.

Jagger headed back to San Francisco in the limousine waiting for him, telling Booth: "I'd like to stay but I've got to rest. . . . I've got to sing—if I had to play the guitar tomorrow I think I'd stay, but I've got to sing."

Jagger was conscious of the burden imposed by adulation, and by the increasing weight of his audience's expectations. To many, he was more than just a singer, more than just a star; he was a leader in training, his songs expressions of a world on the brink of unimaginable change.

. . .

Rock 'n' roll, in its earliest incarnation, had been a primal howl: of sexual need, of dissatisfaction, of satisfaction denied, stymied. As the 1960s progressed, and the musical world shifted, the Stones' work began to obliquely reflect the world around them. To be young was to live out an intimate relation to violence: to the American soldiers fighting in Vietnam, the disaffected young black men and women in the inner cities, the antiwar protesters clashing with police. Around the world, too, from Prague to Paris to Peking, the armies of youth were colliding with the forces of order.

In songs like "Street Fighting Man" and "Salt of the Earth," both from the Stones' acclaimed 1968 album *Beggars Banquet*, Jagger and Richards obliquely addressed the volatility of the era. "Street Fighting Man" was an ode to defiance, less a protest song than a statement of support, set to the thrum of marching feet, for those rebelling against the constricting consensus of the mainstream. Jagger seemed to acknowledge his own remoteness from the conflicts he observed, enlisting himself in the cause with the weapons closest to hand: his voice, and his band.

"Street" was an expression of sympathy that made few promises. Jagger would not be manning the barricades; he would not be fighting in the street. Instead, he would go on doing what he had always done, secure in the knowledge that those doing the fighting would know he was with them. This was compelling, and daring, but it also reflected the fundamental remoteness of the Rolling Stones, better suited as observers than participants. "We take it for granted that people know we're with you," Richards had announced during a tour press conference, his statement perfectly articulating that conjoined sense of intimacy and distance.

Ominous portents emerged over the horizon, and the Stones looked to the horizon with trepidation. If "Street Fighting Man" was a muffled call to arms, "Gimme Shelter," from the band's brand-new album *Let It Bleed*, released the day before Altamont, prophesied unrest to come, with rape and murder, and the intimation of yet worse, just a shot away. The Rolling Stones were not political artists in the fashion of early Dylan, or Creedence Clearwater Revival. Instead, they were mirrors held up to society, their lyrical concerns reflecting those of their fans and compatriots. Something brutish and unrelenting was on its way.

After Jagger had left, Keith Richards remained behind to wander the grounds, soaking in the atmosphere and enjoying a moment of communion with the crowds. There were, as *Rolling Stone* would later report, amateur musicians strumming their guitars, joints being passed around, and impromptu games of touch football under the glare of the stage lights. Campfires dotted the speedway, with zealous fans seeking to ward off the fierce chill of a northern California winter night.

Much of the crowd was living up to the bands' expectation of mellow revelry, but others seemed to embody the dark side of the counterculture. This segment of the audience comprised, as one onlooker would later describe them, "speed freaks with hollow eyes and missing teeth, dead-faced acid heads burned out by countless flashes, old beatniks clutching gallons of red wine, Hare Krishna chanters with shaved heads and acned cheeks." They had hitchhiked to the show with strangers, or been abandoned there by boyfriends on the make. Their eyes were hollow orbs, empty shells decimated by drugs. They were the detritus of the counterculture, their very presence a rebuke to its ideals. Music might not do it after all.

The early word had said one hundred thousand people might make their way to Altamont, but anyone in the Bay Area scene who had polled their friends, or followed the pre-show frenzy, seemingly broadcast twice an hour on KSAN, KMPX, and the other San Francisco rock stations, would have known that the number was likely to be much higher. KSAN had been hyping the concert without pause, spreading the word to the FM-listening cognoscenti about their planned coverage of the earth-shattering concert. The station had plans to cover the concert live, with members of its news crew and DJs broadcasting from the event. Between songs by billed performers like the Stones and Jefferson Airplane, DJs would provide traffic updates for those driving to the show, and even directions for those who had never made it out to Livermore before.

Preparing for the concert, Albert and David Maysles had hired seventeen crews—mostly composed of one cinematographer and one sound operator—to film the show from every conceivable angle. Many had been recruited by Baird Bryant, a highly respected New York cameraman with links to dozens of young filmmakers on the East Coast and in California.

Before the concert, David Maysles had gathered his film crews, in from San Francisco and Los Angeles, and given them a pep talk, arguing that they were about to be in the presence of history. With their cameras and tape recorders, they would capture another turning point in the story of the American counterculture's triumphant march to destiny. This was to be another Woodstock, and the camera crews were there to document the peace and harmony and brotherhood. Albert, taking a slightly different tack, asked the crew to maintain an attitude of inquiry. Stories would unfold before them, and it was their responsibility to follow them.

Most of the film crew was to come to Altamont the morning of the concert, but the Maysles sent out a handful of crews the night before, to film the frantic preparations at the speedway.

Instructions were minimal. Most of the crew were already experienced documentarians, and instinctively understood how to seek out the best story, the freshest angle on a day expected to be a West

Coast re-creation of an event that had already, in a few short months, become a part of living history.

A concert film held little inherent interest for David and Albert. They could not see, just yet, how to make a worthy full-length picture out of a live performance, but something about the collision of the Stones and the American public nagged at them, too fascinating to ignore. What would happen when an enormous, Woodstock-sized audience encountered Mick Jagger and Keith Richards?

Altamont had been, as so many of the Maysles brothers' projects were, something of an accidental convergence of filmmaker and subject. Albert and David were interested in, as one critic had it, finding the regular people inside celebrities or the performers buried inside regular people, and the prospect of a mass rock spectacle, uniting rock gods like Richards with their workaday fans, made for a potentially groundbreaking study of popular culture and its effect on American society. This could be the start of something special.

For Albert and David Maysles, so much of their careers up until that fateful moment had been a matter of serendipity. Albert had never used a movie camera before heading to Russia with a friend's borrowed Leica, retrieved out of hock, and shooting a film called *Psychiatry in Russia*. Its success helped him find work with the dean of direct cinema, Robert Drew, who was just then about to start shooting a film about the tightly contested 1960 Democratic presidential primary in Wisconsin.

Primary erased the distance between politician and constituent, star and fan. Suddenly, we were able to follow so closely behind a candidate for the presidency of the United States that we could almost feel the flap of John F. Kennedy's suit jacket lightly brushing our arms as he maneuvered his way to the next crowd, the next microphone.

After a number of years working with Drew, Albert joined his brother David, who had been working in Hollywood, and started a documentary-production company.

The Maysleses' work, documenting the secret lives of the Beatles, Marlon Brando, and Truman Capote, was intended to offer audiences a peek through the looking glass of celebrity.

1968's *Salesman*, the Maysleses' best-known film, was an exception to their star-studded earlier work, a film deliberately lacking in glamour or romance. At first glance, *Salesman*, which silently observed a team of Bible salesmen as they knocked on doors, cajoling housewives and retirees to buy overpriced Bibles with a mixture of oozing bonhomie and Catholic guilt, seemed a notable about-face from the Maysleses' earlier work. What could be further from the hothouse worlds of the movie colony or rock stardom than the lives of itinerant salesmen? And yet, on closer inspection, *Salesman* was closely linked to its predecessors. What was this film, after all, but another glimpse behind the frayed velvet curtain, peeking at the private lives of professionals whose careers depended on their ability to play a role? We watched the men in a hotel room, practicing their pitches, and came to understand that they, too, were actors, their livelihoods dependent on performing convincingly.

Soon the film they would shoot would become the primary lens through which the vast American audience not in attendance at Altamont would understand the tumultuous events of the day. Without it, there would be little but rumor and hearsay with which to understand the explosive clashes of December 6.

All through that night, fans left San Francisco and Berkeley, beginning the fifty-mile drive east through the all-encompassing darkness in the hopes of arriving at Altamont ahead of all the others sure to come. Woodstock had already entered the cultural pantheon as the culmination of the hippie fantasia: three days of peace and love and music. The counterculture had begun to envelop the mainstream, and it was likely only going to grow larger and more fruitful. With the Grateful Dead and Jefferson Airplane, Janis Joplin and the Hells Angels, Ken Kesey and LSD, the Bay Area had been the birthplace of the counterculture, and it galled the musicians, hippies, freaks, burnouts, druggies, and artists who made up its ranks that some no-name town in upstate New York had stolen its fire. This life was not a Madison Avenue affair, and the upper crust of Park Avenue was not invited to its celebrations. The time had come for the West Coast to reclaim its birthright, and Altamont—already called by some, as they hoped it might become, Woodstock West—was to be its coming-out party.

4. Outlaw Pride

It was a marriage of opposites, the collision of the middle-class rebels of the local music scene and the working-class motorcycle enthusiasts. Each had seen themselves as refugees from polite society, standing in opposition to the enforced consensus of postwar America.

For the bikers, the hippies and musicians were well-liked acquaintances, offering entrée to many of the Angels' favored pastimes. For the counterculture, the feelings were stronger, with the Hells Angels seen as allies in the battle against middle-class bourgeois mores. The counterculture in the Bay Area had long thought of itself as a kind of outlaw posse, living beyond the law and grateful for the company of all who similarly found themselves at odds with the establishment. It believed itself to be a large-tent party, encompassing anyone and everyone for whom the mainstream made no space.

The Angels were crude and impolite and little better than brigands, but they were the counterculture's own designated brigands. They were holy outlaws, and fellow travelers on the road to musical and cultural revolution. Their unruliness was a powerful symbol, the corporeal manifestation of the hippies' idle talk of overturning the system and flouting the law. The establishment was the enemy, and the Hells Angels were the only ones willing to take the fight to them, to risk their own well-being to defy authority. They physically embodied the counterculture's spiritual struggle.

The alliance between the counterculture and the Hells Angels was born of a deliberate ignorance, a desire to romanticize the outlaw. The Hells Angels were desperados, dissenting against the stifling consensus of the mainstream. The counterculture and the bikers shared a common enemy: the stultifying order of the postwar consensus, in which women were happy homemakers and men work-minded breadwinners, living at the office to pay for their families' lives. How could these two groups, each rebelling against the machine in their own manner, not share more than what separated them?

For all their surface differences, the counterculture and the Angels had an overlapping sphere of interests: drugs, free love, and good music. The counterculture supplied a good deal of each, of which the Angels were only too happy to partake. And the counterculture had a vested interest in putting on safe, secure events without involving the local police. Police departments were, they believed, corrupt, prone to outbursts of violence, and innately hostile to longhairs. They had been the ones responsible for the savage beating of protesters at the Democratic National Convention in Chicago in 1968. If a good portion of the counterculture's political energy focused on ending the misbegotten war in Vietnam, the police were seen as the local representatives of the U.S. Army, equally brutal and equally loathed. The Hells Angels were the counterculture's substitute police force, their ramshackle representatives of law and order. The Angels' presence at a concert, providing a protective cordon around a band or guarding their equipment, allowed the counterculture to believe it capably and safely policed itself. The authorities were no longer necessary.

The Hells Angels had had a long and mutually admiring relationship with Jerry Garcia and the members of the Grateful Dead. The Dead were the avatars of the Bay Area scene, pot-smoking hippies with a taste for folk melodies, country instruments, and long, shambling solos. The band cultivated an antiestablishment ethos that it only furthered through its canny association with the Hells Angels.

Garcia preferred hiring the Angels for his band's shows to employing private security, or the hated cops. He treated the Hells Angels with deferential respect, letting them in free to any show they might show up at, and the Angels respected him back. The Grateful Dead were the philosophers and court musicians of the new society, and everyone interested in participating was welcome. The exiles from polite society were gathering, and the Angels were only one colorful patch on the crazy quilt of the counterculture.

Garcia was friendly with a number of the San Francisco Hells Angels, and he regularly defended them against others' reproaches. When others criticized the Angels for their recklessness, Garcia would note that at least the Angels wore colorful garb that instantly identified them as men to be wary of. What of all those others in their identical suits and ties, wolves posing in sheep's clothing? The Hells Angels were wolves in wolves' garb, and when they growled, at least there would be no confusion about just who they were.

The Angels stood in opposition to both the mass of workaday middle-class and working-class drones—whom they referred to, dismissively, as "citizens"—and their fellow bikers, who might have been riding Harleys but were otherwise equally bland rule-followers, lacking the flair and vigor of the Hells Angels. To be a Hells Angel was to be called to live up to an ideal.

In his essential 1967 chronicle *Hell's Angels: The Strange and Terrible Saga of the Outlaw Motorcycle Gangs*, which introduced many readers to the bikers' subculture, Hunter S. Thompson wrote of one Angel nicknamed the Mute who, when stopped by the police and told to remove a jacket with the Angels' famous death's-head insignia, took it off to reveal a second matching jacket with the identical logo. A third death's-head lay beneath it, followed by a shirt with the logo imprinted on it, a similar undershirt, and a Hells Angels tattoo inked on his chest. The officer let the Mute go before he could show off his death's-head emblazoned underwear.

Like the counterculture they now associated with, the Hells Angels had been born out of a desire to sidestep authority, to avoid the constricting embrace of normalcy. For many young men drafted to serve in the Second World War, the war years had been defined by a sense of masculine camaraderie. In the absence of women, in the presence of an enemy committed to their slaughter, these young soldiers found comfort in their comrades. And when the war ended, and so many veterans rushed home to find stability in job and home and hearth, others were interested in prolonging the war's extended leave from workaday responsibility. The war had exposed many of them to heavy machinery for the first time, and where some vets fell in love with hot rods and formed car clubs, and others took up surfing, many found comfort in motorcycles.

Motorcycles were relatively affordable, easily customizable emblems of freedom and speed and motion. Many veterans were mechanically adept and capable of fixing and personalizing their bikes themselves. Some of the bikes these early riders purchased were from surplus military stocks, their riders literally bringing the war home for their own pleasure and consolation. Many cyclists likely suffered from what would later be called post-traumatic stress disorder, whether diagnosed or undiagnosed, and motorcycles were a homeopathic remedy for the ailments of men who had liberated concentration camps, stormed Omaha Beach at Normandy, and survived the unfathomable depredations of the war in the Pacific. They were not ready to throw on their suits and take up the concerns of middle management just yet.

With the end of the war, the country stood on the cusp of a huge surge in the popularity of motorcycle riding. In 1945, there had been only 198,000 motorcycles registered in the United States. By the early 1950s, there were already 500,000, and within two decades, there would be more than 3 million motorcycles on the roads and highways.

The bikers formed makeshift, ragtag associations. Men interested in motorcycles banded together and gave themselves masculine, grandiose names like the Outlaws. They would gather together to putter with their bikes, ride them on local roads and freeways, and drink beer together. It was mostly a working-class activity, one redolent of axle grease and wrenches, like a fleet of alcohol-fueled mechanics trained to work only on their own roaring two-wheeled beasts.

And California was the place to be a biker. The warm weather allowed for year-round riding, and the new freeways were as hospitable to motorcycles as they were to cars. California had more registered bikes than any other state in the union, so naturally, the first bikers' rallies took place in the Golden State in the late 1940s and early 1950s. Motorcyclists would gather in no-name towns like Hollister and Riverside, their drunken antics drawing the attention of the local authorities. The bikers were a direct affront to the enforced quiet of the immediate postwar years of Truman and Eisenhower, a time of panic about saboteurs in the midst and threats to the American way of life. The more that way of life was defined and enforced by the establishment, the more disaffected young men like the bikers would push back against any such designations. "What are you rebelling against?" Marlon Brando's outlaw biker is asked in the genre-defining 1953 biker film *The Wild One*. "Whaddaya got?" he sneers.

The Wild One reflected a slow-burning panic about bikers, and their perceived antipathy toward vanilla American life. What did these bikers want? It was in the nature of motorcyclists to be noticeable. They rode noisy bikes in large groups, often appearing en masse in small towns wholly unprepared for an onslaught of imposing, bearded men in leather jackets drinking beer in their bars and town squares. They did not appear gainfully employed (although in actuality, a good number of them were machinists and other skilled blue-collar workers), nor did they appear to be family men. The authorities were rattled by their presence, often overreacting and sending in their lumbering police forces to counteract the perceived threat. The bikers' actual crimes, at this point, mostly stopped at public urination and drunk and disorderly behavior.

The bikers' groups were what they professed to be: gatherings of enthusiasts with an affinity for motorcycles. And most of them were determinedly law-abiding. As one possibly apocryphal story has it, the American Motorcyclist Association assured a nervous American public that 99 percent of bikers were upstanding citizens, with only the remainder composed of lawbreakers. Hell-raising bikers' groups soon adopted the critique as a badge of pride, and the one-percenters were born: so-called "outlaw" biker groups intent on standing athwart the historical consensus, shouting incoherently. To be a biker was still a hobby and not a profession, nor was it yet an outright expression of criminality. But it increasingly reflected a certain worldview: defiant, pugilistic, crude, beer-soaked, drugged-out, and vaguely patriotic.

A biker named Vic Bettencourt had gotten stranded in southern California in the late 1940s, and started a bikers' group while stuck there. It had begun as an offshoot of another biker group, the Pissed Off Bastards. They called themselves the Nomad Hells Angels, soon shortened to the Hells Angels. The names all evoked a certain frame of mind: ornery, vulgar, redolent of low living and bad manners. They were designed to be at odds with polite society, to keep their distance from all that smacked of bourgeois values.

The future leader of the Oakland chapter of the Hells Angels, and de facto chief Angel, Sonny Barger, had grown up reading Western novels by Zane Grey and Louis L'Amour: hardscrabble, unadorned tales of the frontier, of cowboys and Indians, of two-fisted combat and the romance of the road. In high school, he saw *The Wild One* and was instantly enamored, not of Brando's Johnny Strabler, but of Lee Marvin's psychotic Chino. The frontier was closed, the Indians all slaughtered or penned in on reservations, but the open road remained, and the two-wheeled steeds that could ferry him into the future.

When Sonny was sixteen, his beloved older sister Shirley got married and left home, and his father sold the family's house and moved into a hotel in downtown Oakland. Sonny forged a birth certificate and joined the army. Sonny enjoyed the camaraderie and regimentation of military life, and was disappointed when his commanding officers discovered he was underage and booted him from the service, honorable discharge in hand. He was seventeen years old, a veteran, and uninterested in the workaday world or the cozy domestic life promised by the paragons of American propaganda. He wanted a clan. "I needed a second family," he would later write. "I wanted a group less interested in a wife and two point five kids in a crackerbox home in Daly City or San Jose and more interested in riding, drag racing, and raising hell."

Barger met Vic Bettencourt. His organization's rules reminded Barger favorably of army life, and he joined the Hells Angels. Barger was six feet tall, and a slim 170 pounds, no match for the imposing brutes he associated with. But when Barger spoke, people listened. And the other Angels knew that, in a scrape, he would be the first to enter the fray, whether against a lone, petrified barfly or a passel of armed police officers.

By the late 1950s, the Hells Angels were well known around northern California for rowdy, occasionally deviant behavior. More than anything, the club was defined by its choice of motorcycles. The Hells Angels rode, romanced, and worshipped Harley-Davidsons, and only Harley-Davidsons. They would often buy their Harleys from police auctions, aware though the authorities were not that even bikes deemed to be little more than scrap metal could always be rebuilt. They lovingly restored the bikes and kept them polished to a high sheen. The Angels fetishized their Harleys, "chopping" them to their specifications by cutting off back fenders, switching out the handlebars, and removing the front fenders, then painting them gaudy colors.

Everywhere the Angels went, they attracted the attention of prospective converts to the motorcyclists' cause. Here was rebellion, here was chaos and noise and life on two rubber wheels. Some wanted to join the club. Some wanted to fight them, to test their own mettle. And others just wanted to be in their presence, so they could later tell their friends that they'd been drinking, or riding, with none other than the Hells Angels.

The club was a study in colliding contrasts. They were majestic in motion and tedious in conversation, glorious outlaws and plodding bores all at once. Some, by the reckoning of old friends of the Angels like onetime Digger Peter Coyote, were thoughtful and personable, others outright sociopaths. By 1958, Barger was president of the Oakland chapter of the Hells Angels, and the club rented an old Victorian home they dubbed the Snake Pit. The place played host to an array of parties, meetings, and dances. The club's rules were limited but vigorously enforced: no fighting or swearing at club meetings, no Angels chapters within fifty miles of another chapter (the Bay Area, with two chapters, was a notable exception), and mandatory wearing of the Angels' patch.

The Angels had their own code, and their own patois. Club patches spoke a language of their own, communicating a rude intimacy with the demimonde. Their leather jackets were all emblazoned with the Angels' logo and their bottom rocker, a sewn-on patch identifying their local chapter. A "13" patch, worn by practically every member, indicated a taste for smoking marijuana. Red wings professed the Angel had performed oral sex on a menstruating woman; black wings suggested that he had had cunnilingus with an African-American woman.

Their standard kit could be personalized with earrings and belts made from motorcycle drive chains, and a motley assortment of Nazi paraphernalia purchased from flea markets and gun shops, mostly Luftwaffe gear and death's-head insignias. The Hells Angels were not neo-Nazis, although Barger himself betrayed a certain nostalgia for what he viewed as the discipline and rigor of Hitler's Germany. American Nazi leader George Lincoln Rockwell once approached Barger, suggesting he start a Nazi motorcycle corps for his party, but Barger demurred. Instead, they deliberately scorned the enforced propriety of the era, daring passersby and bourgeois liberals to be offended by their mockery.

The Angels would regularly adopt already existing motorcycle clubs into their fold, sometimes issuing polite invitations and at other times telling them to "wear our colors or no colors." Often, a select group of bikers from a particular club would drift away from the more milquetoast riders in their area and join forces with the Hells Angels. George Christie and Paul Hibbits had attended high school together in Ventura County, and hung out with a group of outlaw bikers known as the Question Marks. Then Hibbits got in trouble with the authorities and wound up fleeing to San Diego, where he

The Hells Angel known as Animal. Note the fox-fur hat perched atop his head.
(Courtesy of Robert Altman)

fell in with the Hells Angels. Hibbits would ultimately venture north to Oakland, to the heart of the Angels' California enterprise. There, he would become better known by another name: Animal. He would wind up playing a crucial role in the unraveling at Altamont.

In 1964 the group first made national headlines, when two members were arrested on rape charges in the beachside town of Monterey. The charges were eventually dismissed, but local newspapers were filled with shocked descriptions of criminal, deviant bikers, their unchecked licentiousness a threat to chaste American womanhood. The outlaw biker became a familiar figure in the American unconscious, feared and envied all at once.

The Hells Angels were hardasses with an occasional soft spot for stranded motorists or lone women. Many in the Bay Area had spotted them at the side of the road, pulling out jumper cables to help a stalled car, or escorting a woman home through the empty late-night streets, and been pleasantly surprised by their gallantry. Without their knowledge or assent, they became the adopted mascots of a counterculture about which they understood little. They were fêted as folk heroes, and included in the celebrations of a movement with its sights set on remaking the country in its enlightened, progressive image. Hunter S. Thompson introduced the Angels to Ken Kesey and his Merry Pranksters, who gave them their first taste of LSD. Thompson believed that the Hells Angels never understood their new friends, or their affection for bikers. They were just happy to be invited to the party.

Given their dress, their proclivities, and their general anti-authoritarian bent, there was an assumption in the air that the Angels and other outlaw groups were essentially hippies on bikes, but this was imprecise at best. The Hells Angels and other biker groups gladly formed alliances with the cultural wing of the counterculture while furiously rejecting its political beliefs. In that, they were representative of a fractured nation.

The country was deeply polarized, torn apart by raging arguments over the war in Vietnam, and over the place of African-Americans in American society. 1969 served as the culmination to a decade of ever-increasing schism. Lyndon Johnson's Great Society had collapsed under the weight of the morass of Vietnam. The preceding year, Richard Nixon had been elected president on the promise of a vague plan to end the war in Vietnam and a pledge of allegiance to the "silent majority" turned off by campus unrest and hungering for the return of law and order—understood to mean a clamp down on students and blacks.

The Republican Party, written off for dead after Barry Goldwater's blowout loss in 1964, had been revitalized, with Nixon peeling off Democrats' support among anti-civil-rights whites. "The Southern strategy," it was called, and it was the harbinger of the nation's fury: over the injustice of racism, or the gall of those who sought to demand their rights while hard-working Americans struggled to make ends meet. "The only consensus," observed Rick Perlstein in his history of the era, *Nixonland*, "was that the consensus was long gone."

Two groups of Americans faced off uncomprehendingly, each flummoxed and infuriated by the other's American dream. "What one side saw as liberation the other saw as apocalypse," argued Perlstein, "and what the other saw as apocalypse, the first saw as liberation." The New Left had seized the nation's attention, which was simultaneously attracted and repelled by the freedoms claimed by the young. Politicians surged in popularity by rhetorically thrashing the counterculture. A hippie, argued Governor Ronald Reagan of California, elected in part on his promises to crack down on Berkeley radicals, was someone "who dresses like Tarzan, has hair like Jane, and smells like Cheetah." The counterculture was ascendant, but the right, led by the likes of Nixon and George Wallace, launched a furious counterattack against what it saw as the potentially fatal threat to the country.

The two sides occupied different countries, with different populaces, different leaders, even different cultures. When one section of the country watched John Wayne symbolically win the Vietnam War in *The Green Berets*, the other, hipper half was, as Perlstein notes, on the next block watching *Wild in the Streets*, in which a rock star becomes president, gives fourteen-year-olds the vote, and places everyone over thirty in an internment camp. The American Dream had splintered into an array of competing fantasias.

"More and more Americans were forthrightly asserting visions of what a truly moral society would look like," argued Perlstein. "Unfortunately, their visions were irreconcilable." And frustration over the shared inability to impose that vision led to an increasing comfort with violence. By 1969, the unfulfilled expectations of the New Left had soured many activists on the possibilities of politics. Nonviolence was a sham, many believed, and the political process was an extended dodge intended to keep radicals from achieving change. Activist organizations like the Student Nonviolent Coordinating Committee and Students for a Democratic Society were succeeded by the Black Panthers and the Weathermen, each intent on proving their bona fides through the symbolic embrace of violence.

The violence, though, was not just metaphorical; it was increasingly present in the communities in which Americans found themselves. In May, Berkeley police had dropped tear gas from helicopters onto protesters demanding access to a spit of land belonging to the University of California they had dubbed the People's Park. Officers there had also shot a student named James Rector to death. Two days before Altamont, Chicago police had killed Black Panthers Fred Hampton and Mark Clark as they lay asleep in their beds. That week, indictments were handed down against Charles Manson and his followers in the deaths of Sharon Tate and four others in the Hollywood Hills. The state's repressive powers were matched by those of the increasingly combative left and the restive right.

Much of the media's attention focused on the splintering of the New Left, but right-wing violence, while often less explicitly ideological, was similarly devoted to delivering a message: that dissent was treason, that contrarian voices would be stifled.

For many Bay Area activists, their first interaction with this new vigilantism had come in October 1965. The Oakland chapter of the Angels, harbingers of a new wave of prowar, anti-counterculture violence, had broken through police lines and disrupted an anti–Vietnam War rally in Berkeley. They beat protesters mercilessly, calling them traitors and beatniks and tearing down their banners. "Go back to Russia, you fucking Communists!" the bikers shouted at the antiwar protesters. The territorial Angels saw themselves as protecting their city from the influx of Berkeley radicals, and were emboldened by the Oakland police's deliberate refusal to protect the protesters. The Hells Angels were the white lower-middle class and working class's spiritual avatars, lashing out physically where the others could only bluster helplessly.

The good tunes and free love and weed proffered by the hippies were all very welcome, but the antiwar rallies attended by many of those same hippies were anathema to many of the bikers. The protesters were cowards, they believed, love-bead-wearing pansies with weak constitutions, physically unfit for the rigors of war. And so the bikers increasingly became identified not as working-class men or veterans, but as a motorized corps intent on dispensing free-floating violence, or at least the impression of same, to their ideological enemies.

Barger once sent a letter to President Lyndon Johnson, offering his comrades' assistance in defeating the North Vietnamese, but the Angels generally betrayed little interest in international geopolitics.

They were haphazardly engaged, primarily enthused about opportunities to wreak havoc. When they gave it any thought, Thompson argued, the club and its members loosely aligned with the unapologetically bigoted ultraconservatism of groups like the John Birch Society and the Ku Klux Klan. And yet, he went on to note, "they are blind to the irony of their role . . . knight errants of a faith from which they have already been excommunicated. The Angels will be among the first to be locked up or croaked if the politicians they think they agree with ever come to power."

The Angels were hardly the only ones to take up arms against the New Left—there were, at roughly the same time, bombings of counterculture groups and newspapers in New York and Berkeley, murders of pacifists in Richmond, Virginia, and more—but they were a reminder that this sotto voce civil war was, as much as anything else, a class conflict, pitting working-class and lower-middle-class conservatives and ultraconservatives against middle-class radicals. Revenge would be taken for the presumptions of the students.

The Hells Angels were vulgar fascists, bored by ideology or doctrine but loosely espousing a belief in order and the rule of force and the inherent transformative force of technology. "The Angels are prototypes," Thompson argued. "Their lack of education has not only rendered them completely useless in a highly technical economy, but it has also given them the leisure to cultivate a powerful resentment . . . and to translate it into a destructive cult which the mass media insists on portraying as a sort of isolated oddity."

No one was badly injured at the Oakland rally, but the day's events galvanized the Berkeley political set. There were genuine enemies within, intent on establishing their patriotic bona fides at the expense of the counterculture. The Angels eventually issued a statement that they would avoid attending, or being in close proximity to, future antiwar rallies because "our patriotic concern for what these people are doing to our great nation may provoke us to violent acts." The Angels, inconsistent as ever, were politically apolitical. They chose to stay out of politics because they were too moved by political issues to stay calm. Moreover, the wording of the statement reflected the Hells Angels' self-image as defenders, not instigators. They would not assault demonstrators, but might nonetheless be provoked to violence by the demonstrators' outrages.

Much of this burgeoning conservatism came from what the Angels and other groups perceived as a governmental attack on bikers. In 1966, the federal government requested that states write their own laws requiring the use of helmets while riding motorcycles. Many motorcyclists, including the Angels, were aghast at the government's seeking to regulate their passion, and took an impassioned stance against the proposed helmet laws. America was a land of freedom, they argued, and as proponents of a furious individualism, they refused to be boxed in by bureaucracy. Their anti-regulation campaign dovetailed nicely with the burgeoning conservative movement, which also sought to limit governmental intrusion into private affairs. Moreover, conservatism's impassioned defense of the war in Vietnam aligned with many bikers' belief in American exceptionalism and military might. To ride a bike was to be free, and freedom had to be defended at all costs.

As loath as they were to talk about it, bikers were often the products of broken childhoods, meager lives, and diminished ambitions. Riding a motorcycle made them feel strong in a world that insisted on their weakness. Associating with a motorcycle club held prestige, too. To ride with a club was to be part of a confederation of real men. Clubs like the Hells Angels were strict about their membership in part to emphasize the desirability of joining, but also to maintain a barrier between themselves and the world they scorned. They were a family, but one that defined itself in opposition to all those other bland families.

The emblem of the new, useless man described by Thompson was a young biker named Alan Passaro. His father, Michael, was an Italian immigrant who had lifted himself up in the world. Michael was the proud owner of a barbershop in San Jose and property back home in his native Italy. His son had dreams of being a lawyer, a force in the world—anything, in fact, other than a barber. But the law required an academic diligence that Alan could not quite muster.

When high school came to an end in 1967, he enrolled in a barber college. He met his girlfriend Celeste while they were both in high school in Santa Clara, and now she, too, prepared for a life of scissors and hair clippings and dryers, taking classes at beauty school. Alan had been the boy she met in art class, the one who made pocket money by painting nativity scenes on the windows of local gas stations. Now, here they both were, in love but on the fast track to lives they did not truly want.

Passaro had a job at a barbershop in Milpitas, north of San Jose, and he and Celeste got married. They bought a two-bedroom house in San Jose. They were living their own modest version of the American dream, and yet for Alan, it did not feel like enough. He found drinking and drugs, elemental American distractions, and then came something even better. Motorcycles were loud, brutal, masculine, unflinching—everything he saw as missing from his milquetoast life. He got himself a Harley-Davidson, chopped it to his specifications, and made a new frame for it. He joined the Gypsy Jokers, a motorcycle club in San Jose. Celeste was not enamored of the motorcycle, or the club, but was pleased her husband had found a pastime. He was a father now, and his newborn son Michael (named after his immigrant father, the barber) needed him clean, needed him present. If motorcycles would smooth the way, it was a welcome diversion.

Soon, Bob Roberts, the president of the San Francisco chapter of the Hells Angels, approached the Gypsy Jokers. If they would voluntarily give up their colors, he offered, he would enroll them en masse as a new San Jose chapter of the Angels. They agreed, and handed over their colors. They were stunned when the Angel leadership summarily turned them down for membership. Roberts, seeking to salvage a fraught situation, told the disappointed former Gypsy Jokers that all sixty of them should come to San Francisco that week for a chapter meeting. There, they would all be accepted as prospects in the San Francisco chapter of the Hells Angels, on the way to full membership.

Roberts saw the new prospects as having already demonstrated their bona fides through their loyalty to their new club. Nonetheless, a certain process would have to be followed. The club was like a fraternity, and there would be some hazing before anyone could become a full-fledged member. Some of it was long-standing Angel practice. The new Hells Angel would attend his initiation in brand-new jeans, and a sleeveless jean jacket with a Hells Angel emblem sewed onto the back. Then he would take them off, and the members would dump a bucket of shit and piss onto the unsoiled clothing, taking care to trudge and plod over them until the filth was irredeemably caked into the fabric. The soiled clothes were the initiate's new uniform, the daily costume of the new Hells Angel.

But there were also smaller tests. Roberts would ask men to go to the pharmacy and pick up tampons for his girlfriend. It was intended to be demeaning, a diminishment of his manhood, to do so, and any red-blooded man would be well within his rights to reject such a task. The men who unblinkingly followed orders, though, would most likely become full-fledged Hells Angels. Masculine bluster and paeans to freedom were the public face of the Hells Angels, but to become a member, such matters had to be put aside, and unquestioning fealty was the order of the day.

For Passaro, though, becoming a prospect, even a Hells Angels prospect, was a demotion in status, one that would have to be remedied by diligence and faithfulness. "I will prove that I'm good," he told Roberts, intent on demonstrating his devotion. When they were not out riding or tinkering with their bikes, the San Francisco Angels liked to hang out at a pool hall on Hay Street. Many of them had grown proficient enough at the game that they had purchased their own cues, which they would bring along with them to the pool hall, and elsewhere.

Try as he might, the straight and narrow eluded Passaro. He had been arrested in 1963 when still a teenager, accused of stealing a car. In May 1968, he was arrested on automobile theft charges once more, and discovered to have marijuana in his pockets. Passaro, like the young man with whom he would soon be forever conjoined, seemed to live in the revolving door between the bedroom and the jail cell, freedom and incarceration. He grew long hair, a beard, a droopy mustache. The look was emblematic of the Angels, but also a symbolic severing of his ties with his past. Who would go to a longhair barber for a trim?

His understanding of who he was changed on becoming a Hells Angel. "I tried all that straight shit, and it wasn't me," he later said. "All my life I wanted to be a Hell's Angel. Like some dudes want to be lawyers and some dudes want to be barbers, I wanted to be an Angel. I can't tell you why. How do you describe love?"

The Hells Angels were a fraternity, a guild of true men, and Passaro desperately wanted to be accepted, to be the truest of the true. Pleasing his new masters, though, meant letting down the woman he had pledged to spend his life with. His relationship with Celeste grew rocky. Alan loved his son Michael, and cared for his wife, but the club came first. Alan ended up moving out of the home they had purchased, crashing on his fellow biker Dennis Montoya's couch. He and Celeste were still close, but they needed some breathing room while each figured out what they wanted from life.

The Hells Angels were proudly exclusionary. There were no women in their ranks, and they were unblinking in their racial preferences. The Hells Angels attracted the bikers too raw, too devil-may-care even for other outlaw groups. For many Angels and Angels-to-be, the bikers were attractive primarily as defenders of an ironclad racial hierarchy. The Hells Angels had a long history of violent outbursts against African-Americans. In one incident reported in Thompson's book, a fight had broken out between some Angels and a seven-foot-tall African-American biker from a rival club. They claimed that he had pulled a knife, and beat him mercilessly while attempting to subdue him. No knife was ever found, and the police let the matter go, seemingly content with the Angels' explanation.

The Angels defined themselves as rip-roaring symbols of white, working-class macho vigor. They were threatened by expressions of black power, whether from rival motorcycle club members, the civil-rights movement, or the Black Panthers, then popular in the black neighborhoods of Oakland. They never expressed it quite so bluntly, but for the Angels, to be black was to be lesser, and any attempt to reorient the balance of power was viewed as an affront. The Angels' long history of violence against African-Americans demonstrated that belief, with fists and boots and pool cues and knives doing the work of reminding them who was boss.

While many saw them as the counterculture's police force, and others noted their propensity for fisticuffs with the authorities, it was possible to see the police and biker gangs like the Hells Angels as fundamentally allied. Bikers and cops may have regularly done battle, but both saw themselves as protectors of order in the communities they patrolled. Each identified a common enemy against whom they stood in unison. The police and the bikers may have squabbled like brothers, but they likely would have agreed that the political radicals, and the African-American community, were common threats.

Biker-led attacks on African-Americans often met with a muted response from the police. Many believed that the Angels and other biker groups functioned as a first line of defense against African-Americans, an unacknowledged paramilitary force. "There were blacks raping our kids, our women," Bob Roberts, the leader of the Angels' San Francisco chapter, would later argue in defense of the Angels' rearguard work. Roberts would walk the length of Page Street, in the Haight, wearing a HUEY P. NEWTON button covered in etched notches affixed to his jacket as a provocation. Each notch stood for a black man he had assaulted in his self-declared mission to clean up the streets of his neighborhood.

An incident that had taken place in San Francisco in September 1969 underscored the Angels' unpredictability, and helped to explain why they were perpetual targets of police surveillance. Moreover, it offered clear evidence of the Hells Angels' racist predilections. On the night of September 8, the SFPD had received a report that three bikers were assaulting a group of African-Americans outside the Angels' clubhouse at 715 Ashbury Street. Police came to the scene, and spotted two men pushing a brown 1959 Pontiac down the street, letting it coast unassisted down a hill. They approached and arrested the two men.

One of the men, Ron Segely, attempted to run, and was knocked to the ground by the police. The second man, already cuffed, sought to choke a police officer with his handcuffs, and was also subdued. Then the bikers massed inside 715 Ashbury took notice of the commotion and emerged. There were forty-five or fifty men, along with an unstated number of women, and they began to pull the police officers off their friends. The Angels told the cops that they had guns and were willing to shoot them to protect their brothers. The police officers pulled their guns, and the bikers and their friends dashed back inside. The SFPD wound up arresting twenty-one men and fifteen women that night, including Segely and Roberts.

The three African-American victims told the police that they lived down the block from the Angels' clubhouse, at 709 Ashbury. They had seen the bikers congregated on the street and approached them, asking "What's happening?" One unidentified Angel had responded by throwing a can of beer at their windshield, and then twelve Hells Angels gathered to pummel their car. They hit the windows with tire irons, breaking the front and back windows, and assaulted the three passengers. When the victims fled, they gave chase, running after them for two blocks. Having failed to catch them, three of the bikers came back to the Pontiac, pushing it away from the Angels' clubhouse and allowing it to drift down the street and crash. Racially motivated antipathy and a misguided desire to protect their space had seemingly compelled the Angels to assault African-American bystanders without provocation.

Sonny Barger argued that the swastikas on the Hells Angels' helmets were mere decoration, with no political significance, but the Angels' behavior indicated a certain affinity for authoritarianism, and for those inclined to take a stand against minority rabble-rousers. The Hells Angels saw themselves as the tip of the spear defending their communities against all potential infractions from African-Americans. It was not accidental that Barger, in his memoir, observed that there had been little crime in the East Oakland neighborhood where he had been raised, shortly followed by his noting that "few blacks lived in East Oakland."

There were two distinct views of the Hells Angels, and of bikers in general, neither entirely accurate. In the first, they were icons of a purer American spirit, their sangfroid and restlessness emblematic of the country's pioneer ethic and its exploration of unknown frontiers. While the rest of the country had grown fatally limp, the Hells Angels still roared across the nation's highways, in search of freedom. In the second, the Hells Angels were beasts with the powers of demigods. They were the dark spirit of Richard Nixon's Silent Majority, a paramilitary force of racist, ultraconservative revanchists intent on stifling dissent and fomenting chaos. The Angels were bits of both, but many of them were also working stiffs with day jobs as machinists and factory workers, and family men with wives and children and mortgages. They were average working-class white men with an interest in motorcycle riding who were so enamored of the masculine, steely, unfettered style embodied by the Hells Angels that they took it for their own.

To be a Hells Angel was to play a role. It was to be the baddest, toughest, most daring, most amoral, manliest man in any room, ready to fight any man or fuck any woman, to be up for any challenge that came their way. They were actors who wore their costumes morning and night, their masks eventually hardening until they had fused with their faces. The Angels performed a role for public consumption and private amusement. The mainstream media were horrified by the Hells Angels, seeing them as the embodiment of all that was wrong with the growing dropout culture, but the Angels could not have taken the form they did without the express approval, and fascination, of the cultural establishment. They needed the media's attention, and even its alarm. They were bogeymen, and demanded to be celebrated and demonized as such. The role fit them like a second skin. "The Angels play the role seven days a week: they wear their colors at home, on the street and sometimes even to work; they ride their bikes to the neighborhood grocery for a quart of milk," wrote Thompson. "An Angel without his colors feels naked and vulnerable—like a knight without his armor."

For all the attention they received, there were surprisingly few Hells Angels in the Bay Area. By the mid-1960s, there were only about 150 Angels in the region, split into chapters in San Francisco, Oakland, and elsewhere. This was due in part to the care the Angels took in selecting new members, with a long and rigorous screening process. It also reflected the Angels' outsized media presence, which gave off a whiff of a shadow army when it was more like an overgrown club.

When the Hells Angels received the call from the planners of a Rolling Stones concert, the rough outline sounded familiar: another free show in Golden Gate Park, much like the ones they had worked for the Grateful Dead, Jefferson Airplane, and others. Everyone involved—the performers, the bikers, and the audience—would likely already be familiar with the venue. The Angels' responsibilities would be minimal, and even with the substantially larger crowds expected, the Stones show would likely involve nothing more than keeping potential mischief-makers away from the generators.

Then the concert venue changed, first to Sears Point, and then to the Altamont Speedway. The chaotic planning left little time to reassess the arrangements already in place, and so the Hells Angels, fixtures of the San Francisco scene, were carried along to the outer reaches of Alameda County, to a place they did not know, and fans they had never met, under what would prove to be unpredictable, anarchic conditions.

Part Two

UNRAVELING

5. The Outer Circle

Fans stood near the entrance to Altamont, anxiously awaiting the opportunity to pounce on an open gate and stream inside. Some had slept in the junked cars that littered the speedway. For at least one couple, the backseat of a rusted Plymouth provided enough privacy for a rushed sexual encounter. At last, dawn came and the speedway opened to admit the crowds, many of whom had spent the night unprofitably seeking sleep outside its gates. An enormous mass of young people began pouring through, wine bottles and joints and LSD tabs gripped in their hands along with their blankets and coolers, resembling nothing so much as an invading army intent on occupying enemy territory.

The line of fans awaiting entry stretched over one hill, and down the next, rise after rise covered with anxious, exuberant concertgoers. To some, they already looked like refugees: tired, bedraggled, and trudging toward a final destination they could only hope was akin to paradise.

One instantly recognizable man carried a sack over his shoulders, like a hippie Johnny Appleseed. He would reach into his sack as each fan passed his way, and hand them a fistful of pills. The concertgo-ers swallowed the mystery pills without finding out what they were, trusting a stranger not to take advantage of their innocent hunger for temporary release from their bodies.

Streams of people poured in through every possible entrance to the speedway, some by car, and others on foot. People abandoned their cars at any wide spot in the highway, sensing that they could get no closer. The new 580 freeway leading from just north of San Francisco to the eastern reaches of Alameda County, still not fully open to the public, became a massive parking lot, with parked cars filling each of its four lanes for miles. Helicopters flying over the site could make out an endless line of cars stopped on the side of the freeway, beginning as far as eight miles away. Each parked car led to dozens of imitators, with drivers sure that others knew something they didn't. Fans parked miles away and trekked on foot through the brisk Saturday morning air, in search of rock 'n' roll utopia. The California Highway Patrol, in a vengeful mood at the incursion of so many hippies, lurked just behind them, ready to begin towing fans' improperly parked cars.

Locals from the nearby town of Livermore drifted over in pickup trucks, promising to usher fans directly to the concert over secret back roads for $5 a pop. Some fans walked along the nearby railroad tracks, sure they would lead to the speedway. Instead, their route took them through the Altamont Pass and beyond it, stranding them on the far side of the speedway. "For once, we're just gonna let it happen," said one of the concert organizers, making his peace with the total lack of coordination over the parking. "If for no other rea-son, for experimental purposes."

Only the night before, the concert had still felt like a privately shared secret. Only the diehards, the professionals, and the true believers had trekked east to Livermore on Friday. Now it was

Saturday, and everyone knew that there would soon be hundreds of thousands of people here.

The country was experiencing, as Morris Dickstein would later characterize it, a new great awakening. After a long era of spiritual lassitude, of emotional frostbite, a new generation was awaking to the glories of the transcendent. New sects formed daily, each professing a direct link to the ineffable. But their devoted followers were found in no church, took no officially sanctioned communion.

A generation of young American men and women had grown up in unparalleled, unprecedented affluence, the beneficiaries of a generation that had overcome a depression and defeated the Nazis—and were disappointed in their patrimony. The older generation, having experienced chaos, wanted nothing but order; their children, having had their fill of order, craved a taste of chaos.

In the mid-1960s, the demographic bulge of postwar children known as the Baby Boomers began to come of age. The youth of America saw themselves as the avant-garde of a coming revolution. No more of the stultifying political consensus of their childhoods. No more of the polite lies of craven art. Everything would have to be reassessed, rethought, remodeled. Nothing was exempt. The model of a middle-class American life—birth, education, employment, marriage, child-rearing, retirement, death—was being rejected by a new generation who demanded something else, something new.

The burgeoning culture of youth loosely split into two overlapping communities. For one, the horrors of racism and the hated Vietnam War demanded an immediate about-face in American politics. They formed groups that argued for a more inclusive, more tolerant, less imperially minded United States, and they agitated fiercely for those ideals. They held conferences and marches and sit-ins and protests.

For the other, a better world was to come from within, not without. The solutions were not to be unearthed in any state capitol or judicial chamber, but inside the self. They discovered marijuana and LSD, found Eastern religions, worshipped in the new youth cathedral of rock 'n' roll. Music was the sound of self-expression, of a generation hungering for experience.

The two wings of youth culture frequently collaborated, their overlapping interests and membership prompting a shared set of ideals and interests, and a shared language. The hippies attended antiwar protests, and the politicos smoked joints and listened to Jefferson Airplane. But the new youth culture was less a unified opposition than a mass of splinter groups ultimately selling conflicting visions of the world. The competition was more than a duel between competing philosophies; it was an argument about how to change the world.

The counterculture was about many disparate, often contradictory things—rock music, copious drugs, political change, newfound sexual freedoms—but it was also about the magic of physical proximity. A rock concert, like a demonstration or an acid test, was an excuse to stand together, to crowd shoulder to shoulder, to be near other young men and women who believed in the destiny of their culture to change the world.

These gatherings were substitute church services for a new generation uninterested in what they saw as the stale truths of tradition. From Ken Kesey's Acid Tests, where the Kool-Aid was spiked with LSD, to the massive antiwar teach-in at UC Berkeley, to the Human Be-In at Golden Gate Park, to the March on Washington and the protests at the 1968 Democratic National Convention in Chicago, to the concerts at Golden Gate Park and Monterey and Woodstock, young people spilled out of doors to express their profound belief in one thing above all: each other.

Each concert—each gathering—was bigger than its predecessor, and each one was a further step along the path to eventual triumph. Everyone knew it. No one wanted to miss a moment. Whether a political rally or an outdoor concert, each new feat offered further proof that there was strength in numbers. Each event was a reminder that the youth of America were not alone, that others were breaking free of the chains of family and obligation and custom that had once bound them. "The utopian meanings might be disputed," wrote Todd Gitlin, one of the fans on his way to the concert that morning, "but it was hard to miss the fact that the young everywhere seemed to be deserting their scripts."

They were not in agreement about what ills needed most immediate mending, or how best to achieve their goals, but there was a shared trust in the wisdom of crowds. Individuals gathered together, whether for a worthy cause or merely for the cause of pleasure, and in so doing they created temporary communities of immense power. This was the heart of the counterculture, the soul of the 1960s. People, together, could move mountains.

The very size of the crowd was a message to be delivered. Altamont was to be universal and parochial, all at once. Everyone gathered once more as a demonstration of the raw power of the counterculture, its steady, unstoppable blossoming. This was happening everywhere, all at once, an ongoing celebration of youth of which this was to be the latest and most glittering demonstration.

The sparsely decorated speedway offered little in the way of ornamentation. A few banners and pennants had been hastily hung up, and a giant plastic dome had been erected by some fans, who invited their fellow concertgoers to step inside their homemade bubble.

Cameramen working for the Maysles brothers were out around dawn to catch the first rays of the morning sun, and the first stirrings of the Woodstock Nation. Young men were slumped over on their way to the porta-potties, and couples wandered about, looking to scrounge up some breakfast. Concertgoers who had planned ahead and packed well broke out picnic baskets while others played catch. Revelers wandered the grounds with sacks of wine already bursting loose from bags, and an endless stream of concertgoers streamed over the hill, in search of a spot to sit and see the bands.

So much of one's experience of Altamont would be geographic, dependent on the conditions on the freeway at the moment of approach to the speedway, or the exact location in the crowd where you wearily plopped down with your supplies for the day. As with any concert of this scope, most of the audience was too far away from the stage to see any of the unrest taking place, nor could they hear many of the announcements being broadcast over the loud-speakers. It would be clear to many that something was off with the concert, given the perpetual interruptions to the show and the thin sound that hardly carried to the farthest reaches of the speedway, but most fans could grasp little more.

Altamont was a story of two concerts. The first, disorganized and haphazard, was nonetheless mostly peaceable. The second was not. The outer circle had little idea of the wildly differing experiences of the inner circle, and would not learn more about that other concert until after they had returned home. The fundamental distinction was this: the fans close enough to the stage to interact with the Hells Angels, or watch their interactions with others, attended a very different show, with very different implications and consequences, than those who maintained some distance from the Angels.

All it took was two hundred feet. The length of one city block. In the normal course of urban life, alert pedestrians would easily be able to spot a disturbance taking place on the next block. But the overwhelming crowding near the stage meant that even two hundred feet was enough to render much of the day's unrest invisible. And the fans yet further back, sitting on the gentle slopes of the

Balloons rising above the Altamont crowd. (Courtesy of Jay Siegel)

speedway, or far off in the distance, could make out nothing beyond a handful of indistinguishable blips. The outer circle comprised the overwhelming majority of the fans in attendance at Altamont, but their perspective was distinctly limited. They could only see what happened directly in front of them.

The first stream of rock 'n' roll migrants made their way inside, and began unfurling blankets and setting up picnic baskets. Everyone was hungry for adventure, hungry for experience, and sure that they were shortly to witness history in the making.

For many fans, a dazzling multiplicity of stories, of overlapping beliefs and ideals and fixations, all fruitfully commingled. Coffee-can lids were being repurposed as Frisbees. Babies were being born, couples were forming and congealing, and donations were being solicited for the Black Panther defense fund by a bubbly blonde Doris Day lookalike, who told onlookers that "after all, they're just Negroes, you know."

Many of the fans wound up settling in for the day in resting places remote from the stage and enjoyed themselves thoroughly. There was sunshine and companionship and good cheer and alcohol and marijuana and other stimulants. There were few serviceable bathrooms and little food available for purchase, but the promised mellow vibes were genuine, for at least some of the attendees. Their pleasure, though, was predicated on their ignorance of events taking place elsewhere at the speedway.

Joan Churchill joined them, relieved to at last be able to find some comfort and get to her job filming the free Rolling Stones show. The sun shined, people smiled, and the unpleasant night was forgotten, an affordable down payment on what would undoubtedly be a memorable day.

Churchill had been up the entire night of December 5. She had shivered through the frigid December night, alone and abandoned outside the Rolling Stones' concert site. The Maysles brothers had assured her that after her work documenting the stage's construction was completed, she would be ushered into a secure area to sleep. The security guards standing watch near the stage chuckled at her when she approached expecting to be let in: "Nobody gets in here until eight o'clock tomorrow morning." Churchill had neglected to bring warm clothing, food, or drink. She spent a sleepless night outdoors, cold, hungry, and thirsty.

That morning, Churchill found some of her colleagues, who suggested she head all the way to the other side of the raceway and film fans arriving in their cars and walking toward the site. Her camera bag slung over her shoulder, she made her way through the never-ending mass of attendees along with cinematographer Baird Bryant and sound operator Peter Pilafian, taking in the sheer enormity of the scene before her. There had never been anything like this before in the Bay Area. Even the Human Be-In of January 1967, where tens of thousands of young hippies had crammed into Golden Gate Park to listen to the likes of Timothy Leary and Allen Ginsberg (along with scheduled performers Jefferson Airplane and the Grateful Dead), had been pitifully small in comparison.

Churchill, still hungry and thirsty after her sleepless night outside the concert gates, accepted anything and everything proffered by the outstretched arms of anonymous fans while she trekked to her new vantage point. She stopped in at the equipment tent with Bryant and Pilafian, and a longhaired, shirtless hippie in cutoff jeans offered a slug from an open bottle of wine. Churchill and her colleagues happily drank. Everyone was so jolly, the sun was shining at last, and excitement was in the air. Everything was free, and everything was joyous. A society could be constructed out of mutual pleasure and kindness.

After pushing her way through the swarming crowds to the other side of the speedway, Churchill finally found an optimal spot for shooting near one of the Altamont entrances, and set up her camera. She pulled out her Spectra light meter to assess the quality of the light, and was taken aback to discover rainbows shooting out of its aperture. "I've been dosed," she muttered to herself. Churchill had had some experience with psychedelics in the past, enough to know it was something she did not want to try again. And now here she was, having been hired for one of the most important professional gigs of her career, facing a lengthy, disorienting trip she had no interest in taking. She had been dosed with LSD. There was no way of knowing just who the culprit had been, but word spread throughout the day of wine spiked with acid.

Churchill panicked, acutely aware that her fragile consciousness would soon be swarmed by hallucinations and visions. She expended the last of her waning energy making her way back to the stage, where she hoped she might find some of her colleagues setting up to shoot the bands. Churchill frantically searched the stage and located her boyfriend and fellow cinematographer, Eric Saarinen, at stage right. She lurched toward him. He was standing on the ground near the corner of the stage, and she crawled under the stage platform, gratefully clinging to his legs as wave after wave of drug-fueled paranoia began to wash over her. Churchill would have an accidental, unwanted front-row seat for much of the pandemonium that would follow.

The music had only just begun, as Santana warmed up the crowd with a zippy rendition of "Evil Ways," but some concertgoers had begun to sense something notably off in Altamont's atmosphere. An ugly feeling hung in the air, born, perhaps, of the copious drugs, and a desire to imitate the magic of Woodstock with all too much precision. If the media narrative of Woodstock had been about taking your clothes off and dancing, then attendees at Altamont would also take their clothes off and dance.

Sometime that morning, one of the Maysles cinematographers filmed an enormous bubble drifting through the crowd, skirting numerous daunting impediments to its survival. The bubble stopped in midair, betraying all the laws of physics, and temporarily stood still, beautiful but terribly fragile.

For those fans positioned an impossible distance from the stage, the musical element of the day was chaotic and inconsistent. The music was so far away as to be rendered almost irrelevant. The show, such as it was, was an afterthought. Many fans could barely make out the music, and were either frustrated by the poor sound or doing their best to enjoy a day of community and communion in its absence.

For the outer circle, the concert did not offer much in the way of actual songs. In its absence, much of the crowd found solace, or entertainment, in drugs. Altamont was, as much as anything else, a clash of differing drugs. Many of the hippies in the crowd were on

LSD, which, when taken in moderate doses, could soften edges and give users a warm glow of love and community. LSD transported its users to a sweeter, more vibrant world of imagination, with every sensation heightened, intense, beautiful. But the concertgoers hardly limited themselves to LSD. "Hashish, LSD, psilocybin," a dealer called out to the crowd, offering his wares to all passersby. Two men in dirty serapes wore cowboy hats with small white cards advertising their merchandise: "Acid $2."

A shirtless African-American man put on an impromptu medicine show for a cheering crowd: "I have in my hands one little purple tab of 100 percent pure LSD. Who wants this cosmic jewel?" This was not exclusively a peace-and-love crowd, and the concert was shaping up to be a full-on bacchanalia. The outer circle of Altamont, blissfully unaware of the violence within, was still wracked by the chaos caused by rampant drug use. Whether because of bad acid, individual excess, or some combination, fans overindulged, and reaped the consequences. There was a lack of control on display, and a desire to lose control, and the two in conjunction made for a concert often marked—even for those at the edges of the speedway—by bedlam.

The audience had proven itself incapable of looking after itself. Where had the forethought been when planning for attending the show? Couples at the show with their babies, taking acid. Pregnant women rendered totally immobile by the crush of people. There was such a thing as too much trust, and too many of the people at Altamont seemed to exhibit a blind faith in the goodwill of others and the organizational abilities of the behind-the-scenes impresarios of rock 'n' roll. Community, for many of the people in attendance, meant a casual assumption that all would be orderly, all would come together, all would be harmonious.

During the afternoon, as Jefferson Airplane, the Flying Burrito Brothers, and Crosby, Stills, Nash & Young took the stage in the far-off distance to little enthusiasm or awareness from the fans in the outer circle, reports of LSD overdoses were widespread, with people regularly approaching the stage to plead with concert organizers to warn people away from the acid. One man came forward hoping to track down a man who had gotten separated from his wife and child while on an acid trip. A Hells Angel had stepped on the child, and there was serious, if momentary, concern for the child's life.

Sam Cutler, guarding the stage from unwanted mood-killers, was having none of it: "We're not making any personal announcements; we've told people where lost and found is, we've told people where the Red Cross is. There will be no personal announcements. I don't care if you die; there's not going to be an announcement." Cutler was ghoulishly intent on preserving the fragile good cheer. As he told another potential complainant, "If you lay successive numbers of bummers on this crowd, by the time six o'clock comes around, they are going to be in a real mood. I'm not prepared to lay bum trips on 150,000 people."

Terrified, Joan Churchill reeled from her own blind faith in strangers and horrified by what had been done to her. She looked down at her hands, and believed she could see the veins under her skin, pumping blood through her body. The veins would then turn into colors, pinwheeling into the sky. She was panicked and exhausted, bearing down on the shredded remains of her tranquility in a desperate effort to tamp down the hallucinations. She wanted to stay as calm as possible and keep away the LSD-infused demons nipping at her heels.

LSD had turned the concert into an assault of aural and corporeal terrors, some real and some imagined. Were the sights all around her the hallucinations of an acid trip, or real? Churchill squeezed her eyes shut, hoping to block out the exterior world and grit her way through this nightmare, but every time she opened them, the vision of some new assault gripped her afresh. Even with her eyes closed, the tattoo of clomping feet onstage, directly above her head, drummed into her brain. And when she opened her eyes, it looked like the end of the world. It seemed wisest to close her eyes again, grip her boyfriend's hand, and wish for time to pass more quickly.

Some of the acid making its way through the crowd was tainted, and many attendees were soon suffering from the same private torments as Joan Churchill. They writhed in agony on the speedway ground, or were led by concerned friends to the medical tent for treatment. They lay down, helplessly flailing their arms in the air, clearly going through the horrors of a bad trip. One acid casualty's bad trip had him dreaming of an impending Armageddon: "We are all going to die, we are all going to die, right here, right here, we've been tricked!" And there was a noticeable lack of compassion toward those suffering concertgoers. One woman, writhing in the dirt, was absentmindedly kicked and stepped on by oblivious attendees insistent that she was "working out her trip." Dozens of LSD cases crouched underneath the stage, their eyes flashing white in the darkness. It seemed like every few feet, someone was handing out chocolate laced with acid, or coffee with LSD already stirred in like so many packets of Sweet'N Low. Nothing was to be trusted.

Churchill would not be the day's only acid casualty. Who would dose other unsuspecting concertgoers with LSD? The impulse was perverse, and yet of a piece with the drug culture of the late 1960s. The lowered inhibitions of Altamont, and the sense of a shared, quasi-magical communal experience, encouraged a small handful of concertgoers to violate others' personal and mental space, with terrifying, if mostly temporary, results. Much of the dialogue around psychedelics revolved around their mind-expanding properties. Acid would make you a better, kinder, more empathetic person, so true believers in the magic of psychedelics might have believed themselves to be doing others a favor by sharing their bounty.

The visual evidence assembled by the Maysleses' crews often indicated otherwise, with drug-addled concertgoers invading others' personal space, harassing and assaulting bystanders in their blissed-out states. The cameras would record LSD takers roaring incoherently, clawing at their friends' faces, and flopping bonelessly on the ground.

When the acid cases began to reach the medical tent, up on a rise west of the stage, they were mostly cared for by Dr. Frank Schoenfeld, volunteering at Altamont for the day. Schoenfeld, still a medical resident, had made a name for himself in the Bay Area by working at the Haight Ashbury Free Clinic, where he had ministered to all manner of drug-related casualties. Schoenfeld and his colleagues were taken aback by the sheer number of cases that came their way, with a trickle at the very beginning of the day turning into a gusher by midafternoon. Concertgoers were indiscriminately taking drugs that had been given to them by unknown others. They did not know what they had taken, nor were they sure how much they had consumed. Schoenfeld and the other doctors in the medical tent grew increasingly concerned, unsure what drugs were being used at the concert, or what their potency might be. Moreover, many patients reported having taken cocktails of drugs, mixing psychedelics with marijuana or amphetamines, or drinking wine on top of a tab of LSD. The baking heat of the midday sun likely also played a role in the condition of many visitors to the medical tent.

The initial plan was to screen arrivals, rapidly assess their condition, and determine a course of treatment. Others would make their way to a tent just off the stage, where individuals incapable of reaching the medical tent could be brought. As the day progressed, and his caseload got bigger, Schoenfeld realized that he was wasting too much of his time hiking down to the secondary tent and seeing individual patients, and the plan was abandoned. There was more than enough work here.

By the end of the day, Schoenfeld and his fellow residents had seen upward of two hundred cases. Where earlier in the day most of the patients were treated with a few moments of personal attention and a gentle tug in the direction of reality, the new wave of casualties required more forceful intervention. One young man came in terrified, entirely unaware of where he was, deeply paranoid and combative. Another—Schoenfeld thought he might have been a teacher—said he had taken as many as six good-sized doses of LSD, and was crawling in the dirt, entirely unreachable by the medical staff. A rapid intervention with medication was enough to help these and other more serious cases, but Schoenfeld was unsettled by their prevalence. He had expected to assist naïve types who got in over their heads, but there were clearly experienced drug users here who were wildly overdoing it, too.

Altamont wanted to be Woodstock, and those in attendance wanted to take a page out of Woodstock's playbook. For some, Woodstock was a political statement, a program to be honored and implemented at its West Coast doppelgänger. Berkeley political activist Frank Bardacke and his friends, who called themselves (shades of the French Revolution) the Committee on Public Safety, wandered the crowd, looking to keep merchants from plying their wares at a celebration meant to be about all that was free. Other radicals took issue with some men selling old Stones concert programs, knocking over their table and telling them, "Better give the stuff away, man, or we'll rip it off in the name of the people."

Bardacke saw the merchants as a symbolic representation of the old guard they were attempting to overthrow. Others might have read Bardacke's half-hearted protest as indicative of something unthinking in the counterculture's consensus. Why did Woodstock have to be aped down to the last detail? And why did the need for ideological purity, for sacred space, trump others' rights to engage in the most vanilla brand of commerce?

The regular interruptions in the music, and the hortatory announcements from the stage, added to the sense that not everyone was enjoying themselves. But it was too hard to see anything. And the sound was so poor that all many fans took in were the interruptions in the bands' performances. The thin sound felt as if it were coming from an impossible distance, and would regularly cut out for minutes at a time before abruptly returning. For some, this was the source of the gnawing feeling in the pit of their stomachs. Something was off—terribly off—but no one could quite say what. Some refugees from the inner circle made their way to the margins, laden with reports of the pandemonium below, but only a small handful of fans heard the news. For many others, this was just another glorious day out. No one was entirely sure what had happened to the Grateful Dead, who had been supposed to perform, but with the Rolling Stones still to play, the best was undoubtedly yet to come.

And the listeners at home were ill-informed about the chaos as well. Stefan Ponek, reporting for KSAN to all the listeners at home in San Francisco, Berkeley, and Oakland, had been calling in to the station all afternoon. He had been reporting on the glorious, Woodstock-like atmosphere, the good vibes, the great music, talking up the Altamont ambiance. It was, he told the thousands of listeners hungering for a glimpse of the concert, a "peaceful gathering." It was unclear whether Ponek was poorly positioned to take in the chaos, or simply chose not to feature it in his reports, perhaps deeming it a sideline to the main story. And yet, Ponek gave his listeners no inkling of what was taking place in the inner circle of Altamont. Perhaps the cumulative pressure of the Woodstock West frenzy made it too difficult to tell his audience just how bad things had gotten.

. . .

By the time Denise Jewkes, of the local group Ace of Cups, and her husband Noel Kaufman got close to the Altamont Speedway earlier that morning, they had to pull off the road and park some distance away, then walk the rest of the way to the concert site. The setup appeared disorganized, but Jewkes, a veteran of the local music scene, was hardly troubled. The community had always come together for these kinds of concerts before, creating the necessary infrastructure for a safe, pleasurable mass gathering on the fly. Surely someone had carefully planned every detail of an event as massive as this, even if the evidence of that planning was hard to discern.

Jewkes and Kaufman wound their way up the hill, through the dense crowd packed onto every square inch of the speedway. They claimed a spot for themselves far above the stage, sitting down and spreading out their picnic. Fans sat shoulder to shoulder, already anxious for amusement. No one was belligerent here, this far away from the action, but there was a dyspeptic quality to the crowd, a frustration that was palpable. Jewkes munched on a carrot, ready for the music to start.

Later, someone would tell Jewkes that they had seen some rowdy bikers in the area behind them, drunken and disorderly. She never got a chance to see them. An empty glass beer bottle, quart-size, came flying through the air from behind her head, and smashed into her temple. It appeared as if it had been lazily lobbed into the air, with Jewkes unlucky enough to be sitting under the final resting point of its downward arc. She felt the bottle crunch into her skull, and she collapsed into her husband's lap, blacking out. Others had already seen Hells Angels chucking beers at fans closer to the stage. They were ostensibly sharing their bounty with thirsty fans, but it appeared even there to have a malevolent purpose, more intent on hitting someone than quenching their thirst.

Jewkes was only out for a matter of seconds, but when she came to, her vision was blurred and darkened. She and her husband began to haltingly make their way down the hill and toward the stage. Seated concertgoers enveloped the ground, jammed in so closely there was hardly room to maneuver between them. The planners had neglected to leave an aisle between sections, making even emergency efforts a time-consuming, physically draining slog. Jewkes took a seat in a station wagon that drove her to the medical tent. A doctor, his hand to her head, asked her if there had been any gunshots nearby, terrifying her. She was rushed to a nearby hospital for emergency neurosurgery.

Jewkes was the rare concertgoer positioned far from the stage to suffer physical harm at Altamont, but if one were to have hovered directly over the crowd on that Saturday, drifting down in the direction of the stage, the thin sound of guitars and drums would occasionally be drowned out by the piercing wails of lone men and women in agony, and the dull crunch of fist and stick meeting bone. As the inner circle of Altamont drew nearer, so did the sense of dread and dislocation. Those residing in the outer circle of Altamont were often in danger from their own poor decisions. Those in the inner circle faced more immediate threats.

6. "Let's Not Keep Fucking Up!"

Puttering in mostly unnoticed among the stream of vehicles making their way onto the speedway grounds, a tan school bus crammed full of young men parked just behind the stage. From the exterior, this bus hardly differed from any of the other ramshackle vehicles to have arrived at Altamont that day. But unlike the majority of people attending, the men in the dun-colored bus had come to do a job. They were bikers, and the bus was owned by the San Francisco chapter of the Hells Angels. The vehicle containing the bulk of the security staff for Altamont rolled to a halt about one hundred yards away from the stage. The remainder of the Angels rode their Harleys—some solo and some with female passengers clinging to their backs—right up to the lip of the stage. The crowd frantically scattered out of the way of the sputtering motorcycles.

When the Hells Angels rode in to a new destination, they always followed a distinct pecking order. The full-fledged members would roar in on their motorcycles first, with the prospects, associates, and assorted hangers-on bringing up the rear. What was true of their entrances was true of all the bikers did. The members would always lead the way. The others, particularly the prospects who hoped to curry enough favor to join the club, would always follow the lead of their superiors.

There would be little oversight of the Hells Angels at the start of the concert, either from the festival staff or the Angels' leaders. Few, if any, bikers present would be concerned with the long-term reputation of the Hells Angels, and how the broader public might perceive their actions. Oakland Angel chief Sonny Barger, perhaps the most respected (and feared) of the Bay Area Angels, was absent at the start of the concert, attending an officers' meeting along with numerous other high-ranking Hells Angels. In their absence, the Angels dispatched many of their younger and more spirited members, along with prospects intent on proving their mettle under battle conditions.

On this day, there were approximately twenty or twenty-five Hells Angels present, with another few dozen prospects and hangers-on with them. The prospects in particular knew that the best way to win the Angels' acceptance was with a demonstration of their unyielding toughness. With little police presence at Altamont, and almost no security presence besides the Hells Angels, bikers had carte blanche to strong-arm the audience. And as fans kept pushing forward from the back, those up front would get dangerously close to the Hells Angels and their motorcycles.

Three hundred thousand people arrived at Altamont over the course of the morning and early afternoon, and the only protection they had from chaos was itself fomenting that very same chaos. There was no visible police presence, and little security beyond the Hells Angels, who, whatever services they might have provided in the past, were clearly uninterested in keeping the peace at Altamont.

As the Angels took their places, a huge contingent of fans was attracted, as if by invisible magnets, into close proximity to the bikers, near the lip of the stage. They were impelled by an unconscious

Fans reclining near the stage at Altamont. (Courtesy of Jay Siegel)

desire to be as close as possible to the Rolling Stones, and by the layout of the speedway itself. Everyone crept closer and closer, and for the people at the front, there was nowhere to go.

The raceway was enormous, and the stage tiny in comparison. From a distance, the figures on the stage were hardly more than dots, and fans who had made the trek from the Bay Area wanted to come home with firsthand reports of having seen Mick Jagger in the flesh. They began to push in. The fans already standing near the front were crunched ever closer to the stage. A tight-knit crowd became standing-room-only, and standing-room-only became not quite enough room to stand.

Some onlookers thought the whole scene resembled a New York subway car at rush hour. There you were, holding on to a strap, breathing in the fumes of someone's wet armpits, and convinced it could not possibly get any more crowded. There simply was not room for another human being in this car. Then the train stopped at the next station, and another crush of human beings shoved their way on. Then the same scene repeated at the next stop, and the one after that. The fifty or sixty yards nearest the stage rapidly transformed into a carpet of people, a breathing mass of undifferentiated humanity too crammed together to separate. It was terrifying to be so closely packed in, to have one's well-being be so thoroughly at the mercy of the crowd.

From the moment of the Angels' arrival, violent conflicts broke out everywhere. Wherever bikers were, violence spontaneously erupted. If you asked the bikers themselves, they would tell you it was because their reputations preceded them. Everywhere they went, there would be someone with a hard-on for a biker, intent on kicking some Angel ass so they could go home and brag to all their friends.

Detractors might argue that the bikers themselves treated violence as a blunt instrument, capable of dealing out punishment, retribution, or a much-needed lesson after a perceived infraction. Altamont was no different. Bikers grabbed women by the hair and assaulted them. They spotted attractive women in the crowd and yanked them up forcibly to the top of their bus. They snatched cameras out of fans' hands and ripped out the film after being photographed without their permission. They threatened to kill concertgoers who accidentally stepped on their fingers. The bikers had established a closed system in which they were simultaneously the criminals and the police force tasked with preserving order. Those looking for justice would find nowhere to turn other than to those who had violated their trust.

Five-foot-seven and 175 pounds, all muscle from his day job as a roofer, "Hawkeye" came with three knives and a .22 revolver, in the mood to party and only too glad to hassle anyone who got in the way of his fun. Hawkeye and his friends from another motorcycle group, the Sons of Hawaii, had come with a fistful of counterfeit $20 bills they had printed at a local copy shop, planning to use them to buy drugs from sellers in the crowd. Upon arrival at Altamont, they realized there would be no need for such elaborate chicanery. He and his friends would steal money and drugs from those displaying their stashes or their bankrolls, and then violently manhandle them when they complained. The victims would almost inevitably head off to find their friends, and when they came back, spoiling for a fight, Hawkeye and his friends would beat them once more. The victims were scared, and desperate for a security presence to resolve the situation, but no authority was higher than that of the Hells Angels. Hawkeye didn't worry about their complaints, or even their fitful attempts to get rough. Unless they came back with an army, they would have no chance at all. He and his friends were pushing people around, kicking ass, and stealing girlfriends, and having the time of their lives doing it.

The only thing missing for Hawkeye and his friends was a pad and a pencil. There were so many free-love girls there, all flashing their breasts and flirting outrageously with the bikers, that he later wished he had gotten some of their numbers for later use. This was a party, and they were the guests of honor. They never wanted it to end. Hawkeye and his friends felt free, unquestioned, even loved. They tossed some overzealous band handlers off the stage, and basked in the glow of the audience's pleasure at seeing this literal leveling. The whole crowd laughed with them, or at least it felt that way for these young men, high on crank—a variant of methamphetamine—and their own authority.

Four or five plainclothes Alameda County sheriffs stood around backstage, their weapons in their holsters. After intervening in one of the early fights between the Hells Angels and fans, they took note of how thoroughly outnumbered they were, and thereafter ceded the field to the Angels. Few fans or performers saw them for the remainder of the day.

The counterculture saw the Hells Angels as they wanted to see them, turning a blind eye to their professed love of violence, their misbegotten politics, and their outright racism. That alliance was in the process of breaking down this Saturday, shattered by the overly ambitious professional demands imposed on the Angels, and a creeping rage toward the music-loving masses.

The bikers' ferociousness, and their remarkable sense of cohesion, made for a notable contrast with the idealism of the crowd they patrolled. The counterculture believed itself to be an organized mass, intent on fomenting change in the United States: ending a war, returning power to the people. But seeing the Hells Angels was a reminder of the counterculture's limitations, embodied in the actions of their foes.

The Angels were violent authoritarians in the guise of bikers, intent on imposing their will on an unruly crowd. They were also a cohesive unit, acting in unison. The Angels had determined who would run Altamont, and what was and was not permissible there, and no one would be permitted to question the new order. This was the day's new reality. The counterculture spoke of unity, but the Hells Angels lived it. It was so powerful in action that it could hold hundreds of thousands in its thrall. What good was a peace sign against someone wielding a pool cue?

Some of the Angels approached Sam Cutler, guiding the action onstage, looking for guidance about how to handle unruly crowd members. This rushed tête-à-tête only further underscored the differences between Altamont and previous concerts, in which the Angels had putatively provided security but rarely interacted with the crowd. "We don't give a fuck," Cutler bluntly told the Angels. "Just keep these people away." Whether or not the Stones and their representatives knew what they were doing in hiring the Hells Angels, they had now given them explicit authority to manhandle the crowd. Passive negligence regarding the show's security had now

Sam Cutler speaking from the stage. (Courtesy of Robert Altman)

become, due to the disinterest of the Rolling Stones and their handlers, an active policy of violence and domination. The Angels were
now patrolling deeper into the crowd, targeting the 18-wheelers
that had been parked next to the stage. The Angels seized fans sitting atop the trucks and flung them off, a dozen or more feet down
to the hard ground.

Once they got settled in, fans began to realize that there would be
nowhere to go for the duration of the concert. The crowd kept inch-
ing forward, steadily filling what had once been pristine observation
points with people. Fans slowly understood that there would be no
leaving until everyone around them was ready to depart, too. They
would have to hunker down for the duration of the day. The furthest they would be able to make it was to the cars parked nearby,
where they might be able to urinate with a modicum of privacy. This
was home now.

Meredith Hunter was one of the thousands of drivers on the highway that day, taking in the sight of the newly sprawling temporary
city unfurling its borders at the edge of Alameda County. He pulled
his borrowed Ford Mustang to the side of the road, tucking it in
behind dozens of other cars on the highway leading to the Altamont
Speedway. Cars lined both sides of the highway, the remnants of an
armored corps reduced to the level of infantrymen. Hunter and his
girlfriend Patti Bredehoft, and their friends Judy (a fellow Berkeley
High student) and Ronnie Brown, joined the stream of concertgoers
trooping away from the highway and over the hills toward the racetrack.

The speedway was already crowded when the foursome made
their way toward the stage, but there was still enough room amid the
crush for them to snag some of the coveted real estate closest to
the stage. Glancing around the concert venue, Hunter may have silently

taken note of how few other black men were present that day, besides himself and Brown. This was, overwhelmingly and unsurprisingly, a white affair. And at least some of the African-Americans in the crowd seemed to be targeted by the Hells Angels. A longhaired biker threw one young man to the ground for no apparent reason, then proceeded to mouth obscenities at the fallen concertgoer. This was undoubtedly a familiar feeling for anyone, like Hunter, who had spent time at the parties and celebrations of the overwhelmingly white counterculture. Perhaps a fleeting thought of the burning crosses his sister had seen on her excursions into the far reaches of the Bay Area flitted through his mind. Were there people in the crowd who hated him with such fiery passion?

As Santana wrapped up its unremarkable set, the bulk of the audience had gotten itself into place, prepared for local heroes Jefferson Airplane. The Airplane had helped to introduce the concept of the free show to the Bay Area, regularly storming Golden Gate Park and surprising fans with an impromptu concert. Altamont was intended to be a steroidally enhanced version of the Golden Gate Park shows, and while the concert had gotten off to a rough start, many in the crowd hoped that Jefferson Airplane would steady frayed nerves.

Jefferson Airplane had provided the soundtrack to the hippie homeland of the Haight, their music the aural expression of the counterculture's rebellious pose. Songs like "We Can Be Together" were anthems of mutiny from the polite consensus, romanticized statements of protest that celebrated, at least metaphorically, the forces of chaos and anarchy.

The band had come together in March 1965, when Paul Kantner, Catholic military-school alumnus turned LSD connoisseur, took the stage at the Drinking Gourd, a folk club in San Francisco, then decided he would rather not play his set after all. On his way out, a painter, singer, dancer, and actor named Marty Balin stopped him and asked if he wanted to start a band together. Balin had seen Trini Lopez play folk songs with an electric guitar, and was instantly transfixed by the combination of tradition and forward-thinking modernity. They were joined by obsessive blues fan Jorma Kaukonen, who had been granted, for obscure reasons, the nickname Blind Thomas Jefferson Airplane. Kaukonen passed on the name to the band, which lopped off the first half and called themselves Jefferson Airplane. Soon enough, the band's savvy management team was making JEFFERSON AIRPLANE LOVES YOU buttons and bumper stickers, and paid young women to pass them out at other performers' shows.

Their sound blended folk, rock, and blues, with a department-store model and finishing-school graduate named Grace Slick joining Balin as the group's other lead singer. The title of their first album with Slick came from the Grateful Dead's Jerry Garcia, who heard one track and declared it as "surrealistic as a pillow." 1967's *Surrealistic Pillow* made them stars, and featured two era-defining hits: "Somebody to Love" and the *Alice in Wonderland*–inspired "White Rabbit." The band played before twenty thousand people at the Polo Grounds in Golden Gate Park at the Human Be-In, celebrated by the *San Francisco Chronicle*'s Ralph J. Gleason as "a statement of life, not of death, and a promise of good, not of evil." For their fans, Jefferson Airplane were the avatars of a better, kinder world to come, and Altamont would be their victory lap as much as the Stones' or the Dead's.

The Airplane was among the most experienced groups of the era at playing massive outdoor shows. They had been at the Monterey Pop Festival in 1967 and at Woodstock, where they had been scheduled to go onstage at 9 p.m. on Saturday and didn't get to start their set until 7 a.m. Sunday morning. They had played before one hundred thousand people at the Atlantic City Pop Festival in

August 1969 alongside the Byrds, Little Richard, and Creedence Clearwater Revival, and had been at the Palm Beach International Music and Arts Festival with the Rolling Stones the week prior to Altamont. They had boarded a 7 a.m. helicopter to the speedway, bedraggled and unkempt, after getting in from Florida at 3:30 a.m. The band was used to facing down belligerent police officers and security guards threatening the peace at their gatherings. "Remember," Kantner told the crowd at one 1967 show in Bakersfield, "there are five of them and five thousand of us." Jefferson Airplane began their set at Altamont with "We Can Be Together," but the message stubbornly refused to take hold. Unity was not the tune being hummed on this day.

There were dozens of fans in the scrum near the stage during the Airplane's set, with elbows and knees making unwanted contact with nearby bystanders. Fans grew unruly, pushing and shoving. Some stormed the stage in their shambling, drugged-out fashion.

The crowd was acting out. They would surge toward the stage in regular waves, and intrepid or foolhardy souls would attempt to climb up and approach the musicians. Rampant misdemeanors, many of them fueled by drugs, notably detracted from the crowd's pleasure of the day, but few crimes required immediate intervention.

One dancer, the music having wormed its way into that deepest place inside of him, the place where his soul resided and dreams of transcendence lingered, cut loose in front of the stage. Or perhaps he had gotten hold of a batch of the good acid making its way around the Altamont Speedway, and visions of sugarplums and fairy dust danced in his head during their performance of "The Other Side of This Life." Either way, the man—young, hefty, Hispanic—had stripped off his shirt and twirled unselfconsciously through the crowd. He waved his arms around and clomped his feet, and inadvertently or otherwise, he was stomping on nearby concertgoers. It was an annoyance, not an emergency.

Then the Hells Angels came roaring down from the stage, dispensing their own brand of mob justice. The Angels selected victims and systematically targeted them, isolating them before pummeling them into submission.

One shirtless African-American man who was at the center of a struggle early in Jefferson Airplane's set attempted to hold off an assault from a phalanx of Angels. Another, a bearded young white man wearing a hat, sought to stave off the bikers verbally, holding up his palms in an instantly recognizable symbol of surrender. The Angels knocked him down anyway, proceeding to calmly smash him with their pool cues. A coordinated, lightning-quick array of blows rained down on his head and chest, an act of extreme aggression far beyond any minor irritation the victim might have caused.

The crowd, hemmed in, found room it did not know existed, collectively surging back to avoid the wrath of the Angels. A semicircle of open space formed around the beating, an empty amphitheater for this symbolic performance of the eternal showdown between the powerful and the powerless.

The crowd froze in shock and fear. No one knew how to respond, what to do to stop the thrashing. The Hells Angels were vastly outnumbered. There were approximately five thousand concertgoers for each biker present, but only the Angels were willing to be so vicious, so unrestrained. Which attendees would be so foolhardy as to put themselves in the path of a vengeful Angel? And so the Hells Angels imposed their will on an entire concert, their brutality making it increasingly unlikely that they would find any opposition. Instead, lone members of the crowd lifted two fingers into the air, forming peace signs that they hoped would mark their intellectual and spiritual opposition to the Angels' excesses. The symbol was empty, demonstrating an inability to wrestle seriously with the enormity of genuine malevolence.

After each Angel incursion, the semicircle of empty space immediately filled in, so rapidly and so thoroughly that some fans were left without room to place both feet on the ground. It was a frenzy, one that had as much to do with the frustrations of the day and the desire to assert some minuscule semblance of authority in a chaotic situation, as with any actual proximity to the musicians.

The crowd was uncontrolled, and growing uncontrollable. There were so many people at Altamont, and everyone wanted to be close enough to the stage to reach out and touch the musicians. They surged forward, pressed shoulder to shoulder, flank to flank, and no organizer, no star, no calming voice was capable of convincing them to stop. The Hells Angels saw themselves as having been hired to do a particular and limited job. The uncontrolled environment made it increasingly difficult for them to provide security.

From the stage, Jefferson Airplane could see the Angels darting through the crowd and clobbering people who approached the stage. The band was frustrated by the rampant violence, which they seemed to condone with their presence.

As the opening notes to "Somebody to Love" rang out, the band's co-lead singer and guitarist, Marty Balin, was visibly annoyed by what he saw as the Hells Angels' provocations, and jumped down into the crowd, in an excess of foolhardy courageousness, to break up a fight between the bikers and a young African-American man. Balin saw the Angels targeting people and insisted that they stop.

The Airplane had spent time with the Hells Angels in the past, and had always been friendly with the bikers, but they were not entirely surprised by the sudden shift in the tone of their interaction at Altamont. To be a musician was to be armed for the unexpected, and to always be prepared for what came next. On this day, the Hells Angels were the problem, and Jefferson Airplane struggled to tamp down the violence already beginning to spread out, beyond the stage and into the crowd.

The Angels gathered near the stage conferred, and they agreed:

something would have to be done. A Hells Angel named Animal was dispatched to speak to Balin, still in the crowd, and plead the Angels' side. "They're pushing on the stage. They're knocking bikes over," he told Balin. "We're not trying to be assholes. We're just trying to protect our property." Balin, unmoved by the bikers' concerns, responded angrily: "Fuck you, Animal." Animal, donning a hat-cum-headdress that made him look like some sort of hybrid beast, half-man and half-predator, shook his head, a tense situation now grown all the more stressful: "Man, don't talk to me like that."

As Balin likely understood, to speak to a Hells Angel with such brazen disrespect invited a fierce and immediate response. The Hells Angels traveled with their own laws, a portable code of ethics that enveloped them like a cloud. The rules were immutable and permanent, and friends and even bystanders were expected to abide by them. Balin, a longtime friend of Animal's, and of the Angels, was a surprising candidate for such blatant disrespect to the Angel code. Another man might have immediately felt the crunch of a fist breaking his nose, but Balin was being offered a second chance to repent, and to tone down his burning anger when in the presence of a Hells Angel. Balin ignored the warning, and tripled down on his original statement: "Fuck you. Fuck you. Fuck you." Animal—a dead fox, eyes bulging open, propped jauntily atop his head—felt compelled to respond in predatory fashion, and viciously cold-cocked Balin, knocking the lead singer of Jefferson Airplane unconscious.

The Angels had changed the rules of their encounters, and their demands of fealty now extended to the entire crowd. If the Angels were willing to beat up a musician in the middle of his performance, what could possibly prevent them from doing the same to an anonymous concertgoer?

"Hey man, I'd just like to mention that the Hells Angels smashed Marty Balin in the face, knocked him out for a bit. I'd like to thank you for that," guitarist Jorma Kaukonen calmly intoned into the

Jorma Kaukonen of Jefferson Airplane arguing with the Hells Angels. (Courtesy of Robert Altman)

microphone, addressing the Angels. His bandmates were terrified, afraid that Kaukonen's attitude had him next in line for a beating. Guitarist Paul Kantner was used to these kinds of situations at Jefferson Airplane concerts. He would regularly march into the middle of an unruly audience, his guitar over his head like a musical halo, intent on breaking up any ruckus that ensued. The guitar served as instant identification, but the threat of being whacked on the head with Kantner's Rickenbacker may have played some part in defusing any tension. Here, though, a guitar would not be enough to calm the audience down, nor would Kantner's presence impose tranquility.

One Hells Angel made his way onto the stage, grabbed one of the microphones, and told off the band for interfering: "Is this on? You talkin' to me, I'm gonna talk to you." Kaukonen replied calmly: "I'm talking to you, man. I'm talking to the people who hit my lead singer." The Angel riposted forcefully but somewhat incoherently,

"They're my people. Let me tell you what's happening. *You* are what's happening." Having witnessed her bandmate's beating, co-lead singer Grace Slick got on the mic and sought to spread the blame around evenly: "People get weird, and you need people like the Angels to keep people in line. But the Angels also, you don't bust people in the head for nothing. So both sides are fucking up temporarily. Let's not keep fucking up!"

Jefferson Airplane's sharply differing responses to Balin's beating were telling. Kaukonen and Kantner blamed the Hells Angels for their violent intimidation, while Slick preferred to depict the crowd as equally responsible for the violence. Was the growing misadventure of Altamont entirely a product of the Hells Angels' presence, or was it caused as well by the crowd's mischief? Slick was sensitive to the Altamont crowd, and the anger and hostility that so many in the audience had felt. But her appeal sounded like a passive acceptance of the Hells Angels' own warped viewpoint, in which they were the arbiters and interpreters of the unwritten law, able to impose judgment on rule breakers at a whim. The fact that so many people—whether due to drugs, alcohol, or just a general desire to act out—clearly did need to be kept in line did not make the Angels the appropriate figures to do so.

Jerry Garcia, his girlfriend Carolyn "Mountain Girl" Adams, and the other members of the Grateful Dead had gingerly stepped out of their band bus to watch Jefferson Airplane perform. The Dead had arrived earlier that morning via helicopter. One of their roadies had driven their bus, which was now parked backstage and serving as the Dead's dressing-room-cum-drug-den. A tent had been pitched nearby for an impromptu hospitality suite. Looking out beyond the stage, and into the vast crowd crawling up the hill, they saw glimpses of the unrest to come, with Angels angrily protecting their motorcycles from the crowd, and handling their security duties with brutal efficiency. The level of hostility between the audience and its putative security force far exceeded anything they had seen in the peaceable San Francisco shows they had headlined, but only after Marty Balin decided to confront the bikers did the Dead fully comprehend the enormity of what they had helped to unleash.

Garcia and his bandmates helplessly took in the grisly sight of their longtime friend Animal, resembling nothing so much, they thought, as an animate piece of roadkill, attack Balin, yanked away by firm hands as he sought to crunch his boot into the face of a musician there to entertain three hundred thousand fans. Garcia blanched, raising both arms, as the band's manager Rock Scully would later describe it, "in an involuntary gesture of keeping back some unseen host of demons."

The Maysleses' cameras would catch up with Garcia on the mostly empty speedway track as he received further reports of Balin's beating: "Oh, that's what the story is? Oh, bummer!" Garcia's tense body language contradicted his bland tone as he nervously glanced around, his eyes pulled away from the camera's interrogating gaze. The band, anxious to avoid being pulled into the violence, hastily beat a retreat back to its bus. The day's bill had the Dead scheduled as the final openers for the Stones, bridging the gap between the opening acts and the headliner. It would be Garcia and his bandmates who would soon have to face the Hells Angels. And there was little opportunity for coordination or planning; Garcia only spotted Jagger briefly as the Stones entourage swept past, exchanging a few brief words and little more.

Balin roused a few minutes later in the band's truck, and was taken aback to see the enormous Hells Angel looming over him again. "I'm sorry, man, I didn't mean to knock you out," Animal told him, "but you can't say 'fuck you' to a Hells Angel. Don't you know that?" Balin, undaunted as ever, responded pithily: "Fuck you." Animal knocked him out again.

7. Whippin'

Jerry Garcia returned to the Dead's bus after Balin's beating and lay down on the floor, his teeth chattering, shaking uncontrollably. Garcia's body unconsciously responded to the chaos roiling near the stage even before his brain could fully compute the import of what he had just seen. "Oh, maa-aan, no *way* are we doing this," Garcia told Rock Scully. "The inmates have definitely taken over the asylum. Rock, go sort it out, man. Talk to the Angels or something." Garcia's girlfriend, Mountain Girl, called out for some marijuana. Garcia's bandmate Ron "Pigpen" McKernan was at the back of the bus, unable to summon a coherent response to the nightmare unfolding outside. Here, the hippie aesthetic of laissez-faire planning slammed into brute reality. Here were the Dead's erstwhile friends choosing one of the biggest days in the band's career to prove a point: that they could not be managed, could not be corralled into playing the part of mascots for peace and love. The vision must have been shattering, and Garcia appeared to retreat within himself, intent on blocking out the spectacle taking place just outside his windows.

Garcia crouched next to Mountain Girl, struggling to understand what he had just witnessed, and increasingly certain of one thing: "No way am I playing, man, no fucking way am I going out there!" The Grateful Dead had not only played a crucial role in the planning and coordination of Altamont, but they also had been the ones to plump for the Hells Angels. Now the utter naïveté of their stance was being exposed with each fresh assault by the bikers they had insisted were peaceful, law-abiding members of the counterculture.

Garcia's bandmate Phil Lesh was the only one on the bus with the courage to part the curtains and peek at the stage. He issued a steady stream of dire proclamations to his bandmates: "Jesus Christ, there's this three-hundred-pound naked guy, and—oh God!—the Angels are beating him to a fucking pulp!" The Airplane's set was coming to a halt, the band doing their level best to play even with Balin now unconscious. But Garcia was not prepared to face the chaos he had helped to unleash. "This show is like some kind of runaway train," he said, "and we best get the fuck *out* of here before it runs into us." Fear had led Garcia and the Grateful Dead to contemplate fleeing from the very concert they had been instrumental in putting together.

The Dead's soundman Dan Healy poked his head into the bus door: "The Airplane are coming offstage, what do you guys want to do?" They hastily called a band meeting. The band was increasingly hysterical, panicked by the vision of hell visible through the parted curtains and fearful of being forced to face the chaos. There were concerns that the encroaching darkness, now only a few hours off, would only worsen the situation, and with the slate of bands having run long, the Stones might not be able to go on until well after dark. Self-preservation was the order of the day, and excuses were hastily sought to keep them from facing the consequences of their poor decisions.

There was nothing the band could do, they believed, to salvage this misbegotten day, and it was now time to seek refuge. The band had not yet even taken the stage; instead they huddled in a defensive crouch, seeking to spin their flight as an attempt to placate the crowd by giving them what they wanted. If this was a Rolling Stones show, they argued to themselves, best to put the Stones on as soon as possible. "Let the Stones go on, this is *their* madness," Lesh argued. Garcia agreed, providing further justification by contending that they would hardly be capable, under these circumstances, of entertaining their fans: "No way we're going to *play* good, anyway. We're just gonna give our enemies more ammunition." The Grateful Dead would happily cede the stage to the headliners.

Whether they intended it or not, the Grateful Dead's decision not to play began a process of erasure, whereby the band that had played a central role in planning and organizing Altamont, and on whose home turf the concert had been scheduled, became the show's invisible men. Their footprints were being deliberately scrubbed, leaving the Rolling Stones as the sole owner-operators of the debacle called Altamont.

The maelstrom instigated by the Hells Angels transformed Altamont from a joyous celebration to a crime in progress, and the filmmakers present believed themselves to have an artistic responsibility to capture it for posterity. People would need to see what had taken place here. As Balin and Animal were having their first tête-à-tête, cinematographer Stephen Lighthill moved from the right-hand corner of the stage to the center, hoping to film their fight. When he returned to the corner, an Angel gruffly told him, "You don't film us anymore." As the situation spiraled out of control, the Hells Angels did not want their reckless behavior recorded. But the Angels were too distracted by the tumult to devote much attention to Lighthill, whose casual, hippie-style clothing and low-key manner allowed him to blend in unnoticed.

Lighthill took in the chaotic scene, increasingly horrified by the Angels' violent raids on the crowd. He was back on the right side of the stage, ideally positioned to film the Angels, but his bulky, shoulder-mounted camera could hardly be hidden. The bikers had already approached Lighthill numerous times, threatening him with bodily harm if he attempted to film them, and he had reluctantly agreed to comply. But his inflexible, bulky camera—the same one that had doomed him to the relatively boring assignment of filming from the stage—had a hidden advantage: Lighthill could close its viewfinder while filming, preventing it from leaking light. To a casual observer, he would appear not to be recording. Lighthill craftily turned away from the scene at his feet, swiveling to chat casually with sound recorder Nelson Stoll. He looked entirely relaxed and nonchalant, even as his camera recorded the turmoil below.

The sheer scope of the task the Hells Angels had been entrusted with—overseeing the conduct of three hundred thousand concertgoers—was daunting for a band of bikers with little experience with crowd control or peacekeeping. The Angels were overwhelmed, the bands having saddled them with work far beyond their capabilities or their numbers. A small crew of bikers was the only separation between the performers and hundreds of thousands of concertgoers, and even Sonny Barger, newly arrived at the concert in the early afternoon, was unsettled by the vastness of their mission. Lashing out was the most comfortable response. The Hells Angels instilled terror in those near them through the unpredictability of their moods. The threat of being hit cowed the overwhelming majority of the crowd. For the rest, there were the pool cues, and the knives.

This was not the day to underestimate the size of the security staff that would be needed to keep the peace. People could be kind and compassionate and decent, just as the hippies were always arguing. But it was probably best not to give a large, unruly audience too many opportunities to lash out, or to empower men like the Angels to keep the peace.

It required courage, and more than a touch of foolhardiness, to confront the Angels. And those who did often found themselves facing the bikers' wrath. Backstage, an Angel, his eyes pinwheeling from methamphetamine, crouched atop a hapless concertgoer, punching him again and again as a crowd of thirty or so people gathered in an enormous circle to watch. No one intervened. No one wanted to be the next to trigger the Angel's temper. Perhaps, too, some spectators enjoyed watching the real-life cage match being staged just a few feet away from them.

Young journalist Kate Coleman, horrified by the violence, leapt forward, grabbed the hulking Angel by the collar, and began to pull him off, telling him, "That's enough, you've made your point. Now let him go." The Angel stood up and turned to face her, his meth-addled eyes slowly meeting hers. He grabbed Coleman, yanked her roughly, and began thumping her into a nearby VW van. He pointedly avoided punching her, his delicacy presumably due to Coleman's being a woman. His chivalrousness did not keep him, however, from repeatedly slamming Coleman's head into the van.

While Coleman was being beaten, some bystanders dragged away the Angel's first victim, moving the bloodied, dazed man to safety. Even as he beat her, Coleman was stunned that no one else exhibited the courage she had in intervening. Why wouldn't anyone attempt to rescue her?

Finally, Coleman was rescued by an elfin journalist for a local underground newspaper, *The Tribe*. She stepped near Coleman, grabbed her hand, and told the Angel, "I'm taking her away now." The Angel, too dumbfounded or drug-addled to reply, let them go.

Fear prevented others from being as daring—or as reckless—as Coleman had been. This backstage moment would serve as a capsule version of the day: a story of violence and domination, of an impassioned minority running roughshod over a cowed majority.

The audience, too, had proven itself incapable of looking after itself. There was such a thing as too much trust, and too many of the people at Altamont seemed to exhibit a blind faith in the goodwill of others, and the organizational abilities of the behind-the-scenes impresarios of rock 'n' roll. Community, for many of the people in attendance, meant a casual assumption that all would be orderly, all would come together, all would be harmonious.

Word of the day's excesses began to trickle back to the Huntington Hotel in San Francisco, where the Rolling Stones were spending a lazy afternoon before flying out to the concert site. What had been a highly anticipated peak to their American tour, and to their careers, was rapidly devolving into a catastrophe, and the band was developing second thoughts about participating. The Rolling Stones would have loved to escape from their commitment to Altamont, but it was simply too late. The show would have to go on. The band began to mentally prepare themselves for what would undoubtedly be an unusually trying day. The helicopter would be leaving soon.

The Stones finally arrived at the festival by helicopter at around 2:45 p.m., accompanied by Albert and David Maysles. As they exited the chopper, a swarm of fans approached, dashing up the hill toward the band, hoping to catch a glimpse of Mick Jagger. Albert filmed one bellicose young man, likely emboldened by drugs, as he rushed the Stones' lead singer and proceeded to punch him in the face. There would be no Altamont honeymoon, even for the day's headliners.

Jefferson Airplane's set was immediately followed by the country-rock stylings of the Flying Burrito Brothers, whose debut album *The*

Gilded Palace of Sin had come out earlier in the year to ecstatic reviews and minimal sales. The band was an outgrowth of the Byrds, led by former Byrds collaborator Gram Parsons and ex-bassist Chris Hillman, and their mellow sound played a role in momentarily calming the overheated crowd. Mick Jagger and Keith Richards emerged from their trailer during the Burritos' performance, briefly taking to the stage and signing autographs for the crowd, on everything from album covers to draft cards. The Hells Angels were there to provide security for the headliners, clearing a path for Jagger and Richards wherever they roamed.

The crowd was like an eyeless beast, thrashing about in its mindless frenzy to approach the stage, and unable to restrain itself in its headlong charge to the front.

As fans pressed forward, they nudged the concertgoers nearest the stage in the direction of the Hells Angels' motorcycles, parked just in front of the stage. The bikes were being toppled, knocked over by the pent-up weight of three hundred thousand people, their pedals and mirrors crushed by the knees and elbows and shoulders of the crowd. Some of the Angels' motorcycles had their wires cut, whether by saboteurs in the crowd or simply from the jostling of so many pressing bodies, no biker could say. The motorcycles were sacred property, though, the physical manifestation of a biker's heart and soul. No Angel would let his motorcycle be manhandled any more than he might allow himself to be maimed bodily. A line had to be drawn.

As with so many crowd panics, the people at the back could not see what was happening at the front and continued crowding ever closer, unaware of the ripple effect of their efforts. The crowd pushed fans back against the Hells Angels' motorcycles, and this time the pent-up force shoved over a wave of bikes, five of the Angels' prized possessions toppling over in one fell swoop.

The Angels righted their motorcycles, but the panic only highlighted their territorial feelings regarding the contested space near the stage. They were not only doing their job; they were guarding their treasures, and no one was going to damage their most precious possessions. The Hells Angels had never been particularly kind, or inclined to treat others gently, but at their previous concert gigs, they had been relatively placid with interlopers and stage trespassers. Perhaps the danger posed to their motorcycles—along with the copious drugs they had already consumed, and the scope of their responsibility, abandoned as they were to the task of providing security for so large a gathering—helped to tip them over in the direction of full-on violent hostility toward the fans they were allegedly protecting. The failures of foresight during the planning for the concert were having disastrous consequences. Why had the planners told the Hells Angels to park their motorcycles in front of the stage, of all places?

The Angels' bikes would not be wrecked by a shoving crowd. The wires could easily be repaired. Minor infractions would have to be counteracted with the threat of overwhelming force. Bystanders who had stepped out of line would be faced with a flying Angel, leaping from the stage to confront them.

To be an Angel was to be inflexible, unwilling to overlook a violation of the rules. It meant denying the power of the rules that governed others' lives while insisting, with niggling precision, on the universality of one's own personal code. To be a Hells Angel was to act out a parodic version of American freedom, where freedom itself was an amoral act, unkind and selfish. It required tuning out the quiet voices that insisted on the inherent dignity of others, and amplifying the ones that demanded that others respect yours.

The Hells Angels lashed out, but were comfortable with others' violence as long as it respected their authority. Stones bodyguard Tony Funches beat two bikers who were fighting onstage, coming dangerously close to the bands' equipment. Funches thought he would head off any potential trouble by finding Animal, whom he rightly judged the ringleader of the biker circus. The fox-head hat was disconcerting, but Funches gamely pressed on. "I'm a dead man," he told him. "I just cold-cocked a couple of your buddies, because they were fighting each other and knocking over the equipment on the stage."

Animal didn't flinch, and didn't shout. He calmly gazed down at Funches and said, "Hey, man, we've got no problem with you. You're just doing your job." Funches treated the Angels—or at least the lead Angel—with deference, acknowledging his authority. The Hells Angels demanded respect, and shows of deference would be the dividing line between those passed over by the Angels at Altamont, and those doomed to face their wrath.

Crosby, Stills, Nash & Young had only reluctantly agreed to take the stage, with David Crosby prodding his bandmates to fulfill their commitment to entertain—or at least pacify—the crowd. It had long since become clear that Altamont was anything but a success. The sound had grown even weaker, and the crush near the stage, worsened by the presence of the Angels, made it even harder for any fans to pay attention to the band's set.

From the second the band arrived at the speedway, the members of Crosby, Stills, Nash & Young felt under assault: from the unsettled atmosphere, from the electronic music booming through the loudspeakers. Graham Nash found the music tremendously annoying, and Stephen Stills was downright spooked.

The group had only existed in its current format for a handful of months. Nash had left the Hollies to join Stephen Stills, formerly of Buffalo Springfield, and David Crosby, formerly of the Byrds, in a new band. They had been encouraged by Ahmet Ertegun of Atlantic Records, who had funded a London recording session for the new trio. "Our voices blended gorgeously on every song," Nash would later observe. "It was as if they knew exactly where to go without having to be told." Crosby Stills & Nash recorded a triumphant first album, and when Ertegun encouraged them to add a fourth member, they initially balked. Neil Young had been Stills's bandmate in Buffalo Springfield, and Stills had found him to be mercurial and frustrating. But the band needed a lead guitarist to take over when Stills played keyboards, and Young's deft charm, and his fistful of new songs, won over his new bandmates. His presence changed what had been a melodious hippie act into something slightly heavier, slightly deeper. They played their first show as a foursome at Chicago's Auditorium Theatre in August 1969, in preparation for Woodstock.

Woodstock was a minor calamity, with poor sound and guitars that repeatedly went out of tune, but CSNY's hour-long set went over well with the audience. Jerry Garcia, who had played alongside them at Woodstock, had reached out and asked them to join the bill for the San Francisco free show as a personal favor. The band had been skeptical, but agreed to play nonetheless.

Stills got out onto the stage, and something about the composition of the audience, or the Hells Angels' behavior, caused him to panic. Even as the band played its brief four-song set, he was convinced that terror was in the air. CSNY played their new song "Long Time Gone," in honor of the assassinated Robert F. Kennedy, and Stills worried that Mick Jagger, too, would be murdered on this day. "Stop hurting each other," Crosby pleaded with the Hells Angels, still frantically assaulting concertgoers, but to no avail. Young led the way with his furious guitar assault on "Down by the River," but as soon as the last note began to fade, the four musicians dashed for their helicopter, in a frenzy to escape Altamont. Word had gotten to them that the Grateful Dead were no longer planning to play, and the Dead's absence from the show they had helped to plan convinced the members of CSNY that this was no longer a show they wanted to associate themselves with.

The stage had gone silent. Injured bodies littered the crowd, and stretchers began to emerge, with the wounded passed hand-over-hand above people's heads and onto the stage, where they could be carried to the Red Cross tent. The headliners were up now.

On their fall tour, the Rolling Stones had played with Ike & Tina Turner, and had grown accustomed to a lengthy interlude between the opening act and the headliner. Ike & Tina's sets, capped by her stunning rendition of "I've Been Loving You Too Long," in which she stroked the microphone stand in a mimed state of erotic bliss while expressing fealty to a missing lover, were so thoroughly dominating that the Stones hardly wanted to compete, and preferred to wait well over an hour before they went on. Ike & Tina were not present at Altamont, but the Stones' sense of drama remained. The band preferred not to compete with the sunshine, and wanted to let the day, and the memory of the other performers, drain away before taking the stage. Moreover, bassist Bill Wyman was running late. He had spent the afternoon shopping for antiques, as he liked to do in his free time, and had missed the initial helicopter flight to the speedway.

This was to be the capper to a day of musical drama. The audience, already deeply impatient, had reached a near-frenzy of impotence and thwarted desire. They had come for history in the making, and had received—at least those in close proximity to the stage—a miserable day of discomfort and fear in its stead. If the Stones would only come on, this day could finally come to a blessed end, and everyone could proceed to forget all about what had preceded it. The Rolling Stones appeared to be operating on an outdated schedule, heightening the drama for a moment unlikely to please most of their fans.

Patti Bredehoft was hardly surprised when Meredith Hunter came back to the car to join her. This concert was a bust, and she was ready to leave, Rolling Stones or no Rolling Stones. She was dumbfounded when Hunter went over to the Mustang, unlocked the trunk, and removed a long-barreled .22 Smith & Wesson revolver with a blue-steel barrel. Bredehoft watched him put the gun in a pocket of his jacket. "Why are you getting that?" she wondered, shocked. "It's just to protect myself. They're getting really bad," he told her, referring to the Hells Angels. "They're pushing people off the stage, and beating people up."

The couple had been among the fans terrorized by the Hells Angels' presence. They had scurried out of the way when the Angels had roared up to the stage on their Harley-Davidsons with hardly a pause; if they hadn't made room for the motorcycles, they likely would have been run over. They watched helplessly as the bikers used their pool cues as truncheons, beating fans who had violated the unspoken rules of proximity to the Hells Angels. Bredehoft was particularly troubled by the bland announcements that came from the stage, asking the audience to calm down and be cool. It wasn't the audience causing the trouble in the first place, she thought.

She had never seen Hunter with a gun before, never heard him talk about weapons or any other sort of serious illegal activity. Bredehoft had spent time with Hunter at the homes of her friends from Berkeley High School, at the park outside school, and in the neighborhood. They had hung out with other high school kids, some white, and some black, but few, if any, engaged in illicit behavior. The teenage couple would drink together, would sometimes smoke weed together, but that was the extent of it. Why would he have brought a gun to a concert? And why take it out of the car now? Bredehoft could not imagine what might have inspired him.

The concert had been disturbing and unsettling, but this seemed like an unnecessary additional step. Hunter likely felt differently, though. Everyone in the Bay Area—everyone black in the Bay Area—knew the Hells Angels were unambiguous racists, and a chaotic scene like this concert could be the perfect cover for an attack on a lone African-American adrift in a sea of white faces. It was better to

Meredith Hunter in 1969, wearing the same lime-green suit he would wear to Altamont. (Courtesy of Dixie Ward)

be protected. The gun, as he had told Dixie, was unloaded, but might be able to scare off a Hells Angel intent on disturbing his peace.

In retrospect, this would be one of the crucial moments of the day. The concert had been a fizzle, the violence had been unsettling and frightening, and neither Hunter nor his friends were particular devotees of the Rolling Stones. Why didn't they try to leave then, as others who had been spooked by the presence of the Angels had chosen to do? Even their friends Ronnie—one of the few other African-Americans who had been standing near the stage—and Judy were leaving, deciding they had had more than enough of the concert. Perhaps Ronnie felt particularly vulnerable in this overwhelmingly white place, surrounded by Hells Angels intent on brutalizing innocent bystanders.

If the situation was uncertain enough to require a gun, wasn't it smarter to simply leave? But to ask the question was to lose sight of something essential about Meredith Hunter: he was an eighteen-year-old boy. He had served time in juvie, but he was still an unformed personality. He was a teenager, not a grown man. In his mind, the gun was enough to ward off any potential threat from the Hells Angels, but little thought was likely given to what the Angels' response to seeing that gun might be.

Bredehoft wanted to leave. Altamont was no fun at all, and she was getting scared. Hunter wanted to stay, and encouraged her to return to where they had been standing. "Come on," he gently told Bredehoft. "Come back with me. The Rolling Stones are finally getting ready to go on." The teenage lovers walked away from the Mustang, and back toward the stage. It was now time for the headline act.

8. Gun and Knife

Darkness came early in the Bay Area in December, and with its arrival, the temperature fell precipitously. Some of the crowd had been overdressed for a warm day in the sun; now, most of the crowd was underdressed for what was proving to be a very chilly evening. It got colder here in eastern Alameda County than it ever did in Berkeley or San Francisco. All across the speedway, small tongues of fire lapped into the sky, with paper bags and trash set ablaze to provide some much-needed warmth. Across a shallow ravine from the stage, there were hills ringed with wooden fences, and fans had begun to disassemble them, tossing the fence posts onto bonfires. The air filled with the oily, acrid smell of burning garbage and creosote.

The concert's hasty setup meant there had not been time to put up the arc lights, the assembly of which required a crane that never arrived. Instead, the boxes containing the arcs had been forgotten under the scaffolding. Now, those same boxes were being ransacked by freezing concertgoers, who tossed them directly onto bonfires to keep warm. The $7,000 arc lights burned unnoticed inside the boxes.

Chip Monck, who had ordered the arc lights, would not know about the damage until they were already serving as tinder.

The wait after the end of Crosby, Stills, Nash & Young's set had extended for an uncomfortably long time. The Rolling Stones stayed in their trailers as darkness fell, and the crowd was left to stew, smoking joints and popping pills and sipping from bottles and cans to keep warm. The hope, unjustified by anything that had taken place so far that day, was that the star power of the Rolling Stones would be enough to calm the tensions in the crowd, to soothe all hurts with the balm of their fame. During the hour-and-a-quarter wait for the Stones, the backstage lights remained off, hampering the efforts of the concert's medical staff to care for the injured. The lengthy delay before the Rolling Stones emerged only worsened the hostility in the crowd, and the sense of siege for those concert-goers trapped closest to the stage.

Two groups of young men faced each other, almost close enough to shake hands, or at least exchange greetings. On the one side, in their backstage trailer, a British rock group selling a persona two parts prince-of-darkness allure and one part hippie goodwill, all held to-gether by a furious two-pronged guitar attack; on the other, surround-ing the stage, a clan of California bikers, increasingly bitter over the thankless job they had been tasked with and sorely tempted to lash out violently. The Rolling Stones and the Hells Angels stared at each other from across a vast gulf, separated by mutual incomprehen-sion. No word went between them, the Stones hoping for an im-provement to the situation in the crowd and the Angels waiting for some hint of what might happen next. In the meantime, the Angels began pushing fans back anew, clearing out about forty feet of space between the stage and the audience.

Soon, more Angels came blazing in on their motorcycles, push-ing concertgoers out of their way to form a path through the over-crowded thicket close to the stage. One fan, presumably thrilled by the Angels' unbridled display of power, clapped each biker on the back as they rode by. One Angel stopped his motorcycle to take a lengthy swig from a jug of wine proffered from the crowd.

The band was still in their tiny, airless trailer, the smell of stale smoke filling their lungs as they grimly assessed the diminishing goodwill of the day. Having stayed up the entire night, Richards was drained and anxious to conclude the show. People poked at the windows, shouting and pining for a glimpse of the Stones. The band hoped to play an abbreviated set, then call a halt to the misbegotten concert and send the fans home. The Rolling Stones asked the Hells Angels to escort them to the stage, but Sonny Barger and the other Angels were turned off by what they saw as the band's antics. Why had they waited so long to play before a clearly violent, dyspeptic crowd? Barger did not like what he saw as an unnecessary delay, intended, as he saw it, to heighten the dramatic tension on an already unbearably tense day. The Hells Angels would no longer serve as bodyguards to "a bunch of sissy, marble-mouthed prima donnas."

Patti Bredehoft and Meredith Hunter returned from the car and made their way back toward the front, where the Rolling Stones were about to take the stage, accompanied solely by their bodyguard Tony Funches. Bredehoft was afraid of the crowds, having already seen the Angels mauling concertgoers, but Hunter was intent on staking out a spot near the band. The crowd was fierce. No one wanted to cede an inch of space. No one wanted to lose out on their hard-fought proximity to Mick and Keith and the Stones, won with an intrepid spirit and the stubbornness that came of standing in the same crowded space the day long, as the sun arced over the Livermore fields and disappeared behind the horizon. Shoves and sharp elbows met their every step, demonstrations of intent by a crowd that had endured more than their share of discomfort and downright terror in the hopes of seeing history in the making.

The Rolling Stones finally appeared, and for a brief moment, a sense of relief spread through the speedway. The Stones would undoubtedly cool off the overheating crowd, get them back to concentrating on the music, and return the focus where it belonged. "Oh, babies," Jagger addressed the crowd. "There's so many of you. Just keep cool down in front and don't push around. Just keep still, keep together." Jagger, resplendent in a red cape knotted around his neck and a ruffled orange-and-black silk shirt, had the presence, and the confidence, it seemed, to instantly reorient the crowd in the direction he wanted.

Astonishingly, the Rolling Stones were still expected, under these alarming circumstances, to play a concert, as if this were another night at the local basketball arena. Richards, his rhinestone-studded orange shirt left unbuttoned, his black sunglasses clipped to his T-shirt, fingered the opening notes of "Jumpin' Jack Flash," and the rest of the band fell in, determined to bash their way through this.

Some fans believed the band deliberately tanked its performance, hoping to deflate some of the frantic energy of Altamont with a mediocre gig, but the Stones sounded fairly solid on this night, given the unprecedentedly adverse circumstances in which they played. Bill Wyman's bass was mostly inaudible, and Charlie Watts's drums were poorly miked, but the night belonged to Richards, who played with a restrained frenzy.

After "Jumpin' Jack Flash" came to its fiery conclusion, a young man with long blond hair tried to climb onto the stage, and was brutally confronted by the Angels, who swarmed around him. They punched him repeatedly, and one Angel kicked him in the face. He was soon motionless, spread-eagled on the ground, surrounded by a crowd so densely packed that there was no room for him to move, or for anyone to assist him.

Mick Jagger and Keith Richards. (Courtesy of Robert Altman)

The Stones' laid into their cover of Chuck Berry's "Carol," a blues rave-up they favored on many of their '69 tour dates, and immediately followed it with Jagger chugging from a bottle of Jack Daniel's placed at his feet. "I'd like to drink one to you all," Jagger chuckled, trying on a broad Southern accent for size. Richards picked up on the moment and launched into the stop-and-start riff of a jagged "Sympathy for the Devil." A young woman next to the stage longingly held up a bouquet of pink roses as an Angel glowered next to her. The flowers still looked fresh, but their leaves—the ones almost touching the biker—were already seen to be wilting.

Even the Stones' performance could not change the composition of the toxic stew down below the stage. The audience, thrilled to spot Jagger, surged forward once more. There were calls to clear the stage of everyone other than the performers, but the Angels flat-out refused, preferring to tell others to move. "*Off* the *stage*," a biker, his eyes rolling back into his head, his teeth grinding, ordered. The bikers formed a wedge in front of the band, primed to leap into the crowd on the slightest provocation. The band, flummoxed in its attempts to move the bikers away, reluctantly pressed the Angels into service for the task of clearing others off the stage. The Angels' excessive shows of force, flinging others from the stage, inevitably led to more scuffles breaking out, both on the stage and elsewhere.

The Angels, and their motorcycles, were still precariously propped up near the stage, and the crowd heaved forward once more, thousands of diehard fans craning for a glimpse of Mick and Keith. One fan kneeled on the motorcycle seat of a San Francisco Angel named Julio, and his weight shorted out the bike, starting a small fire. A thread of smoke began rising up toward the stage, and into the sky. Barger spotted the smoke from his perch on the stage and leapt off to shove the fan away from the motorcycle. Other Angels jumped down to put out the smoldering fire.

The burning motorcycle touched off the day's severest round of violence yet. The proximity of the Angels' motorcycles to thousands of wild fans emboldened by the presence of the Stones meant such skirmishes were inevitable. The Angels pushed fans away from their bikes, once more clearing out a demilitarized zone closest to the stage, and kicked, punched, and trampled audience members in the process. The frustrated crowd threw bottles and grabbed for the Angels' motorcycles, only further agitating the bikers. The Angels surged into the crowd, attacking those they believed had manhandled their bikes and beating them mercilessly. Meredith Hunter was in the thick of the chaos as the Angels rampaged. He reached into his jacket pocket, where he had placed his gun, without removing anything, as if feeling for a totem of protection.

The Rolling Stones, the ostensible stars of the day, perched above the hellish scene, utterly unable to prevent the violence. Guitarist Mick Taylor was stunned by the uncontrolled environment, and found himself incapable of enjoying what should have been a triumphant moment for his new band. He thought about walking off the stage, but was worried that this would only exacerbate the calamity unfolding at his feet.

Sam Cutler approached Jagger with a message about the violence, but Jagger waved him off. The lead singer called out to Richards to halt the song: "Will you cool it and I'll try and stop it."

Jagger asked the crowd to sit down, hoping that if more fans got off their feet, the less pushing there might be, and the sooner calm might be restored. The Angels began flapping their arms, gesturing to those fans near them to sit. Jagger called out to his "brothers and sisters," pleading with them: "Everybody, just cool out!" The crowd reoccupied the space that had been emptied out by the Angels. Watts played drum fills to occupy the silence and Richards fingered his guitar. "All right?" Jagger asked the crowd. "Is there anyone here that's hurt?"

"Something very funny always happens when we start that number," Jagger impishly told the crowd. The Rolling Stones had only been too happy to seize on others' claims of the band's demonic powers, and now Altamont would be further evidence of their dark hold on their audience. The band started up "Sympathy" once more, Richards's guitar shooting off sparks as it let loose. Richards, framed by the darkness, calmly let loose thunderbolts of rhythm. The elegant, woozy riff appeared to have momentarily lulled the audience into tranquility. As Jagger sang of czars and ministers, a dog casually strolled across the stage. The day had entered the realm of the surreal. But the violence had only temporarily abated.

As Richards let loose a beautifully limber solo, fluid and relentless, the music was overpowered by the sound of a horrified crowd. The Angels were beating a young man whose overly exuberant dancing—so daring when in the presence of such violence—had irritated them. An Angel shoved the dancer, and another biker began swinging his pool cue wildly at the crowd. The audience members in closest proximity to the Angels surged away from their reach, and the dancer took the opportunity to run away from the stage. The Hells Angels caught up with him, raining blows on his head with their pool cues and kicking him mercilessly, all for the crime of having momentarily enjoyed the concert.

The Maysleses' cameras caught a goateed young man in a newsboy cap looking at Jagger, silently pleading with him to intervene on behalf of the audience. As Jagger kept dancing, his hands atop his head, his elbows out, encased in his own private world of pleasure, it was clear, to one concertgoer at least, that the lead singer of the Rolling Stones was ill-inclined to help. It was a damning moment. "The Stones' music was strong but it could not stop the terror," Stanley Booth would later write of the scene. "There was a look of disbelief on the people's faces, wondering how the Stones could go on playing and singing in the bowels of madness and violent death."

One young woman, close enough to rest her fingers on the stage, nodded her head as tears ran down her cheeks. Meanwhile, the fan next to her smiled beatifically, thrilled by his proximity to the Rolling Stones. It was a study in contrasts, with the unrest and uncertainty of the day parceled out unevenly and inconsistently. Some fans were overwhelmed by the chaos, while others were intent on boxing out all such distractions from the music.

A close look at the Maysles' footage would also later reveal a brief glimpse of a young black man in a black shirt and lime-green suit, surrounded by the crush of fans near the stage. Meredith Hunter would appear for about eight seconds in his penultimate appearance onscreen, looking mostly calm and untroubled, even as he stood in the eye of the oncoming storm. He raises his head, the wide brim of his black hat ascending to reveal his face. He is sticking out his tongue, his eyes lifting to take in the stage, but the most telling detail is just how close he is to the Hells Angels. The burly biker in the black watch cap and the Angels jacket would seemingly only need to briskly shove two young women out of his way to stand chest-to-chest with Hunter.

The Angels were not merely the accidental purveyors of fear; they were studied practitioners of low-grade terror. By the Angels' warped logic, their opponents understood violence would be the bikers' response to all assaults on their honor. Altamont, by this logic, was less a mistake, or a wildly excessive counterattack, than simply a larger stage for what the Hells Angels had always done. The Angels were intent on dominating and terrifying all opponents, real and imagined; today, their enemies ran three hundred thousand deep. "Who's fighting, and what for?" Jagger asked the crowd. "Who's fighting, and what for? Why are we fighting?" "The fuckin' Angels," shouted a disembodied voice in the crowd.

Keith Richards, never as enamored of hippie romanticism as Jagger, harbored no illusions about who was at fault for the disorder in the crowd. "Listen, man. Either these cats cool it, man, or we don't play," Richards announced from the stage, taking a notably more confrontational stance than Jagger had by pointing directly at the Angels below him. The stern warning, clearly directed at the Hells Angels, had little effect on the chaos below. An Angel grabbed one of the microphones and implored the crowd to calm down, as if they had been the instigators of the chaos: "Hey, if you don't cool it you ain't gonna hear no more music! Now, you want to all go home, or what?" Stones roadie Ian Stewart frantically called for a doctor to approach the stage, and Sam Cutler made an announcement about a five-year-old girl who had gotten separated from her parents. Jagger conferred with Animal, still highly visible in his fox-head hat, who seemed to be keeping the Stones singer informed about disturbances in the crowd.

Patti Bredehoft would have been just as content to leave, having had more than her fill of the festival ambience, but Meredith Hunter was intent on staking his claim to the Stones, and she was there because he wanted her to stand with him. In the ongoing melee near the stage, Bredehoft was separated from her boyfriend, but still able to see him. She could see Hunter, like many other concertgoers positioned near the stage, still aggressively attempting to lay claim to his own space. He had climbed onto one of the speaker boxes set up just next to the stage, in search of the best view, and the modicum of protection it granted.

"Let's play cool-out music," Richards told Jagger, uncoiling a languorous blues melody on his guitar. Sonny Barger later claimed that, at this point, he approached Richards and pointed his pistol at him. Keith would play his guitar, he claimed to say, or he was dead. "He played like a motherfucker," Barger crowed. But Barger could not be seen next to Richards in the film footage shot that day, nor was his bragging entirely believable. If Barger had pointed a gun at Richards, the Rolling Stones would have had a legitimate claim to playing Altamont as hostages to a hostile, armed force, compelled to play by the threat of being maimed or killed. The Stones never made such a claim, nor did they ever mention it in the years and decades that followed. Barger likely confused fantasy with reality here, mistaking his undoubted verbal intimidation of the day's headliners with a more physical brand of assault.

"If we are all one," Jagger announced, "let's show we're all one." "Preach it, brother," a voice called out from the crowd, and Jagger called on the crowd once more to sit down, hoping to cool some of the overheating tempers on the speedway. Jagger called for a doctor to come up front, next to the scaffolding, and Mick Taylor snuck a quick drag off the cigarette stuck into the fretboard of his guitar before launching the languorous melody line of "Under My Thumb." The song felt stretched out now, elongated to encompass the crowd, the night, the enormity of this moment. Here was the Stones' moment of triumph, feted and adored in front of a crowd of hundreds of thousands.

As the drums entered once more, and Jagger repeatedly intoned the line "I pray that it's all right," another space ominously began to clear in the audience below. The huge mass of people near the stage, pressed together so tightly that they had practically formed a single, many-limbed organism, *Homo rockismus*, was now disintegrating, crumbling under the weight of the fear sweeping its ranks. The Hells Angels swooped into the crowd, a leather-clad phalanx wading into the morass, and the fans in their vicinity rapidly backpedaled, seeking daylight from whomever or whatever had sparked the Angels' ire.

The Rolling Stones had initially instructed the Hells Angels that their main responsibility was to keep the audience off the stage. The Angels had devoted much of their day to throwing fans off the stage, often with more enthusiasm than the bands might have envisioned or desired. During the Stones' set, too, the Angels intended to keep the stage unoccupied. Their charge, as they saw it, extended beyond the stage to the bands' equipment. One of the people in the crowd standing on a speaker box was Meredith Hunter.

A hefty Hells Angel jerked roughly on Hunter's ear and hair, chuckling all the while at his daring as he yanked Hunter down from the speaker box and onto the ground alongside him. Hunter shook off the Angel, and the Angel grabbed him by the arm and hand. Hunter pulled back, and the Angel punched him in the mouth.

When Bredehoft glanced in his direction, having missed the opening beats of the skirmish, she thought she saw Hunter turning around and being approached by first one Angel, and then two or three more. The Angels knocked Hunter to the ground, and he leapt up, intent on defending himself against their assault.

Hunter attempted to flee into the crowd. The Angel then leapt off the stage and chased after Hunter, joined by four of his fellow bikers. They stepped on bystanders' fingers and feet in their haste to pursue him. Five bikers surrounded one teenager, assaulting him without justification or fear of interruption, as on so many other occasions that day. Meredith Hunter pushed the crowd away from him in his desperate flight from the Angels, looking fiercely at his tormentors in a doomed attempt to scare them off.

Meredith Hunter was in flight from the Hells Angels who had beaten him. He had watched the pool cues raining down on concertgoers all day, had seen the manic glee with which the bikers had beaten others for the crime of enjoying themselves. He had undoubtedly noticed, as well, the viciousness with which the Angels had singled out other African-Americans. What thoughts must have surged through his mind in the moments during which he desperately sought to escape their frenzied grip?

Perhaps, too, the methamphetamine Hunter had taken during the day had lowered his inhibitions, and dulled the innate caution that anyone would have when surrounded by weapon-wielding bikers. But Hunter was not just another concertgoer. He was a black man amid a sea of white faces, and perhaps his reckless calculation was predicated on the knowledge that he had already been singled out for punishment by a group of white men known to target black people.

Reaching into the pocket of his suit jacket, he pulled out his .22 Smith & Wesson pistol and held it up in the air. Both his arms were spread, with his left hand, clutching the gun, outstretched in the direction of the stage. Bredehoft shouted at Hunter not to shoot and pulled closer to her boyfriend. She grabbed at Hunter, then turned, spun around by the momentum of the fracas. Hunter was still running away, even as he began to lower his gun. A short, stocky Angel wearing a sleeveless light-brown vest with a FRISCO patch over the left breast jumped on him from behind, grabbing at his arm. The biker almost rode on his back as he raised his arm over his head and brought his knife down in a long, curving arc, stabbing Hunter twice. Bredehoft was now alone in the empty circle cleared out by the fearful audience as Hunter was carried away from her.

If we were to pause here, we could picture a moment when the clash might have been resolved in markedly different fashion. The danger had been mostly checked. The gun had likely already been wrenched away from Hunter, and even if it had not yet been, he was hardly in any position to fire it anymore. If the Hells Angels had believed in good faith that Meredith Hunter was a threat to the Rolling Stones, or to the crowd, they might have hauled him away, and dispatched one of their men to call the police. The threat would have been defused, and Hunter might have been taken to the hospital, his wounds serious but quite likely, given their location, not life-threatening. Meredith Hunter might have eventually been arrested, and charged with possession of a deadly weapon. But this was not the story of the day, nor of the men tasked with protecting the crowd. Vengeance, not justice, carried the day. Punishment was dealt out swiftly and brutally. The momentum of the scuffle carried Meredith Hunter toward the nearby scaffolding, where he disappeared from sight, surrounded by Hells Angels intent on teaching him a lesson.

The Hells Angel stabbed Hunter no less than four more times, his knife repeatedly piercing his back. Hunter, wounded, dropped to his knees. The Hells Angel gripped him by the shoulders and kicked him in the face, over and over. The Angels surrounded him in a loose circle, pounding him with their boots until he collapsed face-forward. The Angels punched and kicked Meredith as they dragged him away from the stage and toward the scaffolding. Hunter fell to the ground, and bumped against some part of the scaffolding, perhaps its pillars. Hunter softly told his attackers, his strength already beginning to fade, "I wasn't going to shoot you."

Bredehoft watched as a small group of Hells Angels surrounded Meredith and pummeled and stomped him, their boot-clad feet and fists surging into his helpless body with terrifying relentlessness.

She screamed at the Angels, pleading with them to stop: stop the fighting, stop the assault on her boyfriend, stop the madness. Bredehoft grabbed the jacket of one Angel near her, attempting to pull him off her boyfriend, but he simply threw his arms back, shrugging her off without lifting a hand to her. The Angels were now locked in on Hunter, and Bredehoft's efforts were incapable of distracting them from their vigilante justice.

Meredith Hunter was in front of them and under their feet, and something had enraged them, something had set the Hells Angels into a frenzied motion that would not be sated. Any threat that Hunter's gun might have posed had long since been quelled, but the assault went on until he was battered and bruised and completely still.

"Look, we're splitting!" Keith Richards angrily shouted into his microphone. "If those cats don't stop beating everyone in sight. I want them *out* of the way!" A Hells Angel instantly approached Richards, and began tugging on his arm. "Hey!" he yelled at the Stones' guitarist. "The guy's got a gun out there and is shooting at the stage." The story of Hunter's shooting at the stage, however implausible, was spreading from the moment of the encounter with the Angels. (How had Hunter fired his gun in the crowd without hitting anyone or anything? And where had the bullets that had supposedly been fired gone?)

Hunter was now down on the ground under the scaffolding. One of the Angels grabbed a cardboard garbage can with a metal rim and proceeded to bash it against Hunter's skull. He then dropped the garbage can and, joined by his fellow bikers, kicked Hunter repeatedly in the head. The Angel who had stabbed him, not yet done with Hunter, stood on top of his battered head for a full minute before finally stepping back. "Don't touch him," he told a bystander who had been watching the fight. "He's going to die anyway."

Giving up on fighting off the Angels herself, Bredehoft stepped out from under the scaffolding and approached the nearest members of the crowd. Please, she asked, would somebody help out her boyfriend? No one moved. They had seen what the Hells Angels were capable of, and were frightened of becoming their next victims. They moved back, still able to see a fellow audience member being assaulted by the bikers, but out of the reach of their fists and pool cues. They warned her to get back, otherwise she might be the next one hurt.

Bredehoft attempted to break through the tight circle of bikers, hoping to pull Hunter out to safety, but a burly Angel stopped her, telling her that he was not worth it. "He was gonna kill us," the Angel told Bredehoft. "He deserves whatever he gets." Why was she trying so hard to help him, anyway? The Angel appeared not to realize that Bredehoft was Hunter's girlfriend, assuming, perhaps, that she was merely a well-intentioned hippie girl hoping to intervene to protect a stranger. He shoved Bredehoft back, and an onlooker caught her before she crumpled to the ground.

Bredehoft gave up. She had tried to stop the fighting herself, and had futilely attempted to enlist the help of others in fending off the Hells Angels. Nothing had worked. She could do nothing. She sat there crying, pleading with them to stop, watching helplessly as they pummeled her boyfriend. She was still begging them to stop, but the hope she had had, only a few minutes prior, that she might convince them to behave rationally had dissipated into despair. They would not be done until they said they were done—until they had extracted payback from Meredith Hunter for his perceived crimes against the collective body of the Hells Angels.

The whole scuffle, from start to finish, had taken not more than five minutes, but for Bredehoft, it felt like an entire lifetime had passed—an eternity of bearing helpless witness to a terrifying assault. At long last, when most of the Angels moved on from Hunter, and the beating came to a halt, she made her way over to him. An

Angel stepped into her path and asked her where she was going. She told him that she was going over to help Hunter, her boyfriend. "You shouldn't be crying over him," he responded. "He was gonna kill innocent people and he should be dead."

The Angel stood in her way, and would not let Bredehoft approach Hunter. She remembered that earlier in the day, she had spotted a first-aid station nearby. She stumbled over to the Red Cross tent, hysterical but resolute, and pleaded with them to help. The Hells Angels had beaten someone up, and he was lying nearby, just around the corner.

A pair of bystanders, including a young man who called himself Paul Cox, and had witnessed the entire ordeal, helped flip Hunter onto his stomach, hoping to clear the blood away in order to assess the severity of his wounds. He had wounds at his temple, and on his upper and lower back, and Cox had the horrifying sensation of looking directly into another human being's lacerated body. The wounds were at least an inch deep, and soon enough, Cox was soaked in Hunter's blood. A doctor examined Hunter's wounds and asked the Rolling Stones to call for an ambulance.

Cox picked up Hunter's legs and attempted to remove him from the scene with the help of Sam Cutler and some other onlookers. They thought they might carry Hunter onto the stage, hoping to capture the attention of the Rolling Stones, and thereby stop the concert. The Hells Angels would not let him through, and Cox thought that they might have been calculating that Hunter would soon be dead.

Cox began carrying Hunter in the other direction, away from the stage, hoping to get to the medical tent. Audience members close to Hunter held up bloody hands in the fervent hope that Jagger would see them, and respond. Whether moved by the sight of bloodied concertgoers, or because word of the stabbing had reached the stage, Jagger took to the microphone and pleaded with the audience to make room: "We need a doctor here, now! Look, can you let the doctor get through, please. We're trying to get to someone who's hurt."

Bredehoft waited in the tent while the Red Cross volunteers ran off in search of her boyfriend. The sound of the crowd receded, and she was left to sort out the disordered swirl of thoughts and feelings and hopes that raced around her mind. After fifteen minutes, Cox reached the Red Cross tent. Hunter was placed on a metal stretcher.

In the medical tent, Bredehoft noticed for the first time Hunter's condition. His suit jacket was bloody, and he was unconscious. She realized that something more must have happened to him than the punches and kicks she had seen, something she had been unable to spot in the din and frenzy of the fight. Surrounded by onlookers, Bredehoft was continually being reassured that Hunter would be fine, that all would be well, that there was nothing to worry about.

In truth, medical staff saw that little could be done for Hunter. He was still breathing, but his pulse was weak, and his body had gone completely limp. Hunter's nose was so thoroughly crushed that he gasped for air, attempting to breathe through his mouth. He had deep wounds on his lower and upper back and his left temple. Dr. Richard Baldwin, the head of medical services at the festival, believed that Hunter's wounds were so severe that even if he had been stabbed in a hospital operating room, he still would have been likely to die.

The Red Cross workers rushed Hunter into a waiting station wagon, and urged Bredehoft in to accompany him. They took him the half-mile to the speedway's racetrack, where a helicopter might be able to take him to the hospital. "Don't let him die," Bredehoft pleaded, with everyone and no one. "I don't want him to die." A man standing next to her under the helicopter tried to console her: "They're gonna do everything in their power." "I have to go with him!" she pleaded.

The plan was to evacuate Hunter by helicopter to a nearby hospital, where he might be able to receive the lifesaving care he needed. A doctor and a number of other medical personnel examined Hunter at the gates of the speedway track, giving him mouth-to-mouth resuscitation and cardiac massage, but their efforts were fruitless. Meredith Hunter was dead. There was no need for a helicopter.

Patti Bredehoft was escorted back to the first-aid tent. She was surrounded by the other, less serious casualties of the day: the broken bones and the drug freakouts. She was given a tranquilizer to calm her frayed nerves, and reassured not to worry. Hunter would be fine. He was undoubtedly receiving the best of care as they spoke. Only a few minutes later, two new figures, a man and a woman, approached Bredehoft. They confirmed what a part of her had already known: Hunter had not survived.

For some time—she could not say how long, but it felt like centuries—Bredehoft sat alone. She was surrounded by her fellow Americans, her fellow Bay Area residents, her fellow music fans, and she was abandoned. No one could aid her, no one could rescue her from the abyss she had invisibly stumbled over. A day to see the Rolling Stones and hang out with friends had turned into the last day of her boyfriend's all-too-short life, and there was no undoing the notes of the song, no lifting the needle from a skipping track and resituating it at the outer edge of the black vinyl circle. Meredith was dead, and she was alone.

"Under My Thumb" should have been the conclusion of the Stones' set. But unsurprisingly for this day of fizzled opportunities and disastrous encounters, the Stones dutifully chugged on. Amid the murderous frenzy, the Rolling Stones kept on playing, hoping to preserve what they mistakenly hoped might be the tattered remnants of a fragile peace. "Hells Angels, everybody," Jagger implored the crowd. "Let's just keep ourselves together. You know, if we *are* all one, let's fucking well *show* we're all one."

The band debuted their new song "Brown Sugar," which they were playing live for the first time. They tore through "Satisfaction" and "Gimme Shelter" before wrapping up with their customary closer "Street Fighting Man." The violence never stopped; during "Live with Me," a naked woman sought to climb to the stage, and was assaulted by a team of Angels, who kicked and punched her with brutal abandon until she fell back onto the crowd below.

Keith Richards's guitar loped and rattled, expressing Richards's commingled fury and elegance. Mick Taylor eschewed the stage dance between Mick and Keith, preferring to pose seriously between the Stones' two stars while silently wielding his guitar.

"Street Fighting Man" was a perversely appropriate closer, a celebration of bare-knuckled violence that served the day as an anthem of praise for the very men who had dashed the Stones' dreams. An Angel stood on the stage, flinging flowers into the crowd with gleeful abandon. The Hells Angels were not just defending themselves from a hostile and aggressive crowd; they were actually having a blast while doing so. This was their party now.

Throughout the Stones' set, the majority of the crowd was only aware of a series of interruptions to the music, and Richards and Jagger's complaints about unspecified behavior near the stage. Most Altamont attendees didn't learn a fellow concertgoer was dead until they heard the news on the radio that night, or later that weekend. The further you were from the stage, the less likely you were to have any idea what might have happened. While Meredith Hunter was dying, hundreds of thousands of other young men and women, separated from Hunter only by their relative good fortune, continued to party obliviously.

The counterculture for which Altamont was intended to be yet another coming-out party prided itself on its political progressive-mindedness, devoted as it was to ending the war in Vietnam and advancing the cause of civil rights. But even at their own celebration, the counterculture could not prevent another outbreak of violence. More than that, it remained unaware of the violence even as it happened. Hippie culture was devoted to the idea of the maximization of personal bliss. Music and drugs and sex were gateways to pleasure, the royal road to a gentler, kinder America. But the brutish corners of American life lingered, even in the very epicenter of hippie ecstasy, and no amount of wishing away the bloody reality of racially motivated hatred and discord rampant in American life with paeans to harmony could make it otherwise. The counterculture was idealistic but blinkered, and Altamont was its metaphoric nadir. One young black man died while thousands of white concertgoers carried on enjoying themselves, unable to see or hear the news of his brutal fate.

Part Three

CARRYING ON

9. Last Chopper Out

The last notes of "Street Fighting Man" drifted out from the stage, over the fans still packed in like sardines, over the Hells Angels wielding blood-spattered knives and pool cues, out past the Altamont audience, mostly still blissfully unaware of what had taken place, and on into the darkened and barren nightscape beyond. The music had at last come to a halt, and the debacle known as Altamont was now complete. The Rolling Stones had attempted to hold off the chaos that threatened to envelop their jury-rigged utopia with music, and whether due to their own personal failings, or those of the culture they represented, they proved woefully inadequate to the task of warding off disaster. Now everyone was free once more—free to escape, free to return home, where civilized virtues still took hold. The primary actors on this temporary stage began to disperse, each on their own trajectory away from Altamont.

The concert was over, but people still lined up outside the oozing, festering porta-potties. Many fans waited for the speedway to begin emptying out before they slowly trudged back to their cars. It was simply too crowded to even consider leaving. And the unsettled atmosphere made the cooped-up fans wild. One irate (or drug-addled) concertgoer smashed a full gallon jug of wine against a car seeking to escape the speedway, cracking the windshield and terrifying its inhabitants. And the CHP's overly energetic ticketing and towing earlier in the day meant that once fans did leave, many people would mistakenly believe that their cars had been stolen or misplaced. Some had to spend an unpleasant night at the speedway, or cadge a ride back to the Bay Area with friends or strangers.

The Rolling Stones fled from the stage and up the hill toward the helicopter waiting to whisk them away. It would be the first leg of their escape from America, and a continent that had welcomed them so gratefully only a few months prior. The band and their handlers tore through a hole in the cyclone fence around the speedway and piled into two vehicles—one car and one ambulance—anxious to make their escape. The drivers leaned on their horns, steadily parting the teeming crowd as they made their way to the helicopter. The Stones and their minions boarded, seventeen people in total. Jagger's assistant Jo Bergman would later compare it to the "last chopper out of 'Nam."

The helicopter landed at the nearby Livermore airport, where an airplane waited to fly them back to San Francisco. Richards was furious about the Angels' hijacking of what was to have been their American apotheosis: "They're sick, man, they're worse than the cops. They're just not ready. I'm never going to have anything to do with them again." Jagger sat on a wooden bench nearby, his eyes, Stanley Booth wrote, "still hurt and angry, bewildered and scared, not understanding who the Hells Angels were or why they were killing people at his free peace-and-love show." "How could anybody think those people are good, think they're people you should have around?" Jagger wondered.

"I'd rather have had cops," Jagger muttered, and the Flying Burrito Brothers' Gram Parsons, who had joined the Stones on the helicopter, shared his sentiments. The Angels had spent much of the afternoon attempting to shove Parsons off the stage, and he was fed up with their callous behavior: "The Angels are worse than cops. They're bozos, just a bunch of bozos."

"Some people are just not ready," Richards kept repeating to himself. He was anxious over the absence of two of his prized jackets, both left behind at the speedway, and had to be cajoled onto the airplane with assurances that someone would go back for his lost coats.

A fleet of limousines waited at the San Francisco airport to usher the Stones back to the Huntington Hotel. The televisions in their suites were tuned to the news reports of the concert, and the band members wondered nervously about whether they might be summoned back to California to testify in a future court case. Richards smoked a joint and assisted Parsons with deciphering the French-language room service menu. "If Rock Scully don't know any more about things than that, man, to think the Angels are—what did he say? Honor and dignity?" Richards fumed. "Yeah, man. He's just a childish romantic. I have no time for such people." The Angels, he declared, were "homicidal maniacs," and should all be in jail.

Jagger encountered the film's producer Porter Bibb at the hotel, and the Stones' lead singer sounded deflated over the prospect of a concert film: "I don't want—it's not that it didn't happen, I don't want to try to muzzle it, but I don't see any sense in trying to exploit what happened." Only a few hours after the concert's end, remorse was setting in: "I didn't want it to be like this." Drummer Charlie Watts would later call it "an event waiting to go wrong."

Jagger, doing a radio interview, tried to put the extraordinary, unimaginable chaos of the day into halting words. "If Jesus had been there," he archly told the interviewer, "he would have been crucified." The food finally arrived, and Richards, Parsons, and Booth ate silently, stripped of language with which to encompass or explain what they had seen and experienced. "We had been through a shattering experience," Booth would later write, "in a way the experience we had been looking for all our lives, and none of us knew what to say."

As the Stones had played, the Grateful Dead fled for the headliners' helicopter, not even staying for the entirety of the final set. The Dead's departure was ignominious, lacking the resolve of the Rolling Stones, who, whatever their other failings of planning or execution, or their lack of compassion for what their fans were experiencing, faced the crowd and did their level best to calm the furies. The Dead merely left.

Could the Grateful Dead, by performing, have done anything to halt the violence? In all likelihood, no. The unrest was too far advanced, and the Hells Angels already too unhinged, for any one performer or participant to put a stop to it. But of all the bands at Altamont, the Grateful Dead unquestionably had the longest relationship with the Hells Angels, and arguably had accrued the most goodwill with Bay Area rock fans. If they had taken the stage and pleaded for calm, or approached the Angels and asked them to halt all hostilities, it could possibly have gone some way toward cooling the tensions at the speedway.

Instead, the Grateful Dead chose to abscond, determined to protect themselves first. The decision should not be castigated lightly. Given what they saw and heard, and what had befallen Marty Balin, it was not unreasonable to conclude that taking the stage might very well mean putting their lives at risk. But it is entirely possible that had the Dead taken the same stance as the Rolling Stones, and taken the stage, some of the later horror might have been mitigated.

Later that same night, the Grateful Dead stopped by the Fillmore West, where they had been scheduled to play a gig. The word about the Altamont debacle had rapidly spread, and the audience had stayed away, sure the Dead would not show their faces. Jerry Garcia, Rock Scully, and drummer Bill Kreutzmann were backstage, taking hits of nitrous oxide from a tank specially designed by Ken Kesey's Merry Pranksters, when the notoriously voluble proprietor of the Fillmore, Bill Graham, stormed in. Graham had also heard about Altamont, and railed against the Dead for their bungled planning. They were the ones, he believed, responsible for the turmoil. "And you especially, Scully," Graham shouted, "you're a fucking murderer!" Scully, still high on nitrous oxide, grabbed Graham and threw him down the dressing room stairs. It was an undignified end to a discomfiting day for the Grateful Dead. What better response to being accused of failing to protect their fans from an outburst of wholly predictable violence than another act of violence?

Crosby, Stills, Nash & Young flew south to Los Angeles for a show that night at Pauley Pavilion, home of the defending national champion UCLA Bruins. Stills, overwrought by the day's exertions, fainted.

Sam Cutler had been left behind as the sole representative of the Rolling Stones, in charge of returning the speedway to its formerly pristine state. Cutler was frustrated with how little all the talk of brotherhood and spiritual communion actually extended to tangible efforts like picking up the mountains of trash. The day after the event, a police photographer went out to take pictures of the concert site, with some observations recorded for posterity: "1. The field located east of the race track was covered with debris, papers, bottles, food, etc." Only fifteen people stuck around after the show, remaining behind to sort through thirty tons of litter. Cutler issued fruitless pleas over the radio for attendees to assist with the cleanup.

The Rolling Stones spent Sunday leaving the country, with

Jagger departing for Geneva with the take from the tour in his suit-case, and Richards, after a breakfast of cocaine and Old Charter bourbon, returning to London with Charlie Watts and Mick Taylor. Jagger was on his way to the south of France, where he would begin looking for a house to rent. They loosely planned a band press conference for Friday, but nothing was organized yet.

The Stones' manager, Ronnie Schneider, stayed behind in the United States as the band went back to Europe, and from his perspective, the story immediately began to shrink in importance. Altamont was a major headache and a frustration, but the band had not pulled the gun, or wielded the knife. The Rolling Stones were not culpable, or even involved. This was a matter between Meredith Hunter and the Hells Angels, and the media coverage was already twisting the story beyond recognition. Moreover, where was the outrage regarding the Grateful Dead? The Stones had headlined the show, but the Dead, Schneider argued, had come up with the idea for it. The Bay Area was their home turf, and their status as hometown heroes might—just might—have been enough to dial down the day's violence.

The Stones camp preferred to see the chaos of Altamont as being less about evil bikers or thwarted assassination attempts than the story of two bands—co-planners in this free concert—who had taken dramatically different responses to the day's events. The Rolling Stones had confronted terror and uncertainty, and gone out to meet it with little more than their guitars and their authority. The Grateful Dead had faced the same moral dilemma and chose to turn tail and flee. Two bands had shown their true colors that day, and the Rolling Stones had been the courageous ones.

Most of the crowd had hastily departed after the show, eager to leave Altamont behind them and return to the Bay Area and civilization.

But some stragglers remained behind, content to keep the party going for a few more hours. The men whose ranks included Meredith Hunter's killer stuck around at Altamont, in no hurry to leave.

Sonny Barger and some of the other Hells Angels remained at Altamont until the last embers burned out, as if this were another of the bikers' overnight campfires, and there was no hurry to leave until every last pill had been swallowed and every last beer can crushed. There was no urgency, no need to craft a response to the reckoning sure to come. Instead, the Angels were angry at having had so much asked of them, and of having to contend with a frazzled, unhappy crowd for the entire day.

The Rolling Stones had left the Angels to fend off what they saw as an angry mob of agitated, disruptive, potentially murderous concertgoers without so much as a thank you. The least the Stones could do, they saw, was to offer some parting gifts for their service. The Hells Angels decided to make off with one of the rugs that had adorned the Altamont stage.

When the show ended, some of the Angels rolled up the carpet and stuck it onto one of their pickup trucks. Chip Monck spotted them and, already disgusted by their behavior, decided to make a point of denying them this small satisfaction. The rug belonged to the Rolling Stones, and should not lie on the floor in some Angel's living room as long as he had a say in it. As the Angels drove away, Monck grabbed hold of one end of the rug, and held still as it dropped into the dirt at his feet. He had not taken into account the two Harley-Davidson motorcycles resting atop the pilfered rug, which also came flying off the pickup.

So much of the day's terror had stemmed from the damage inflicted by concertgoers on the Angels' prized, hand-built motorcycles. Now here was an employee of the hated Rolling Stones, unexpectedly seeking to not only steal from the Hells Angels, but to wreck their choppers. Monck, speaking quickly, kept the ensuing dialogue almost civil for about fifteen minutes. Ultimately, the Angels settled the brouhaha the same way they had so many others that Saturday, and smashed Monck in the mouth with a sawed-off pool cue, knocking most of Monck's upper teeth out. The ground at Altamont was soaked with another man's blood—perhaps the final violent act of the day.

After assaulting Monck, the Angels smoked joints and drank beer until it was, at last, time to go. They found old tires and pieces of wood and built themselves an enormous bonfire. The sight of the blaze attracted other stragglers, and the Angels carried out their frustrations on the interlopers, the beatings continuing deep into the night. Just before midnight, a convoy of motorcycles roared out of the speedway, taking the 5 to Interstate 680 back toward Oakland. Terry the Tramp, another Angel, ran out of gas on the way home. Barger "pegged" him the rest of the way home, leaning their bikes together and placing his foot on the front peg of Terry's motorcycle to keep them conjoined. That was what brothers did for each other. They protected each other from the hazards of the world. Bikers did not leave their motorcycles behind, nor did they abandon their compatriots. A Hells Angel defended his brothers against all assaults.

The day after the concert, Chip Monck, toothless and bloodied but demonically focused on recouping his rug, purchased a case of brandy and paid a visit to Sonny Barger in Oakland. Proffering the brandy as a blandishment, and apologizing for the blood still leaking from the stumps of what had once been his front teeth, Monck asked for his rug back once more. Without it, he told the Hells Angels chieftain, he would lose his job. The Stones had failed them all yesterday, he acknowledged, and while he knew that none of the chaos at Altamont had been Barger's fault, his initial absence had led to a concert whose security was being provided by the chaff of the Angels, and not the wheat. The Rolling Stones were young and callow, but their future held promise, and Monck wanted to be there for all of it. Barger grunted his reluctant agreement: "Take your fucking rug."

The furor over Altamont, which the Angels' studied nonchalance could do little to tamp down, revolved around the propriety of the Hells Angels' presence as a security force. Who had agreed to hire them, and how had they been permitted to act with so little oversight? Most onlookers believed that what Altamont needed and lacked was properly trained security, which would have adequately guarded both the audience and the performers.

There was also the closely related question of whether the Alameda County sheriffs, only minimally present at the concert, should have intervened to protect the crowd from the Hells Angels. It is hard to imagine how four or five officers, even armed ones, might have successfully fended off dozens of Angels, but why hadn't the local police been summoned to restore order? The conspiracy-minded speculated that the local authorities had wanted to see the concert fail, and the hands-off policy did give off the impression of a dangerously laissez-faire attitude toward the health and well-being of the day-trip visitors to Altamont.

The rhetoric of the Hells Angels played down Hunter's death, and their role in fomenting the chaos and hysteria of the day. "Afterward," Sonny Barger would later write, "I didn't feel too bummed about what had happened at the concert. It was another day in the life of a Hells Angel. I did feel it was lucky more people—including the Stones—hadn't been shot dead by this guy, Meredith Hunter. I felt as though the Hells Angels had done their job."

The Angels crafted a narrative that transformed their victim into a potential assassin, and reframed their violent outbursts as a heroic act of diligence. Barger's response was a shrug, as if Altamont were no different from a barroom brawl or a roadside stomping. "Altamont might have been some big catastrophe to the hippies, but it was just another Hells Angels event to me," Barger wrote. "It made a lot of

citizens dislike us, but most of the hippies and journalists and liberals didn't like us anyway. When it comes to pleasing the right people
at the right time, the Hells Angels never came through." The Angels
were proud of their own obtuseness, happily content to walk away
from Altamont with hardly a second thought.

Hidden in Barger's critique was a peculiar, and charged, concep-
tion of his own organization. Altamont concertgoers were expected
to have known the rules of engagement with Hells Angels, even though
many may very well have never encountered a biker in person
before. The rules regarding Angels' motorcycles, and their physical
persons, were treated as holy writ. The necessity of swift punishment for any such violations was as self-evident to the Angels as the
police's arresting a person suspected of committing a crime. Violating the Angels' law had consequences.

The Hells Angels' blind spot regarding their own actions shifted
the blame onto the crowd they had terrorized. The concertgoers had
provoked the Angels by their inability to follow rules they had not
been aware of. "Flower people ain't a bit better than the worst of
us," Barger would write. In Barger's estimation, the only relevant
orders were those issued by the Rolling Stones, who had told them
to sit on the stage and drink beer, and their self-proclaimed right to
protect their own property and well-being. No one else counted.

It was crucial to remember, though, that the Hells Angels were
performers as much as the Rolling Stones or any of the other bands
at Altamont, acting out their fantasies of male potency and vigor. Being a Hells Angel meant inhabiting a role with such conviction that
one no longer remembered the costume could be removed. The ho-
hum response to the violence they had helped to unleash was a part
of the performance, as well, with the Hells Angels playing the role
of hardened street-fighting men, their senses dulled to the crack of
wooden pool cues on skulls or the impact of steel ripping human
flesh. Whether or not they felt, in their deepest inner recesses, any

remorse over what had taken place at Altamont was secondary to the performances they gave, in which Altamont was treated as merely another day at the office.

Moreover, they believed, the fault for Altamont lay squarely with the Rolling Stones, who organized the disastrous concert and failed to protect their fans. "Say what you want," Barger later wrote, "but I blame the Stones for the whole fucking bad scene. They agitated the crowd, had the stage built too low, and then used us to keep the whole thing boiling." The Hells Angels felt burned. They had been subject to the mingled fascination and opprobrium of the media since at least the Monterey rape trial of 1965, but after Altamont, most of the bikers' defenders melted away. Suddenly, the Angels were alone on the American stage, there to stand trial for what the bikers believed were exclusively the sins of the counterculture, particularly the rock bands that co-opted some of the bikers' devil-may-care insouciance without any of their ability to stare down trouble.

Patti Bredehoft still waited in the first-aid tent, frozen in place. Meredith was dead, and she did not know where to go, who to speak to. Ronnie and Judy had long since headed back to Berkeley. She was alone, the enormity of what had taken place only belatedly beginning to sink in, now that the tranquilizer was starting to wear off. She believed that the police had taken away Hunter's body, but where was she supposed to go now?

Eventually, George Hodges, the Red Cross volunteer she had encountered earlier in the day, came around in his white station wagon. He took Bredehoft and some of the other stranded concertgoers and drove them back to Berkeley. Bredehoft was dropped off outside her parents' house just before 1 a.m. She took out her key and opened the door, thinking of the words she would have to say, the heretofore unimaginable events she would have to describe. She woke up her parents and told them what had happened to Meredith, and soon after, the phone began to ring. More people would be looking for Hunter—Ronnie, Meredith's family—and someone would have to tell each of them the horrific news.

The radio was on at Meredith Hunter's sister's house that evening. Dixie Anderson Parker was ministering to her three fatherless children. She was waiting for her brother Meredith's return, hoping that he would come and visit, if not that night, then later that weekend. The children loved their uncle, and in the absence of their father, they craved his presence. Reports spilled out that a crazed man had been killed at Altamont, but what could that have to do with Meredith's excursion with his girlfriend? He was not the type to start any trouble, not likely to tangle with any rough types.

The family's Christmas tree was already in place in the living room at Altha Anderson's house, its branches drooping down toward the floor like a weeping willow. Soon, there would be tinsel draped around the tree, and presents covering the ground beneath it, totems of a happy and fruitful year to come. At two thirty in the morning, the telephone rang at Altha's. It was a family friend, looking to commiserate over the terrible news. This was how the family first heard of Meredith's death. Meredith's sister Gwen frantically made calls to local hospitals and police departments in Livermore and Santa Rita before confirming that Meredith was dead. His body had been taken from the mortuary in Livermore, where it had been delivered earlier in the evening, to the morgue in Oakland, close to their home. At three-thirty that morning, Gwen left for the coroner's office to identify her brother's body.

At the morgue, Hunter's shirt was open, and when his body was turned over, his coat was riddled with cuts. Underneath the suit jacket, there was a large bandage, evidently placed there during the fruitless efforts to save his life. The coroner's report would ultimately detail a total of six wounds to Meredith Hunter's body. Five were found on his upper and lower back, and a sixth in front of his left ear. All were stab wounds. A toxicology report would ultimately show that Hunter had tested positive for a modest amount of methamphetamine and amphetamines. In his drug use, he hardly differed from a substantial percentage of Altamont concertgoers, who had engaged in their own recreational drug-taking that day. (The autopsy did also note track marks on his arms, likely evidence of a pattern of regular crystal-meth use.)

Meredith Hunter's funeral took place four days after the concert, at the Skyview Memorial Lawn in East Vallejo. Only thirty people attended, partially because the funeral notice had not been published until Wednesday, the day of the funeral. Patti Bredehoft was among the mourners present, as was George Hodges, the Red Cross volunteer who had ushered her home.

Dixie Anderson Parker had lost both her husband and her brother in the same year, and the feelings it stirred up were less outrage than a dull, burning grief. She was numb, keeping herself busy with the planning for the funeral and looking after her mother, who seemed to be headed for an emotional collapse. She wasn't angry, although everyone kept asking her if she was, implying that she should be. Instead, Meredith's death merely added another scarring experience to a life already crammed too full of mounting, inevitable loss.

The family could not afford a gravestone, so the final resting place of their son and brother would remain unmarked for decades to come, a symbol of the forgetting already taking place. Meredith Hunter's name would be a footnote to music history, but its link to the real young man who had lived, not just died, disappeared under the earth, with no marker to serve as a reminder.

The beige 1965 Mustang Meredith had borrowed from his mother's boyfriend Charles Talbot had been parked on the side of the road next to the freeway, its occasional driver never to open its door again, never to put the key in the ignition or turn around, exhausted but exhilarated, to head in the direction of home. The police eventually towed the car to an impound lot, and Dixie would have to drive out to Alameda County to retrieve it. It was a curious and empty feeling to reclaim the property of your dead brother, to know that his possessions were no longer his. Dixie drove her car behind the Mustang, a mourner in a procession headed not for the graveyard but for their native Berkeley. What words could describe the void left by death? The Mustang, its two front wheels hefted into the air, returned home, a strong and beautiful machine now without its last driver. It chilled Dixie to watch it, and think about all the places it would never go with Meredith, all the streets it would never trace with its wheels, all the people who would never fit themselves into the contours of its seats.

Sometime in the days that followed—it was hard to separate out one day from the next, as they congealed into a single formless mass of sadness—Patti Bredehoft came to Altha Anderson's house to visit. Hunter's family was civil, but they had never known his girlfriend all that well. And now, a buried question lurked under the surface of every polite exchange, every attempt to attend to the raw feelings of those who had loved and lost their son and brother. Had Bredehoft somehow said or done something that had caused Hunter to lose his life? Had she unconsciously instigated the fatal scuffle between Hunter and the Hells Angels? Bredehoft looked and listened and felt judged. She felt she was being asked to justify herself, to somehow prove the unprovable—that Hunter's death was not her fault, that she had not provoked it, that there had been nothing she could have done to prevent it.

After the funeral, Anderson mingled at home with family and friends numbed by grief and vibrating with rage. Hunter's teenage friends were there, many of them consumed by anger at the pointlessness and brutality of his death. Who had allowed Meredith to be taken away from them? How could a young man full of energy, full of love and life and future, be nothing but a memory now? There had to be some meaning, some answer to the question of Meredith Hunter's death.

Dixie listened as they talked about the Black Panthers—their fierceness, their dedication, their stalwart defense of African-American lives. Dixie was distinctly unenthusiastic about the Panthers, seeing them as unrepresentative of her own political beliefs, but it made a kind of symbolic sense that Hunter's friends, contemplating the horror of his death, were drawn to them. Their militarism and their aura of fierceness made them a more politically minded African-American analogue to the Hells Angels, defenders of an abused minority with an unyielding belief in physical conflict as the ultimate arbiter of American right.

The family seemed unable or unwilling to grapple with the details of Hunter's death. That he had died was already too much. For them, the story and its complexities—rock bands and outdoor concerts and security arrangements—only distracted from an elemental American story, still maddeningly unexceptional in 1969. A black man had gone somewhere he was not supposed to be, with someone he was not supposed to be with, and he had been killed for his presumption. The rest was commentary.

Days and weeks passed, and no one in Meredith Hunter's family had heard from the Rolling Stones, or any of their employees, or representatives. This did not surprise them, exactly; what white man, what famous person, was likely to feel compassion over the death of an African-American teenager?

Journalists were interested in Hunter's family where the bands were not. *Rolling Stone*'s Greil Marcus found Meredith's seventeen-year-old sister Gwen, a student at Berkeley High School, at home and willing to speak with him. She was surprisingly composed and articulate for someone who had so recently suffered the brutal shock of her brother's death: "The Rolling Stones are responsible, because they hired the Hell's Angels as police and paid them. But they don't care."

She would call the police "incompetent" when speaking with another journalist, this one with local radical paper the *Berkeley Barb*, and observe of Altamont that "the majority of people there were white and a white person's not gonna help a black person." For Gwen, her brother's death expressed in miniature the story of race in America: "The Hells Angels are white men. The difference between them and other white men, those white men identify themselves by jackets that says Hells Angels. . . . They're not gonna be stopped. The police never do nothing to them and they're not gonna start to do nothing to 'em, just another black man dead to them."

Patti Bredehoft would also speak with the *Berkeley Barb* in the days after Hunter's death, telling the story of his tragic encounter with the Hells Angels. The news had not yet fully sunk in, even for the young woman who had witnessed her boyfriend's death; in speaking of Hunter's essential gentleness, Bredehoft still used the present tense to describe him. She told the story of Hunter's fatal encounter with the Angels, emphasizing whom she believed was responsible for instigating the fight: "He pulled a gun after they started to beat him. They beat him to the ground and then he got up . . ." The Angels had jumped Hunter, with Hunter only seeking to protect himself from their assault. Nonetheless, Bredehoft concluded that Hunter had not been targeted because of racism. "I don't blame it on race," she told the *Barb*, "because like they were hasseling [sic] white people as much as they were hasseling [sic] black people."

It would not be until six weeks after the concert, six weeks after their son's death, that the first person tangentially related to Altamont paid a visit to Meredith Hunter's family. Chip Monck wandered the streets of Berkeley, stopping bystanders and asking if they knew where Meredith Hunter had lived. Monck, who had had to install the three-foot-high stage designed for the Sears Point site at Altamont, understood why the Stones had immediately departed for England after the concert without a word to the media or anyone else. It would hardly be safe, he thought, for the band to walk the streets of San Francisco after such a calamity. But another part of him wondered if the lack of response to the death of one of their fans was itself part of the show.

Was Hunter's unplanned and unanticipated death now incorporated into the Stones' ongoing PR campaign? Was the death of an eighteen-year-old, hardly more than a boy, at their concert the best possible proof of the Stones' own vaunted fierceness? The scheduled press conference had been canceled, and the Stones seemed to be adopting a policy of silence regarding the concert. Monck was troubled, more than anything, by the idea of the empty bed at Altha Anderson's home. Even if the Rolling Stones were not personally culpable for Hunter's death, Monck wondered, shouldn't someone have the decency to call his mother and offer their condolences? And what did it say about people who could have, and chose not to?

He stopped by the neighborhood police station to ask if they knew where he might find Meredith Hunter's mother. Monck had stabbed no one on that day in Altamont, nor had he hired the people who had, but he felt a nagging sense of responsibility and dismay over the absconding of all other parties. Monck believed someone ought to express their condolences to Hunter's mother for the loss of her son. If the Rolling Stones, and the concert's promoters, were not going to do it, then he would.

The first time he visited Anderson, she threw her tea in his face. The second time, she refused to let him in. The third time he came back, she said, "Oh, it's you again," and let him in. Monck told her, "I thought somebody should say how terribly sorry I am, and I'm sure they are as well, at the death of your son." Anderson calmed down some and offered Monck tea. "Not in my face again, thank you," he wryly responded. The visit was short, but Monck had communicated his message. What else could you say to someone whose son had been murdered?

The sheriff's department had received their first call about a stabbing at Altamont at 6:25 p.m., but the crowding at the site meant that it took ten minutes for the first police cars to arrive at the scene. Seven officers canvassed the site, taking notes and measurements, making drawings and pacing off the distances between the stage and the tents and trailers backstage. They jotted down a name, presumably gleaned from the victim's girlfriend—"Murdock Hunter."

Among the first witnesses they encountered were speedway owner Dick Carter and police science student Frank Leonetti, who had administered first aid to Hunter. ("Also present were a variety of Hippie types," the deputies' notes read.) Carter and Leonetti told the police that some Hells Angels had stabbed a man near the stage. According to Leonetti, the victim had pulled a gun, and the Angels had rushed him to subdue him. During the fracas, the victim had been fatally stabbed.

The police tracked down the '65 Mustang Meredith Hunter had driven to the show, still parked on the freeway about one hundred yards west of the San Joaquin County line, and commenced to move it away from the concert site. The two-door beige convertible was towed just before seven o'clock to a garage in nearby Livermore, where its contents were sorted and detailed: a tape deck, six tape cartridges, one black glove, one pair of sunglasses, and one metal comb.

Witnesses had led the police to believe that Hunter's body had already been taken away, presumably via helicopter. But in fact, Meredith Hunter's body was still at the speedway, abandoned and forgotten by the authorities. It would be more than an hour before the police learned that no one had taken away Meredith Hunter's mortal remains. A representative of the coroner's office accepted his body at 10 p.m., and a sheriff's department ambulance took Hunter's corpse away, bringing it to the Callaghan Mortuary in Livermore.

The police had been aware from the very outset of their investigation that the culprit they were seeking was likely a member or associate of the Hells Angels, with whom they had had numerous run-ins in recent months. The search had rapidly focused on the death's-head insignia on the jacket of the Angels. The death's-head led Alameda County sheriff's sergeant Robert J. Donovan to the Hells Angels, and the relatively small insignia on the stabber's jacket indicated that the Angel in question likely belonged to the San Francisco chapter.

Eyewitness testimony put the onus on the Hells Angels for the attack on Meredith Hunter. Numerous accounts pointed to a man wearing an Angels jacket, but given the sartorial similarities between the bikers at Altamont, and the lack of cooperation forthcoming from the members of the Hells Angels, it was a challenge for the police to determine who had been responsible for stabbing Hunter.

The sheriffs also worked to track down evidence that had been assembled by the journalists and filmmakers covering the story. Word trickled out of a firsthand account acquired by *Rolling Stone* with an eyewitness who called himself Paul Cox for their forthcoming Altamont issue, and of film footage that might have captured the fatal encounter between Hunter and the bikers. *Rolling Stone* editor John Burks told the police that he had thrown away Cox's phone number immediately after he had called him, setting back their efforts to track the witness down.

They also reached out to the Maysles brothers, threatening them with criminal prosecution if they did not produce any footage they might have of Hunter's killing. David Maysles agreed to fly out to

California to cooperate with the investigation, with Stones manager Ronnie Schneider joining him for the trip. The two men smoked a joint in their first-class seats (a flight attendant threatened them with arrest if they did not immediately stub it out), and used the six-hour flight to hash out a deal. The Maysles brothers agreed to make a feature film out of their Altamont material.

After a meeting with David Maysles at the Mark Hopkins Hotel in San Francisco, the police screened the raw footage at Francis Ford Coppola's nascent film studio American Zoetrope on Folsom Street in San Francisco. (Coppola's American Zoetrope partner, and future *Star Wars* filmmaker, George Lucas had been one of the cinematographers at Altamont.) The Hells Angels visible in the footage may have been familiar figures to the authorities, but the counterculture as a whole was not. A note scribbled in one of the police reports read, "Marty Balin—who is he?" The officers were similarly puzzled by a sign spotted at the concert site that read FREE SUNSHINE ACID. The ways of the hippies were foreign to the uniformed men investigating the goings-on at their bacchanal.

The police visited San Francisco Hells Angels president Bob Roberts at his clubhouse. Even in Roberts's telling, the Angels were far from blameless. Hunter had, he said, attempted to climb onto the stage, where eight or ten Angels were congregated. One of the bikers had pushed Hunter down, soon followed by a second Angel. Fighting back, Hunter took a swing at one of the bikers. He pulled a gun and waved it around, and approximately six Hells Angels, joined by three other onlookers, pounced on him.

Roberts told the police that he had no idea who had stabbed Meredith Hunter, but that Hunter was "very militant," and that "he kept pulling up the waist of his pants and acting tough." The implication was that a drug-addled black man had acted out at a concert under the Angels' watch, had forgotten his proper place, and had to be subdued in response. (The irony of a Hells Angel calling out a concertgoer for being stoned was likely lost on Roberts.) The police also heard that the San Francisco Angels had taken possession of Meredith Hunter's gun. After claiming that he had no knowledge of its whereabouts, Roberts eventually turned over the .22 he had taken with him from the concert.

The parallels between Altamont and the Ashbury Street assault from September were eerie. An encounter between a group of armed, belligerent Hells Angels and African-Americans; an unexpected ratcheting-up of the encounter into extreme, and potentially excessive, force; and a belief that race drove the Angels' violent response. No one had died outside 715 Ashbury, but the Hells Angels had demonstrated a profound indifference to the personal well-being of African-Americans. The Ashbury incident appeared to have been set off by the Angels' anger at the black people occupying the hallowed space outside their clubhouse. Could white resentment and territoriality have accounted for the calamitous encounter at Altamont?

Tips came in about bikers from Vallejo to Venice who had been bragging about being present at Altamont. Soon, the police had put together a list of the Hells Angels present at Altamont, which included representatives from the Oakland and Los Angeles chapters. They had thirteen names, but even that was not much to go on. Where, exactly, could they, for example, find an Oakland Angel named Rat?

It would take over a month to track down Paul Cox, who came in for questioning on January 15. He saw the Smith & Wesson .22 that had been handed over by Bob Roberts, and confirmed that it looked similar to Hunter's gun. It also matched the description he had given John Burks for the *Rolling Stone* interview.

They asked Cox to tell them what he had seen, and his story confirmed the account *Rolling Stone* was set to publish, with the Angels instigating the fight and stabbing Hunter *before* he pulled out his gun. Cox was not entirely sure, but he believed there might have been two men responsible for Hunter's stabbing. He had spotted a man with a high forehead, his straight hair combed back, and thought he might have taken part in the assault.

Cox's description of Hunter's assailant eventually led the Alameda County sheriffs to Alan Passaro. Passaro was already in Vacaville prison, serving two to ten years on charges of grand theft, vehicle theft, and possession of marijuana with intent to sell. Four days after the concert, Passaro had been pulled over in a car in San Jose with two other Angels, Danny Montoya and Ron Segely (who had also been involved in the Ashbury Street attack). The police found burglary tools in their car, and arrested the three men on charges of burglary and armed robbery. Passaro also had a knife sheath attached to his belt, and a knife that matched the sheath in the backseat of the car. There were what appeared to be traces of blood on the blade and handle. Was it possible that the Hells Angel who had stabbed Meredith Hunter was brazen enough to be driving the streets of San Jose with the very same knife, having failed to even give it a thorough scrubbing?

Passaro agreed to waive his right to an attorney, and immediately sought to deflect the police's line of questioning. He had been at Altamont, and had been down in front, near the stage, with his fellow Angel Segely. In truth, Passaro told them, he remembered little of what had occurred at Altamont. He had smoked copious amounts of marijuana that day, and much of it was a haze. At first, Passaro denied that he had a knife with him at Altamont, but later in the conversation (perhaps after being reminded that he had been arrested with a knife in his possession), he acknowledged that he did. It had been a long-bladed hunting knife he regularly carried with him, and he said he had pricked his finger with it earlier in the day while cutting some meat. (Passaro also admitted to carrying a .25 caliber automatic under his jacket, which would go mostly unmentioned in the months to come.)

Alameda County sheriff's lieutenant James Chisholm believed a test would confirm the traces on the blade as blood. Moreover, if the blade was removed, there might be more blood congealed under the hilt. The signs pointed to Passaro's weapon having been used recently, likely in the assault on Hunter. Traces of blood were also found on the barrel of Hunter's gun, just in front of the forcing cone. There was not enough, however, to determine the blood type or make any kind of definitive statement about its origins. Circumstantially, though, the presence of the blood indicated that the gun was still close to either Hunter or his assailant when Hunter was stabbed.

Witnesses were brought in to see if Alan Passaro could be conclusively identified as the Hells Angel they had seen stabbing Meredith Hunter at Altamont. Patti Bredehoft selected Passaro's picture from a selection of potential assailants, but said she was unsure if he was the man she had seen. She insisted that she had not actually seen her boyfriend's stabbing. She did, however, identify Hunter's gun, noting that the .22 before her was the same one she had seen him bring to Altamont. Others' recollections were more vivid, with Paul Cox and others picking out Passaro's picture from the spread of mug shots.

In mid-March, Passaro consented to take part in a lineup. Both Patti Bredehoft and a second witness, Denice Bell, were unable to identify him conclusively as Meredith Hunter's attacker. Paul Cox, however, spotted him immediately. On March 24, Alan Passaro was arrested and charged with the murder of Meredith Hunter.

The arrest of Alan Passaro had marked an end to the police investigation, but it did not provide satisfactory answers to the deeper questions of how and why the fatal encounter between Meredith Hunter and the Hells Angels had taken place.

Had Meredith Hunter been singled out because of his race? It was hard to say. By no means had they only picked on African-Americans at Altamont, nor did Meredith Hunter's initial treatment, however egregious and brutal, differ substantially in tone or vigor from that of numerous other victims of the Angels' abuses that Saturday. And yet Meredith Hunter was the only one of the Angels' victims to be stabbed, the only one to die at Altamont.

The Angels and their supporters would point to Hunter's gun as the aggravating factor, and undoubtedly that was true to an extent. But questions remained. Had it been necessary to kill Meredith Hunter in self-defense, or merely expedient? Paul Cox's eyewitness testimony suggested that the Angels had been the ones to escalate the situation, and the first to strike. Had the Angels truly seen themselves, as they would later argue, as defending Mick Jagger and the Rolling Stones from an attempted assassination in that era of murderous assaults on celebrated figures, or was Meredith Hunter's gun a convenient excuse to lash out even more furiously at the black man the Angels perceived as uniquely and terrifyingly violent?

Assassination was in the air in the late 1960s. And artists had not been immune from the homicidal impulse; Andy Warhol had also been shot in 1968, wounded by a mentally unstable extremist intent on peddling her misandrist manifesto.

Meredith Hunter, though, had never expressed interest in Mick Jagger or the Rolling Stones before Altamont, preferring soul and R&B on the whole to rock. Nor had he been particularly political, articulating little in the way of an ideological point of view. While he had a lengthy juvenile record, he had never shown any inclination for the kind of violent crime of which he was being accused. It seemed unlikely that he would have brought in a gun, as the Angels claimed, with the express purpose of killing Jagger, nor would it have been clear why he might have targeted a British rock star and sex symbol as the source of his ire.

Instead, Hunter had likely brought along his gun in the hope of bluffing his way out of any potential trouble. A .22 would not be the ideal weapon to wield in a moment of true danger, and Hunter had told his sister that the gun was not even loaded.

It had undoubtedly been misguided of Hunter to pull out his gun, even in self-defense. Regardless of who had begun the fight, Hunter's gun had escalated it. But the Angels had been the ones who had targeted Hunter first, and they had seized on his mistake to end his life. Their intent, likely unpremeditated but no less ferocious for that, was to kill him, and they kicked and punched and stabbed him until they accomplished their mission. The punishment did not in any way match the crime, and the crime—brandishing a weapon— had itself been prompted by their own assault.

Hawkeye believed Hunter's race was a stroke of good fortune for the security-minded Angels. If Hunter had been white, he would have been one anonymous face in a sea of young white faces as he fled. It had been the color of his skin that allowed the Angels to find and pursue Meredith Hunter, the whiteness of the audience the ideal backdrop for the Angels' hunt for a lone black man. Meredith Hunter had no rights, Hawkeye would later observe with a laugh. There was no law at Altamont.

Bredehoft, confused and numb with shock, initially told police that she thought it was entirely possible that Hunter had been picked on because he was black—an opinion she would later revise in her comments to the media. She had noticed Angels looking at the couple, and at Ronnie and Judy, all day long, and been spooked by their attention, which boded evil intent. Hunter had been singled out by the Hells Angels as a black man, she believed, and moreover, a black man with a white girlfriend. This last point, at the very least, seemed debatable, given that the Angels beating Hunter had not realized she was associated with him.

It was unlikely that the Hells Angels would have decided, in deliberate fashion, to kill Meredith Hunter. Instead, the day's cycle of violence would be carried out, in intensely focused fashion, on Hunter himself. Meredith Hunter had made the mistake of attending a concert while black, first attracting the Hells Angels' attention. Then, perhaps, the presence of his white girlfriend had intensified their focus. Finally, and fatally, Hunter had sought to defend himself with a weapon of his own after being assaulted, thereby justifying, to their minds, their counterattack. A white man with a gun who made the mistake of pulling it on a Hells Angel might very well have been stabbed and beaten to death, as well. The Angels' racism only went so far as an explanation of their actions. But perhaps the Angels might never have singled out Meredith Hunter in the first place, tempting him to head back to the car for his gun, if he had not been African-American.

10. Dupes

"300,000 SAY IT WITH MUSIC," read the newspaper headline that went out to the Bay Area the day after the concert. Inside the Sunday edition of the *San Francisco Examiner*, word spread of another successful mega-concert, about peace and harmony with an accompanying musical soundtrack. The stabbing of Meredith Hunter was briefly noted, but the news was muted, a fleeting moment of sobriety amid the delighted talk of the counterculture triumphant: "But for the stabbing, all appeared peaceful at the concert. . . . The listeners heeded the advice of the Jefferson Airplane: 'We Should Be Together.'"

More than just another story about the Woodstock vibe spreading inexorably across the country, this was a cozy newspaper account of a miracle. The lion had lain down with the lamb, and the spirit of harmony had convinced even the legendarily terrible bikers of the Hells Angels to put aside their own belief in violence as social lubricant: "The action brought a gentle rebuke from the Jefferson Airplane. One told the fighters over the public address system: 'Violence isn't necessary.' Others told the Angels: 'Hostility isn't part of this. Don't spoil the day.' The Angels backed off. Their leaders told them to 'cool it.' The rank and file Angels did.''

In the late 1960s, the *Examiner* and its primary Bay Area rival, the *San Francisco Chronicle*, published a joint Sunday edition to cut costs. The arrangement between the *Examiner* and the *Chronicle* placed the *Examiner*'s staff in charge of the Sunday news coverage, and the *Examiner* had sent out a veteran reporter named Jim Wood, with years of experience covering rock 'n' roll and Bay Area youth culture, to write about the concert.

Wood's voice would be the one that San Francisco readers would hear over their Sunday-morning eggs and orange juice, but the tight production deadlines for the newspaper limited how much he would be able to tell them about Altamont. In order to produce the four-pound brick that would be dropped onto doorsteps early the next morning, the newspaper had to close far earlier than for the weekday paper. And so Jim Wood arrived at Altamont early Saturday morning armed with the knowledge that he would only have a few short hours in which to assemble local color, interview concertgoers and performers, and form an impression of the concert as a whole.

At the appointed hour, sometime in the midafternoon, Wood found his car and driver, got into the backseat, and sped the fifty miles back to San Francisco, his blue portable typewriter perched on his lap. As the car wound its way past the streams of cars still heading east to Altamont, Wood furiously pecked away at the typewriter's keys, hoping to file a legible and honest summary of the brief portion of the day for which he had been present. Wood had been covering these events for years, as his old friend John Burks well knew, and knew how to fill out a spotty firsthand experience with a good reporter's sense of fullness.

Soon after Wood made it back to the *Examiner*'s offices, he would have to file his story, leaving little room for error. But as a veteran reporter, he knew the routine, and was confident that the Rolling

Stones' extravaganza was destined to be an enormous success. Any small snafus he might have spotted would likely be long forgotten by the next morning.

Not only did the Bay Area take in Jim Wood's brief foray at Livermore as gospel; so did the rest of the United States. After being published, the *Examiner* duly filed its story with the Associated Press, which leaned on reports from local newspapers for its coverage of national events. The *San Francisco Examiner* had been the closest paper to Altamont, and after a brief, light edit, the AP posted Wood's story to its wire, giving affiliated newspapers across the country the opportunity to publish the Altamont summary. As far as most Americans knew, Altamont had been a raging success— albeit one at which a concertgoer had been stabbed to death. But then hadn't people also died at the already legendary Woodstock?

One of the few voices to counteract the growing mass of huzzahs for Altamont emerged from one of the papers that had published Wood's account. *Rolling Stone* veteran Ralph J. Gleason, who had played an inadvertent role in the free concert through his diatribes against what he perceived to be the Stones' price-gouging, weighed in on the failures of Altamont in his *San Francisco Chronicle* column.

"Is this the new community?" Gleason asked. "Is this what Woodstock promised? Gathered together *as* a tribe, what happened? Brutality, murder, despoliation, you name it. . . . The name of the game is money, power and ego, and money is first and it brings power." Gleason saw the free concert as a sham, one whose bad faith was being passed along from the con artists to the marks: "The Stones didn't do it for free, they did it for money, only the tab was paid in a different way. Whoever goes to see that movie paid for the Altamont religious assembly."

Gleason went further, bluntly calling out Mick Jagger, Sam Cutler,

Rock Scully, and Emmett Grogan as the culprits responsible for Meredith Hunter's death. The mood was righteously contemptuous, and yet it was telling that Gleason referred to Hunter as "that black man," a rod with which Mick Jagger and his associates might usefully be whipped and little more.

Unlike the *Examiner* or the *Chronicle*, *Rolling Stone* was a publication of the counterculture, as interested in analysis and polemic as reportage. While Wood assembled his impressions, *Rolling Stone* managing editor John Burks had been walking the grounds at Altamont, mentally cobbling together a list of contributors. Much of the *Rolling Stone* crew had been at the show. Some had been there for professional reasons, having been asked to cover the concert for the newspaper, while others had been there just to see the Stones. And as Burks wandered the speedway, taking notes and conducting interviews, he also kept an eye out for friends and contributors he might have a brief word with. Burks would pause and ask each of them the same thing: "Get in touch with me after this is over." He had already spotted Greil Marcus, Langdon Winner, Lester Bangs, Michael Goodwin, and many other *Rolling Stone* stalwarts, steadily updating his mental roster of writers and photographers he could call on to round out his portrait of Altamont.

In the hours after the concert, Burks sought out all of his troops. He called the writers whom he had seen at the show, and fielded calls from others he hadn't spotted while making his rounds. For each of them, he had a single request: "Give me what you've got." Burks wanted to hear everything: any memorable run-ins with concertgoers or musicians or bikers, any fleeting journalistic color they might have noted, any conclusions they might have reached about the day's events.

Film critic Michael Goodwin mentioned that he had brought along his tape recorder, and used it to record Jagger's comments. Soon after the violence had begun in earnest, Goodwin had realized that readers would want to know what the likes of Mick Jagger were saying from the stage. It was too loud, and Goodwin was too far from the stage, to record Jagger directly, even if he held his recorder over his head. Instead, Goodwin listened intently to Jagger's announcements, and repeated them directly into the microphone of his tape recorder. The worse the day got, Goodwin believed, the more crucial this material might turn out to be. As it turned out, he had been the only one of the assembled journalists who had thought to record Jagger, and possessing a record of the Stones singer's simultaneously anguished and anodyne pronouncements would be essential to telling the story of Altamont.

Greil Marcus's day had begun with a hippie angrily rejecting his proffered food, shouting, "I don't want any of your fucking sandwich." Marcus had camped out near the stage, amid a sullen crowd so intent on protecting its hard-won territory that it refused to let him put both feet down on the ground after an Angel incursion into the crowd. He had to be lifted above the audience's heads and carried onto the stage, from where he could retreat to more hospitable turf.

Later in the day, Marcus ran into Burks. Marcus was frustrated and drained by the free-floating tension hovering just above the crowd, and he was rethinking the maximalist plans *Rolling Stone* (then a newspaper) had for covering the concert. Perhaps they would be better off limiting the coverage of Altamont to a bland one-column concert review. How better to express their contempt for this failed spectacle than to treat it as a non-story: "Rolling Stones Play Concert"? The lack of coverage could serve as their final word on the subject. Burks agreed to consider the idea.

Marcus returned to the stage area, where he claimed a spot atop a VW van. Marcus's line of sight was blocked, but sound carried easily over the noise of the Stones' amplified guitars. Screams of undiluted terror regularly split the air. The sense of dread was downright unbearable, like watching a horror film in which unspeakable things happened to the helpless characters just outside the frame, and nothing could be done to save them.

The screams were the distilled essence of Altamont, piercing cries of absolute panic and displacement. To Marcus, they were more than just expressions of bodily fear. They were shrieks of existential dismay, wordless expressions of terror at having ended up in this place, at this moment. They were not the kind of screams that expressed concern. They were out-of-control screams, expressions of living through a waking nightmare from which one could not awake. And the screams kept coming, each one a reminder, in case one was needed, of the dire situation down below.

Watching the counterculture pull itself apart had been a wrenching experience for Marcus, exposing many of the comforting lies that it had peddled for too long. There was no community here, only the self-interested and self-absorbed. And there was no peace, only the illusion of comity, pierced at the first outbreak of chaos. Marcus got back to his car, and his radio had been ripped out of the dashboard. He wasn't upset, or even surprised. It went without saying that a day like today would end with an invasion of his privacy, another assault on common decency.

Marcus left Altamont disgusted by the excesses and obtuseness of the counterculture, so determined on self-congratulation it had failed to anticipate, or even acknowledge, the traitors in its midst. The media's coverage of the concert only worsened Marcus's sense of shock. In their telling, Altamont had indeed been another Woodstock. The Rolling Stones had successfully pulled off a coup, and the counterculture would march grandly into a future of its own making.

Everyone associated with Altamont—the bands, the concertgoers, the journalists covering the show—had wanted a triumphant story, and collectively, they insisted on the story, even when the facts demanded otherwise. To Marcus, this was only further evidence of the rot spreading through the innards of the counterculture.

The counterculture had invited its own worst enemies into their celebration, and had allowed them to hold a crowd of hundreds of thousands hostage to their puerile, totalitarian whims. This story—not the comforting fairy tale that had made its way around the country—would have to be told.

Burks, a vet of *Newsweek* and the daily-newspaper grind, saw himself as a newspaperman covering the rock scene. Burks, with the additional time gifted to a biweekly publication that a daily like the *Chronicle* or the *Examiner* lacked, began to assemble the disparate stories streaming in from his contributors, and it was increasingly clear to him that there was a very different story about Altamont than the one being peddled by the *Examiner*.

As was the habit of everyone in the Bay Area clued in to the hip life, Burks tuned in to KSAN the day after the concert, and caught Stefan Ponek's post-Altamont call-in show. Ponek had been present at the concert on Saturday, delivering a steady stream of real-time reports about a show that had not, in actuality, taken place: placid, fun, peaceable, triumphant. Ponek undoubtedly realized he had bungled the story, and took advantage of a typically low-key Sunday to mull over what had taken place.

"Tower Records Presents a Saturday Afternoon at Altamont Speedway," the program was called, and the anodyne name, like something out of ABC's *Wide World of Sports* or a 1950s television series, belied the furious urgency of the conversation. Before the concert, Tower Records had purchased the rights to play back recordings of the show for a next-day special. The recordings had been made, but all plans to relive the musical memories were overwhelmed by the pent-up desire on the part of those who had actually been present at the concert to talk through what had gone wrong at Altamont (which everyone involved with the broadcast insisted on calling, with a Spanish lilt, "Altamonté"). Before the conversation began, a Tower Records ad reminded listeners that the Stones' new *Let It Bleed* was now on sale for $2.77.

The tone of the show began in confusion and stumbled chaotically in the direction of anger and self-recrimination. "A lot went on Saturday afternoon at Altamont Raceway, and there are probably about three hundred thousand or more different opinions as to what exactly *did* happen there," Ponek blandly noted in his introduction, but his tone rapidly sharpened. "At Altamont, there was a miniature society set up of three hundred thousand and upwards people. It was supposedly a society of the new generation, the love generation, the brave new world, the children of the future. As far as I can say, I don't want to live in a society like the one I saw yesterday."

For four hours, Ponek fielded calls from boldface names and faithful listeners. There were accusers and defenders, storytellers and pundits. Everyone had an opinion or an anecdote, everyone had a position they sought to stake out about this latest gathering of the tribes.

Ponek enumerated the failure of the San Francisco papers and the *Los Angeles Times* to do justice to the story of Hunter's death. He took particular umbrage with Wood's story, which resembled "a cookie-cutter Woodstock story . . . it didn't sound like anybody had really gone there."

Even as injured concertgoers were being treated, Ponek argued, people were blindly pushing and shoving: "I didn't feel any sense of community with many of the people there . . . they weren't my people." If there was a single vibe to Altamont, the participants agreed, it was "the hell with you, brother." Callers immediately jumped in with anecdotes illustrating that sense of faux brotherhood: women getting dragged by the hair, concertgoers hit by bottles, people kicked and stepped on by oblivious attendees.

What, precisely, had gone wrong at Altamont? One caller saw it as analogous to the story of Kitty Genovese, where thirty-seven on-lookers had been said to have watched as their neighbor in Queens was brutally murdered in 1964. Another caller believed the bur-geoning cult of the counterculture superstar had doomed Altamont. By "trying to get as close as possible to these superstars," the crowd had proved they "aren't so different" from the "so-called Hollywood culture" they disdained. Another caller, concert planner and Digger eminence Emmett Grogan, guided listeners through the planning for the show. He cast blame on the Stones' New York office for the failure to secure a suitable location or adequately prepare for Altamont. The free San Francisco concert was a utopia that "turned into a Fran-kenstein."

Burks, identified as a *"Rolling Stone* heavy," wound up calling in, and began with some musical observations: "I tried disengaging myself from all the rest of it, just listening to the Stones as a band per-forming, and goddamn, they were fine. . . . it is just as great a rock 'n' roll band as the finest thing anybody ever said about them. . . . that part of it is good. I don't know. Let's do this Socratically, man. What do you think people went there for?" "I don't know, man," Ponek responded, giggling nervously. "Let me interview you, OK?"

The observers were joined by the participants, already defensive about their roles in a rippling disaster. Pete Knell from the San Fran-cisco Hells Angels called in to clarify how his group had first been summoned for Altamont. Sam Cutler and the Stones' crew had been "a little nervous about the crowd. They had a little trouble in Flor-ida and so on. What they did was, they asked us would we come and keep people off the stage. They didn't want nobody grabbing the microphone."

In Knell's description of the concert, the Angels had participated in a few minor scuffles with fans before settling in to the business of protecting the Stones: "There's a lot of people that get it because they're looking for it. . . . I thought it went pretty good."

Knell's clueless response only contributed to the growing collective sense of the Angels as a band apart from the counterculture, intent on defending their prerogatives above all. Ponek, treading with exceeding caution, summarized callers' denunciations of the Angels' behavior as a polite critique: "Hey man, you didn't have to be so rough." Another speaker audibly repeated the word "rough," and chuckled, as if taken aback by the cop-out word Ponek employed for the sheer unalloyed brutality of the Hells Angels.

Sam Cutler's complaints about the paucity of concertgoers who had stuck around to clean up after the show were soon followed by a deliberate refusal to take sides: "I myself feel that the Hells Angels were as helpful as they saw that they could be in a situation which most people found very confusing, including the Hells Angels."

Not content to leave it at that, Cutler asserted that the Angels' behavior was a matter too furrowed with complexity for him to judge: "If you're asking me to issue a general putdown of the Angels, which I imagine a lot of people would only be too happy to do, then I'm not prepared to do that. . . . Fifty percent of the people will dig what they did and fifty percent of the people might not dig what they did. . . . As far as I'm concerned, they were people who were here, who tried to help in their own way, right? If people didn't dig it, I'm sorry."

Oakland Angel chief Sonny Barger followed Cutler on the air, and after pointing out that he had been "pretty loaded" and a latecomer to the show, stuck at a Hells Angels officers' meeting until the midafternoon, deflected criticism of his group by simultaneously praising the crowd's cooperation and calling out the loudmouths who had engaged with the Angels. "We come through, and, like, the people there were out of sight," said Barger of his members' entry on their motorcycles. "They just stood up and moved their sleeping bags and everything and stepped out of the way and done everything to let us through."

Barger, who would later acknowledge that he was high on cocaine during the broadcast, fumbled through a series of explanations and clarifications, repeatedly mentioning that he and his fellow bikers had parked where they had been told to park, before arriving at what he saw as the heart of his argument.

A biker's heart and soul was his motorcycle, and the concertgoers at Altamont had made the mistake of disrespecting the Angels' bikes, snapping off their mirrors and damaging their pedals. "I don't know if you think we pay $50 for these things, or steal 'em, or pay a lot for 'em, or what," Barger noted. "But most people that's got a good Harley chopper's got a few grand invested in it. Ain't nobody gonna kick my motorcycle," Barger fumed. "And they might think 'cause they're in a crowd of three hundred thousand people, that they can do it and get away with it. But when you're standing there looking at something that's your life, and everything you've got is invested in that thing, and you love that thing better than you love any thing in the world, and you see a guy kick it, you know who he is. If you have to go through fifty people to get to him, you're gonna git 'im. You know what, they got got. And after they got it, then some other people started yellin'. And you know what, some of them people was loaded on some drugs that it's just too bad we wasn't loaded on."

Drug-addled fans had come racing down the hill looking to do battle with the bikers, but "when they jumped on an Angel, they got hurt." No one could mess with the Angels, or their motorcycles, without suffering the consequences. The Angels' rules governed all situations where outsiders came into their presence, and anyone foolish enough to cross them could not plead ignorance as a defense.

The Angels defended their interests with an iron fist. "Sonny, you got it," Ponek told him, implying that his concerns about the Angels' behavior had been assuaged by Barger's rambling and bellicose monologue, which he and the other hosts had failed to interrupt or derail on a number of occasions.

Ponek took the mic for some tentative closing words: "We gotta leave it. I think there's no conclusions to be drawn except this has been a very weird experience. To give this much attention to a rock 'n' roll show . . . it's brought out a couple of good things out of it." He argued that the failures of Altamont reflected less on the concert's attendees than on its planners, who had accidentally provided others with guidelines for how not to put on a concert in the future. Interestingly, for all the discussion of the Angels and the Stones, little was said about the Grateful Dead, who were already starting to disappear from the narrative of Altamont.

Jann Wenner had read the Sunday papers, seen Wood's coverage of the show, and put it out of mind. *Rolling Stone* would undoubtedly cover the show, but there did not appear to be anything of particular note that had taken place at Altamont. On Monday morning, Wenner, founder and publisher of *Rolling Stone*, arrived at their offices at 746 Brannan Street, located upstairs from the print shop that put out their newspaper, settled in for the weekly editorial meeting, and was stunned to hear his staff's starkly divergent take on the show.

The concert, according to his writers and editors and photographers, had not only *not* been a triumph; it had been an epic debacle, one whose contours were only beginning to come into focus. It was more than just a bad trip. It was a roadblock laid in front of the careening counterculture, and a reminder, as Greil Marcus saw it, that there was a death wish here every bit as profound as what might be found at any Nixon rally or John Wayne movie. The horrors of Altamont evinced a moral insanity that profoundly unsettled him. Marcus was torn between competing instincts: the first, to simply ignore Altamont, to treat it as unworthy of mention in the rock 'n' roll newspaper of record, and the second, to surround the story, to cover its every contour and poke into every crevice to emphasize to the naïve youth of the country the myriad ways in which idealism could turn to rot.

Wenner sat at the conference table and listened to the testimony from his staff as the noise of hot lead being hand-set in the type shop below drifted upstairs. Taking in the reports of what they had haphazardly assembled during the concert and in its immediate aftermath, he knew the answer to Marcus's conundrum. "We're going to cover this thing from top to bottom," Wenner announced, "and we are going to lay the blame." It would not be enough to simply report what had taken place during the concert; *Rolling Stone* would also unambiguously point the finger at the culprits it saw as being responsible for Altamont's failings.

Burks wholeheartedly agreed with Wenner's decision. Having listened to the KSAN broadcast, he was taken aback by the recriminations and threats already being fired back and forth between Hells Angels, crew members, musicians, and fans. There would need to be an impartial—or relatively impartial—arbiter, one well informed enough to seriously cover Altamont, and able to stand apart from the fray. Burks passed out assignments, asking for reportage, observations, and local color. They would also need some more reporting muscle. *Rolling Stone* was many things, most of them good, but other than Burks, there were not many traditional shoe-leather reporters on staff. Marcus suggested calling in his neighbor, a Berkeley alum and soon-to-be graduate student named John Morthland, to assist. Morthland had attended the concert, where he had been too far away to see the Hells Angels, or even to hear much of the music, but had been galvanized by the KSAN broadcast and its sharp contrast with the good vibes of the television news reports from the concert.

For Wenner, the calculus of covering Altamont was complex. His newspaper was so enamored of Mick Jagger and Keith Richards's group that it had been named after them, and a hefty part of its appeal was its unfettered access to the Rolling Stones. The counterculture that *Rolling Stone* covered and reflected often preferred cheerleading to critiquing. What would happen if Wenner's investigation wound up identifying the Rolling Stones as the villains of Altamont? Wenner thought it over, and decided to take the risk. His relationship with Jagger would survive this, too, even if Jagger would be greatly surprised and displeased by criticism from *Rolling Stone*. And truthfully, Jagger would likely be upset by coverage of Altamont of any kind, so Wenner might as well push ahead with the special Altamont issue he had in mind.

John Burks had become a journalist in the fabled *Newsweek* organization, which trained its young writers and editors to serve as cogs in an all-knowing, all-seeing system. Burks had, without even being entirely aware of what he had been doing, been echoing the *Newsweek* house style by assembling files on Altamont, asking his friends and contributors for material on what they had seen and heard. Instead of rewriting and reworking all the raw material from the files, Burks considered merely assembling them and folding them together into one lengthy, deliberately cacophonous story.

Along with Morthland, soon to become a permanent member of *Rolling Stone*'s staff, Burks began making calls and tracking down leads. Morthland called hospitals and police stations. He interviewed doctors who had worked in the Altamont medical tent, and spoke with Sonny Barger. He attended a follow-up press conference at Melvin Belli's office. He called Dick Carter, the owner of the Altamont racetrack. Having also attended the show, Morthland did some on-the-scene reporting, drawing from his own experiences at Altamont.

Burks, meanwhile, had been speaking with representatives of the Stones' and Grateful Dead's camps, Sears Point employees, and others who had been involved in the early planning for the free Rolling Stones show.

Stories and story ideas and leads went up on Burks's corkboard wall. As the issue's deadline approached, the air at 746 Brannan took on a bluish tinge from the cigarettes being puffed at desks by the harried editorial staff and writers. Wenner would occasionally pop his head into one of his editors' offices, asking how the story was progressing.

Burks and his team had assembled some remarkable material in only ten days, from some surprising sources. After much painstaking legwork, Burks had tracked down an eyewitness to Hunter's killing. Staff writer Ralph Gleason had been dispatched to negotiate with the young man. The witness wanted to tell his story, but he also wanted to avoid the wrath of the Hells Angels. Gleason promised him that he could tell his story without divulging his name in print.

When the call came through, Burks turned on his tape recorder and let Paul Cox speak: "I didn't know his name or anything, but he was standing alongside of me. You know, we were both watching Mick Jagger and a Hell's Angel, the fat one. I don't know his name or anything, he reached over—he didn't like us being so close or something, you know, we were seeing Mick Jagger too well, or something. He was just being uptight. He reached over and grabbed the guy beside me by the ear and hair, and yanked on it, thinking it was funny, you know, kind of laughing. And so, this guy shook loose; he yanked away from him."

Burks asked the questions and the witness shared what he saw during the moments Meredith Hunter's life came to an abrupt close. Crucially, Cox asserted that he had seen Hunter stabbed *before* he had pulled his gun—a claim that would come under intense scrutiny in the months to come. The interview was both the most newsworthy material Burks and Morthland had uncovered, and also the reportage that most closely resembled what they had in mind for their folded-in story, in which a multiplicity of voices would jostle for attention, each with their own version of the day's events.

Burks believed that they had found their opening, and the interview, edited only lightly, wound up serving as the bravura opening of the *Rolling Stone* story. It thrust readers immediately into the fear and chaos and violence of Altamont, without even an initial question to clarify what they were hearing. There were no identifying names for the interview, just a series of questions and the disturbing answers that followed. The context would follow.

The finished story ran more than twenty-five thousand words, occupying the bulk of *Rolling Stone*'s January 21, 1970, issue, which hit newsstands about six weeks after the concert. The cover image was surprisingly stark: a black-and-white shot of concertgoers, some standing and some sitting, some looking off into the distance and some glancing at the ground. Sunlight streamed through the gaps between the fans, with a trio of rays forming a triangle around the central cluster of concertgoers. For all its formal beauty, the picture is telling primarily for what it lacks: enthusiasm, bonhomie, or even a shared focus. The counterculture was fractured, unable to agree on what it valued, or what it preferred to look at—or look away from. The cover's tagline put it simply, mincing no words: "THE ROLLING STONES DISASTER AT ALTAMONT: LET IT BLEED." Wenner was proud to have sidestepped what he saw as the more commercial impulse to splash a garish, blood-spattered image on the cover, or to have used a headline like "MURDER AT A STONES CONCERT."

The result, a feat of commingled reportage, editorializing, and analysis, incorporated firsthand accounts from the likes of Sam Cutler, Mick Taylor, David Crosby, and Emmett Grogan. It took readers from the confines of Melvin Belli's office to the Altamont stage, from the excited planning meetings at the Grateful Dead's offices to the tragic hush in Meredith Hunter's home. Bill Graham chimed in to blame Chip Monck, for constructing an unacceptably low stage, and Mick Jagger, for bilking his fans. The article jumped around in time as well as space, going from quotes from the morning-after KSAN broadcast to detailed reports of the frantic last-minute efforts to prepare the speedway for the concert.

Burks's folded-in style, which eschewed the use of individual by-lines, gave the impression of the newspaper speaking in a single voice. Rather than a series of jumbled and disordered impressions, this was *Rolling Stone* standing on its hind legs and insisting on its authority to issue a definitive ruling on the missteps of the counter-culture. The Altamont issue sought to honor complexity by telling the story out of order. We jumped in at the very moment Meredith Hunter was about to be killed, and then proceeded to leap backward and forward in time until we took in a kaleidoscopic view of the Altamont landscape.

Given the short time frame, numerous errors slithered into the final version. Perhaps most significantly, *Rolling Stone* told its readers that Hunter had been killed during the Stones' performance of "Sympathy for the Devil," and not four songs later, during "Under My Thumb." (Marcus would later entertain the idea of a different cover for a future issue, one intended to clear up the mistake that *Rolling Stone* had helped to propagate. This issue's cover would read "NOT 'SYMPATHY FOR THE DEVIL'; 'UNDER MY THUMB.'")

Rolling Stone and many concertgoers present at Altamont were convinced Hunter was killed while the Rolling Stones played "Sympathy for the Devil." They would tell journalists that the tragic encounter had happened soon after Keith Richards had played the opening chords, or as Mick Jagger had sung the first lines, or right as the song reached its frenzied pinnacle.

The impression that "Sympathy" had been playing as Hunter

died came about because, as Greil Marcus later put it, it was simply too metaphorically perfect to not be the soundtrack to murder. Audiences in the late 1960s heard Jagger and felt a dark shiver, a sense of Jagger's summoning unambiguous evil in all its black-mass majesty. "Sympathy for the Devil" was a character study and a pocket biography, a highly compressed vision of the history of evil drawn to the scale of a pop song: Christ's crucifixion and the violent deaths of the Romanovs and the Kennedys, all metaphorically summoned by this silver-tongued demon. No other song would serve, no other song would summarize with such devastating aptness the Stones' dangerous dalliance with the dark side, which had ultimately, many believed, cost a young man his life.

For all these reasons and more, it simply *had* to be "Sympathy for the Devil" playing when Meredith Hunter was stabbed. The song allowed for the symbolic transfer of authority from the Hells Angels to the Rolling Stones. It had been a Hells Angel who had stabbed Meredith Hunter, but by playing "Sympathy" when it happened, the Stones had wrenched open the gates of Hell and allowed Beelzebub, or his minions, to reach out and curse Altamont.

This was a kind of magical or religious thinking, in which infernal powers superseded human authority, but it was also a form of wish fulfillment. The fans really did want Mick Jagger to be powerful enough to summon the Devil. They wanted the Rolling Stones at the center of this story, even if the events of the day left the band as little more than helpless bystanders, having set in motion forces they were unable to control. If "Sympathy for the Devil" was genuinely an evil song, with the ability to curse an entire concert, and kill Meredith Hunter, it meant that rock 'n' roll was powerful enough to change the world. Altamont had been irrefutable evidence, in this mindset, of rock's power. The metaphorical rightness of the communion of a band, a song, and an event had been not just about the

Rolling Stones' bona fides as musical sorcerers, but of the sincerity of rock as a force in the world.

Mistakes like the juxtaposition of songs notwithstanding, the result of Burks and his colleagues' efforts was unexpectedly fierce, a no-holds-barred piece of journalism that saw fit to clobber the Rolling Stones for their failures. There was anguish, too, and a sense of misguided hero worship, only belatedly recognized: "Well, fuck Mel Belli. We don't need to hear from the Stones via a middle-aged jet-set attorney. We need to hear them directly. Who *really* cares whether they're going to lay some bread on Meredith Hunter's family? It isn't going to bring him back to life. But some display—however restrained—of compassion hardly seems too much to expect. A man died before their eyes. Do they give a shit? Yes or no?"

Both Burks and Marcus were modestly disappointed with their work, convinced that the folded-in story was insufficient to the task of explaining Altamont. For Marcus, the final result was unsatisfying, lacking some essential but inexplicable quality that might have more accurately captured the madness of Altamont. Burks recalled a letter that British prime minister Winston Churchill had sent to one of his generals during the Second World War. At the end of a ten-page, single-spaced letter detailing his plans and thoughts and ideas, Churchill closed by saying he wished he had had the time to write a shorter letter. Burks believed that more time would have given him the chance to compress and shorten the unusually long piece into something more cohesive. But there had only been a ten-day sprint to put together the entire issue, and there had been no time for a shorter letter.

The *Rolling Stone* special issue began the process of revising the misguided story initially peddled by Wood, the San Francisco papers, and the AP. "The media of the San Francisco Bay Area, with a few exceptions, were programmed strictly for Woodstock West,"

Rolling Stone argued. "They knew what to expect and whatever happened they knew what their story would say."

Unlike those other sources, *Rolling Stone* was instinctively trusted by the counterculture as a whole. (One wonders how perceptions might have changed had the roles been reversed, and *Rolling Stone* had served as Altamont's defender while the mass-circulation press called it an unmitigated disaster.) Having put its imprimatur on the story of Altamont's failure, it reoriented the collective understanding of the concert—a process eventually to be joined by the arrival of the Maysleses' documentary film. Altamont had become, just as its organizers had hoped, an instantly recognizable symbol of the counterculture—only not in the fashion they had intended.

11. "We Only Want Beautiful Things"

When Charlotte Zwerin spoke, the editors working for her would have to lean in closer to hear her, anxious not to miss any stray bits of wisdom from the soft-spoken wizard of the editing room. She was not a public figure like Albert Maysles, not a raconteur like David. No one would catch her hanging out in Mick Jagger's hotel room. For Zwerin, the cinematic process only began in earnest once the film cans started to arrive in the editing room.

For Zwerin, documentary filmmaking required an ex post facto casting process, in which the mass of undifferentiated footage would be scoured for stimulating storylines and compelling faces that might hold the interest of audiences. Thoughtful fiction filmmakers might devote months to the question of casting: who would play the heroine? Who would take the meaty role of the villain?

Susan Steinberg, one of the young editors on the Altamont project, watched carefully as Zwerin, third of the codirectors on the film, made similar choices about how much time the audience for the Maysleses' Altamont film might spend with the likes of Melvin Belli, carefully calibrating the film to balance its mingled storylines, and the clash of its competing interests. Documentary filmmaking began in the field, but it lived or died on the basis of the decisions made in the editing room.

When Charlotte Zwerin was five years old, in 1936, she had been taken to a show called "Big Band and a Movie." The musical act was nice, but the film itself had caught her attention and sparked her sense of wonder: just how was this magical artifact made? Zwerin, who was born in Detroit, attended Wayne State University, where she founded the school's film society. After graduating, she made her way to New York, where she found work at CBS as a librarian for the documentary series *The 20th Century*, in pursuit of her goal of becoming a director herself. Documentary film, with its more engaged, political bent, was more hospitable to female filmmakers than Hollywood, and Zwerin eventually was hired by Robert Drew's company Drew Associates. While there, she ran in the same circles as Drew's cinematographer Albert Maysles. Zwerin rapidly developed a reputation as a gifted editor, able to burrow deeply into complex or gnarled material and emerge with a fleet, sleek story.

When Albert and David Maysles began making their own films together in the mid-1960s, they brought Zwerin along with them as an editor. She edited *Meet Marlon Brando* and *With Love from Truman* for them in 1966, but 1969's *Salesman* established her bona fides. She found that her physical and psychological removal from the material—she had not accompanied Albert and David on their shoots, or ever met the film's subjects—allowed her to pare away the inessential. "I think this removal from the scene," she argued, "helped my judgment and helped me to understand more clearly what the viewer would feel." Given *Salesman*'s runaway success (at least by the hothouse standards of the documentary film world), it was only natural that Zwerin would rejoin Albert and David for their Rolling Stones film. Zwerin was traveling in Europe when the Maysles brothers were shooting at Altamont, and staying at a hotel in

Paris when she received a letter from David, expressing his enthusiasm for the footage they had shot and asking her to join them in New York.

As the unusually frigid winter of 1970 left icicles and streaky trails of condensation on the windows of the Ed Sullivan Theater building at 1697 Broadway in Manhattan, the editors of the Altamont documentary huddled inside, consumed by a series of technical difficulties all orbiting a central challenge.

All involved parties understood that the death of Meredith Hunter changed the equation of how to transform the raw footage from Altamont into a film. "We only want beautiful things," David Maysles had told his crew on the day of Altamont, a pronouncement that was itself a kind of expression of hope. But the unremitting violence, and the tragedy that had marked its nadir, prodded the Maysles brothers to consider the prospect that they had accidentally made another kind of film entirely. And luckily for them, their crews had not listened to David; one cinematographer whom he had castigated went right on filming the drug-fueled panic attack of a disoriented young woman that had initially prompted David's concern.

Hunter's death had upended the entire intended function of the film, which was to have served as a privileged glimpse inside the rarefied world of the Rolling Stones, and a tantalizing opportunity for music fans to bear witness to one of the most hyped concerts of the decade. The Altamont film could no longer just be about the music, or about the Stones. It was a concert film ultimately not about music, but a murder mystery whose key piece of footage lasted less than ten seconds, a story of celebrities whose celebrity might very well be permanently tarnished by the film in which they starred. The death of a fan would have to take precedence, but how could it avoid making the entirety of the film feel misleading, or in poor taste?

The filmmakers worried over a technical matter that was itself an aesthetic and moral quandary: how could the footage be slowed down enough for audiences to see it, without being too jarring an editorial intrusion? It was the film's blessing and its curse that it had captured the moment of Meredith Hunter's killing. Hunter's death made the Maysleses' film so much more than another concert film, but it also forced the entire film to hinge on a single blurry and confusing sequence. Seeing it once, at regular speed, an audience would only be confused by what it had been shown. The lack of a voiceover providing guidance—a direct-cinema no-no—would only make it all the more disorienting. Who were we looking at? Who was the attacker, and who the victim? Hunter's killing cried out for a kind of contextualization that direct cinema was philosophically disinclined to offer.

A cursory glance might have suggested that the issue of structure was irrelevant, too obvious to consider. This was a film, after all, mostly about a single concert, on a single day. The bulk of the film would have to take place in chronological order, culminating in the Rolling Stones' set and the death of Meredith Hunter. But what kind of film would introduce its most important moment at the very end, with no warning, and little in the way of resolution?

Zwerin was the glue that held the Maysleses' work together, with an uncanny knack for taking all the brilliant moments their crews had captured in the field and assembling them into a narrative with a beginning and an ending. But this film proved an immense challenge, with an explosive climax that threatened to undercut everything that preceded it, and that was nearly impossible to foreshadow. The editors working under Zwerin took note of her calm—a calm only further underscored by the air of near panic trickling through the hallways of 1697 Broadway.

The filmmakers were sitting on a snippet of film unlike any they had ever filmed in their careers, and yet the prospect of making a functional feature film out of it grew ever more remote. Only Zwerin's quiet focus soothed the jangled nerves of her colleagues. Albert and David trusted her completely, sure that she would find the resolution they all needed. The Maysles brothers had embraced collaboration as a working style in keeping with the tenets of direct cinema, but it also allowed them to bring in a partner whose strengths made up for their weaknesses.

In the eyes of many of her colleagues, Zwerin was the true director now. Albert and David had done yeoman work in finding the material, but they were now secondary figures in the process of assembly. Neither Albert nor David could shepherd a film as complex as this one through the editing process by themselves. It would require the editing skill, and infinite patience, of Charlotte Zwerin to transform the Altamont footage into a workable film.

Zwerin was known for her incredible stamina, with weeks and months of late nights and unceasing toil marked only by the growing pile of crushed cigarette packs accumulating in the editing room's wastebasket. Zwerin was capable of superlative feats of editorial wizardry when necessary, able to trim together a montage as smoothly as any editor working in documentary—or Hollywood, for that matter—in order to shift a mood, or silently convey a message that might otherwise not make it onto the screen. She understood composition and form, and was a faithful servant of the material, allowing it, and not her own work, to speak loudest. But to edit a work of direct cinema was less about editorial pyrotechnics than about expressing a fundamental respect for the forms and patterns that reality took.

Zwerin would regularly interrupt her work during that long winter, leave her desk in her editing room, located down a corridor from David and Albert's conjoined desks, and lie down on a mattress on the floor. She was resting her bad back, getting off her feet to ward off another flare-up of lower-back pain, but there was likely something else happening, also. The puzzle of Altamont pulled at

The crew of *Gimme Shelter*, taken the morning after the festival. (Courtesy of Eric Saarinen)

her, demanding resolution. The film was a line, plodding diligently down the path from one event to the next, and it needed to become a circle. How could Meredith Hunter's death be resolved? Zwerin never spoke much, did not do much explaining of her train of thought, but the younger editors could see the wheels silently spinning, calculating the angles and searching for a solution.

Immediately after the concert, Albert and David asked two of the cinematographers they had employed at the show, Joan Churchill and Baird Bryant, to pick up the raw footage from the lab in Los Angeles where it had been processed and do a rapid search for the moment of Meredith Hunter's death. Churchill had been renting a cantilevered house in Laurel Canyon from Bryant and his wife, Johanna Demetrakas, and the two filmmakers brought the footage back to the house to search through it. Passing through the potted plants dramatically strung from the exterior walls and into the house's cool interior, Bryant set up camp in the editing room, and Churchill worked on a Moviola editing machine she had borrowed from her father.

Churchill and Bryant were understandably unsettled by the morbid task, their jitters only further underscored by the steady stream of anxious phone calls originating from New York. The Maysleses were rattled by the Hells Angels' pressure campaign, demanding to see the footage shot at Altamont. Their panic had Churchill convinced, every time she looked through the house's large windows onto Willow Glen Road, that Sonny Barger himself was prowling the canyons in search of rogue documentary editors. Churchill would sit at the editing desk, scrolling through footage, and picture packs of leather-clad Angels combing the hillsides for her and Bryant. Paranoia was in the air, borne on the wind by the murderous spree of Charles Manson and his acolytes through these same canyons the preceding year. Death, they felt, just might be stalking them, too.

Churchill and Bryant were unable to locate the footage in question, perhaps misled by the faulty information then circulating about when during the Stones' set Hunter had been killed, and the larger team of editors in New York took over the job. The film came in to the Maysleses' editing room in midtown Manhattan in magazines, each containing approximately eleven minutes of footage. Glimpsed from a certain angle, the movie had been a straightforward production—a three-day shoot, practically, with almost the entirety of it shot over the course of a single day, in a single location. And yet, the challenge of turning the mass of raw material into a polished film had only just begun for the three filmmakers.

The rush was on to find the footage of the encounter between Hunter and the Hells Angels. Editors dug through boxes and hastily cued up footage on their Steenbeck editing machines in the hopes of being the one who found the moment that transformed a concert film into a criminal investigation.

David Maysles told editor Janet Swanson that he was sure Hunter had been killed during the Stones' performance of "Sympathy for the Devil." Swanson spent five full days painstakingly syncing picture with track, only to find nothing related to Hunter during the song.

The idea of seeing the moment of a man's death was so fraught with drama that even experienced film editors expected to find something monumental, an image invested with the weight of its significance. Instead, once the editing team realized that Hunter had been killed during "Under My Thumb," not "Sympathy for the Devil," they rapidly located the stabbing. It unfolded so quickly that even a trained eye might not notice what had just taken place. From the back of the stage, Baird Bryant had shot the footage over the shoulders of the Stones and out into the crowd, where a brief scuffle could be glimpsed in the front rows. In it, a young African-American man appeared to lurch away from a passel of bikers, reaching into his suit jacket and pulling out a gun. One of the Angels then leapt onto him and proceeded to stab him twice before both men disappeared from sight.

It was, on close inspection, unquestionably Hunter, although the camera seemed to arrive after the encounter between him and the Hells Angels had already begun, the footage too herky-jerky and brief to provide any definitive conclusions. Nonetheless, it was, as the directors instantly knew, the most important footage that anyone had shot on that day.

Now that the filmmakers had confirmed the existence of a filmed record of Meredith Hunter's killing, their paranoia about the Hells Angels' threats rapidly amplified. The Angels were naggingly aware that the material shot by the Maysles brothers and their crews might not only reflect poorly on their character, but also serve as incontrovertible proof of criminal activity. With no way of knowing just what the film had captured, the Angels—or some of their colleagues—were concerned about being blindsided by the Maysleses' work. A New York branch of the Angels reached out to Albert and David through mutual acquaintances with a threat: there was a contract out on the two directors' lives. If they were so foolhardy as to release their film, they would both be killed.

David had already been assaulted by an Angel at a meeting in California some days after the concert. He and Albert had brought some footage to show the Hells Angels, hoping to film them watching it. They refused, telling the Maysles brothers that the film had to be destroyed. Alternatively, they could pay the Angels $1 million as a release fee to cover the costs of their performance. David had been summoned to a back bathroom to talk further and encountered one of the Angels. He hoped to speak sensibly with them about cooperating with his film, but had instead been on the receiving end of a beating.

One day not long after the discovery of the footage of Hunter's death, none other than Sonny Barger showed up at 1697 Broadway. He had heard the rumors that Albert and David might be in possession of potentially incriminating footage of one of his members, and he came to do what the Angels did: intimidate their enemies into silence. "You people better not do us dirt," he threatened as he stalked the editing rooms, which suddenly felt airless, and coated with menace. Barger hardly had to make his threats any more explicit. He knew he was speaking to people who spent their days watching what happened to people who crossed the Hells Angels.

Albert and David were understandably terrified, and immediately made efforts to protect their film. They made duplicates of all the footage shot at Altamont, and placed it into safekeeping to keep it out of the hands of any marauding Angels.

No one gave serious thought to the idea of shutting down the film, or soft-pedaling its footage of the Angels' violence. Direct cinema was about honestly reflecting the world without undue filtering or interference. It did not always live up to this ideal, but here, when it appeared as if their lives would be put at risk to test their allegiance to the form's demands, Zwerin and the Maysles brothers stayed true. The film would depict Altamont as they had seen it, and as their crew had filmed it. All other considerations were secondary.

Others believed the threats from the Hells Angels were less terrifying than they might have initially appeared. The death threat had come from a New York branch of the Angels, not their more ferocious California colleagues. Coming from so distant an outpost, and one lacking the fearsome reputation of the Bay Area Hells Angels, it seemed easier to believe the death threats were mere bluster. How much easier, though, to dismiss a death threat when it was not being made against your own person.

Even in its unformed state, the film was an object of fascination, a totem intended to prove a case, make an argument, or take revenge on enemies. One day in the spring of 1970, some of the members of Jefferson Airplane, led by Marty Balin, visited the editing offices. Balin had famously been knocked unconscious by the Hells Angel named Animal at Altamont, in a moment captured by the Maysleses' cameras. The bikers' attack had scuttled his band's focus, ruined his starring turn, and damaged the band's standing in the counterculture. Balin had been cheered for standing up to the Angels, but had also had to suffer the indignity of publicly losing a fight he hadn't been entirely aware he was part of.

Balin wanted to see the footage leading up to and following his being knocked out by the Hells Angel called Animal, as if to confirm his own undoubtedly hazy memories of the event. More than that, he wanted to impose his unbending stance onto the filmmakers, concerned that the Angels' threats of violence might cause them to soften their portrait of the rampaging bikers of Altamont. Jefferson Airplane paid a visit to ensure that the filmmakers followed through on their mission to accurately depict the concert. Their film had to be an unsparing indictment of the Hells Angels' duplicity, viciousness, and callousness.

Word of the footage of Hunter's death had made its way to the offices of *Life* magazine in New York, who called with an offer. The magazine's editors would pay $50,000 for the right to publish one frame of the film—a very substantial offer at the time, and a significant one for a penurious documentary film production. The film's producer, Porter Bibb, was overjoyed, and began to make plans for the windfall. Fifty thousand dollars could go an incredibly long way in promoting a concert documentary, potentially driving audiences who might otherwise never hear about the film into the theaters. To Bibb, this was a no-brainer. After all, not only would the Maysleses not be giving up any of their material, they would be receiving much-needed cash and invaluable free publicity for their film.

But both of the Maysles brothers adamantly opposed the idea. How could they sell their footage to a national magazine when it would give away the ending of their film? Bibb was flabbergasted. It wasn't like any of their likely audience would attend a film about Altamont without knowing what had taken place there. All they would have had to do would be to pick up a copy of *Rolling Stone* to read the entire story.

Albert and David, unmoved, told Bibb that as an equal partnership, the two founding members of Maysles Films would outvote him. Perhaps, though, some of Albert and David's discomfort with the idea of their work appearing in the pages of *Life* had to do with their justified fear of the Hells Angels, and a concern that publicizing the Hunter footage might cause the bikers to violently lash out. The *Life* deal was squelched. Bibb, disgusted, sold his one-third share of the Maysles Films partnership back to Albert and David and dropped out of the project.

All the while, another threat lurked: the other music documentary being edited in Manhattan during the winter of 1970. The Maysles brothers and Zwerin were shadowboxing with a ghost, attempting to guess what the documentary Michael Wadleigh and his team were making about Woodstock might be like, and adjusting accordingly. No one wanted to be the second arrival at the party. But if *Woodstock*, which had also served as a poaching ground from which young editors like Susan Steinberg and Mirra Bank were brought in to work on the Altamont project, was likely to recalibrate expectations about the critical and commercial potential of music documentaries, how might the Maysleses' project distinguish itself, and not just emerge as a pale imitation?

In the Maysleses' editing suite, the stacked work prints rose in teetering piles that almost reached up to the ceiling. David and Albert sat at facing desks, able to communicate with only a glance. Albert would idly retool his Arriflex camera, while David would smoke one cigarette after another as he worked the phones, making connections, hunting down leads, and looking for business. Albert would occasionally pop into the editorial room to check on Zwerin's progress. David had spent a great deal of time with Jagger over the course of shooting the film, and had grown enamored of the Stones singer's panache, style, and sulky charm. Jagger seemed to him the epitome of what a modern man could be, his slinky cool a major component of what attracted him to making a film on the Rolling Stones.

During the editing of the Altamont film, David had ditched his Brooks Brothers attire and started dressing in Jagger-esque clothes, letting his famous friend's dark-prince aesthetic creep into his wardrobe, all swirling scarves and shaggy hair. He would show up in long-sleeved T-shirts, resplendent in pastel colors like peach and apricot, paired with tight bell-bottoms. David found that Mick Jagger reminded him of his cousin Alan, a bon vivant and World War II fighter pilot who had died tragically young. The editors would pore over footage of the Maysleses' encounters with the band, and would get to see and hear David's interactions with Jagger, which seemed to betray a closeness at odds with the filmmaker-subject relationship. Speculation started to creep around the office: did David have a crush on Mick Jagger? Were David and Mick actually having an affair? The likelihood of the latter seemed vanishingly remote, even to those who glimpsed the intensity of David's affection firsthand, but it was a telling question nonetheless. Had the filmmaker grown too close to his subject? And had that closeness eroded the necessary artistic distance to tell a truthful story?

Moreover, an inherent suspicion clouded the Maysleses and Zwerin's project, long before anyone caught a glimpse of a single frame. If this film had started off as a kind of promotional film for the Rolling Stones, how could it ever shed its PR trappings and become a work of art willing to stake out a critical stance vis-à-vis its subjects? A sense of skepticism set in about the film, a belief that whatever its final form, it would be the fruit of a poisonous tree. How could anyone trust the filmmakers to do something so radically different from what they had first set out to do? Moreover, how would a film about a rock band be affected, consciously or otherwise, by the knowledge that the band would financially benefit from the film?

Zwerin's calm inspired a kind of diligent craftsmanship in the editors working under her. Four separate editing rooms were at work at all times at 1697 Broadway, each one wrestling with its own challenges, its own invisible demons to slay. Joanne Burke had been working on the film for months as an editor and silently wrestled with the same questions as Zwerin. She had yet to see the entire film, concentrating her efforts on the segments she was working on, but she had the sense that the film lacked a core. Some segments were absolutely brilliant, she believed. The footage that had come in from Altamont had demonstrated a focus and ingenuity that was downright remarkable. But there were so many strands of narrative to follow, so many threads to account for, that Burke could not imagine how this could ever become a film. It was simply too episodic to work. There was no way to knit it all together.

Many evenings, Zwerin would take a dinner break before returning to the office and continuing her work. She would repair to her nearby apartment, which she shared with her boyfriend, editor Kent McKinney. McKinney would devote six months to the editing of a single song, the bravura slow-motion take on the Stones' "Love in Vain." Zwerin and McKinney would often be joined by Albert and David, and by younger editors like Burke and Mirra Bank. Glasses of wine would be poured, and the day's challenges mulled over at leisure. Charlotte and David had once dated, as well, and though they were no longer a couple, with David having just started to see Judy Verhagen, who would soon become his wife, they had remained close. It was obvious to all the crew working by their side that a deep emotional connection still existed between the two filmmakers, only hastened by their mutual love for the technical, moral, and emotional challenges of the filmmaking process. They were joined in advancing toward a shared goal that they could see far off, in the distance.

The problem, as Zwerin saw it, was that the Rolling Stones needed to be confronted with the proof of their own failures. They had to *witness* the havoc they had caused. But the Stones had fled Altamont immediately after their performance, leaving the scene of the crime without ever seeming to have acknowledged the disaster. Moreover, direct cinema required that filmmakers only seek to shape the material that came to them. They were to be simultaneously passive and active: passively gathering footage without interfering in events as they unfolded, and then actively shaping that raw material into a narrative.

Zwerin saw a way through the tangle of complications, but it required skills more in keeping with David Maysles's strengths. David would have to pull a rabbit out of a hat, and convince the putative criminals to return to the scene of the crime and face a cinematic tribunal. What possible reason could Maysles give the Rolling Stones for following up the mistake of appearing before their cameras at Altamont by doing it again?

Maysles approached the band with an argument, and a plea. The film he and his partners were creating, he argued, and that the Stones would own half the rights to, was a monument to the Rolling Stones in adversity. To abscond without comment, to fail to place their imprint on the story, would be both shameful and a notable missed opportunity. David and Charlotte suggested a brief final shoot, this time in London. A skeleton crew would travel to England to film the Stones watching some of the footage from Altamont, and capture their responses to the death they had perhaps inadvertently caused. Looping in the Rolling Stones, allowing the story to begin and end with the band, would close the circle.

This would not be the Maysleses' first attempt to add context and nuance to the film by flying out to see the Rolling Stones. A few months prior, they had flown to London to film the final mixing for Get Yer Ya-Ya's Out, the Stones' live album from the '69 tour. They bantered with the band about potential titles for the film (Jagger suggested Naughty Ladies 70, while David, riffing off the famous Stones song, proposed Jumping Jack Maysles) but none of the footage wound up in the finished film.

Zwerin's plan was audacious, not only for its desire to recruit the

Stones into responding to the disaster they had so scrupulously sought to avoid, but also in its bending the unofficial rules of direct cinema. Direct cinema was intended to stand back and observe, to capture the world as it was, not to interfere or intervene. Nor was it supposed to script reality, pushing its characters—for even documentaries had performers—to appear in scenes of the filmmakers' devising. Zwerin was coming dangerously close to violating direct cinema's insistence on critical distance in order to solve the challenge keeping this project from becoming a unified whole.

Charlotte and David asked Mirra Bank to accompany them on their trip to London.

Bank had studied film in London and knew the city. She got along well with both Charlotte and David, and had also played a crucial part in finding the footage of the killing. The filmmakers were staying at the Londonderry Hotel, where Zwerin was dismayed to be staying in a dark, small room upstairs, while Albert and David shared an enormous suite facing Hyde Park. Zwerin's room had no bookshelves, and her cramped room was filled with the Steenbeck editing machine and other bulky equipment. She kept the film reels on the open windowsill, and a surprise snowfall one evening had the three filmmakers spending much of the next day drying out wet film stock.

The London footage would provide a context for Altamont, a frame in which it could be seen. It would be, as Bank saw it, a necessary climax to the story. The film was about more than Hunter's death, but without this confrontation, it would be difficult, if not impossible, to make the film work. Watching the Rolling Stones take in the tragic results of their misbegotten concert would provide a genuine moment of reckoning that was otherwise lacking here, a moment of discovery and potential catharsis that the film sorely needed.

The filmmakers had approached all the Stones about appearing onscreen, but ultimately only Mick Jagger and Charlie Watts agreed to participate. Charlotte and David were more than satisfied. Jagger was both the Stones' superstar and the band member that had been the most closely associated, however unjustified, with the debacle at Altamont. It would be his response that would be closely studied.

In his paisley button-down shirt with black collar tabs, black coat, and white scarf, Jagger was an emblem of effortless rock-star chic as he entered the Maysleses' London editing room, but his bandmate Charlie Watts, nervously fluffing his hair, was already anxious: "It's really hard to see this." The filmmakers played portions of the KSAN radio broadcast for Jagger and Watts, and the Stones' drummer could not help but smile when describing the forcefulness with which the Angels had cleared a path for the band as they made their way to the stage. "That's just the way they did it," Watts enthused, before pausing and taking stock of the day: "Oh dear—what a shame." Albert particularly liked these quiet moments; in these moments of silence, he thought, character revealed itself.

An unspoken, unacknowledged tension hung in the air as Bank began to spool the reels of film on the Steenbeck, favored by Zwerin for its sharp, bright screen. The filmmakers needed the cooperation of Jagger and Watts to finish their film. The Stones would have to sign off on the use of their images and on the release of the film, as the band retained the rights. The Maysleses had never gotten releases from the Rolling Stones and were aware of the risk of alienating the band. (Their earlier film on the Beatles, *What's Happening!*, had been denied an audience when the band, about to star in *A Hard Day's Night*, refused to sign their releases.) Albert and David tried to put it out of mind, but in reality Jagger could pull the plug at any time, and all their work would be for naught.

David was deeply concerned about Jagger's reaction. He considered the Stones' front man a good friend, and worried that this would spell the end of their relationship. Moreover, he worried about Jagger lashing out at any perceived affront, or implication that his band was responsible for Hunter's death, and shutting down the film.

The more time Albert and David invested in this effort—and the more time David and Charlotte put in editing the film—the greater the potential catastrophe if the Rolling Stones pulled their coopera-tion. Everything would ride on the trip to London, not only for ty-ing the film together, but for assuring its eventual release.

While there had been newspaper reports on the concert, and nu-merous photographers, including *Rolling Stone*'s Baron Wolman and Robert Altman, had snapped iconic pictures of the day, the Maysleses' documentary was the only filmed footage of Altamont. Jagger was in the unusual position of controlling the rights to public exposition of what appeared to be highly incriminating footage of his band's most shameful moment. It might be pleasing to be thought of as the Devil's guitar-slinging minions; it was assuredly less so to be seen as ineffective planners, publicly held hostage by a gang of demented motorcyclists.

Jagger was particularly adamant at the outset about not wanting Meredith Hunter's death to appear in the film. However, Jagger knew he would have to reimburse the Maysles brothers for the costs of producing the film if he chose not to allow its release, and the threat of a six-figure payout stilled his natural impulse to stifle the film.

Although Zwerin had prepared a rough cut of the entire film in preparation for the London meeting, she only screened some of its footage for Jagger and Watts before showing them the killing. There were ten or fifteen minutes of footage on the reel, with numerous takes of certain scenes included. The filmmakers wanted to make sure Jagger and Watts would be able to see Hunter's death, and also understand the malevolent forces that had led to the moment when the Angel's knife had penetrated his back. Interestingly, they did not show Jagger and Watts the eight seconds of footage of Meredith Hunter from a few minutes prior to the fatal encounter the cameras had captured—or at least did not include it in the final cut of the film. An opportunity to humanize Hunter had been overlooked, or ignored.

The resulting sequence was a landmark in the history of the documentary film. The brief, blurry footage was marshaled as evidence in a cinematic trial, with Albert, David, and Charlotte as judges, Jagger and Watts as cooperative defendants, and the audience as jury. The purpose was not to punish, but to witness the acknowledgment of responsibility.

The film broadened the definition of direct cinema by pushing it into territory we might identify, from the perspective of the twenty-first century, as a kind of reality television *avant la lettre*. Zwerin (who would go on to work on the first American reality television series, 1972's *An American Family*) set up a scene for the cameras to film, hoping to capture a revelatory moment that they had themselves planned. Their subjects' responses would be genuine, but to what extent was genuineness undercut by the prefabricated aura of the moment? If this was still direct cinema, it was a highly flexible model that allowed its filmmakers to insert themselves into the reality that they were filming.

There had been no coaching, no preparation before the scene. The camera caught genuine reactions. David told Jagger and Watts that he had the moment of Hunter's death on film, and Albert filmed them as they watched it.

In the version included in the final film, the audience was thrust into the action at Altamont before being roughly pulled back, reminded that what appeared on the screen was being filtered through the presence of the men watching the action. "People!" an Angel on the screen called out into one of the microphones onstage after

Hunter was stabbed. "Let's be cool!" Sam Cutler began imploring people to move back. Without warning, we were interrupted, yanked out of the moment by the voice of Mick Jagger: "Can you roll back on that, David?" As Maysles rewound the film, the moment of Hunter's stabbing was now framed in the editing machine's screen, mediated by the very fact of the editorial process. This was not reality so much as a film earnestly attempting to document that reality. Moreover, the story being told by the film was still in the process of unfolding, with Jagger and Watts's spectatorship folded into the narrative. David asked Jagger if he had been able to see anything of Hunter's stabbing while he had been performing. "No," he responded, "you couldn't see anything. It was just another scuffle."

Intriguingly, Maysles felt comfortable asking Jagger a question here, his direct-cinema scruples notwithstanding. Perhaps the question itself was more conversational than interrogative, or perhaps David believed the answer was an absolute necessity for his film. Either way, the rules were bent once more to accommodate the Maysleses' needs. And there would have been no reason to behave otherwise. If the filmmakers were willing to fly to London for this quasi-artificial encounter, it stood to reason that Jagger could be asked what he knew at the time of Hunter's killing.

Mirra Bank watched Jagger closely, his eyes glued to the screen, and thought she saw an intensely devastated man viewing the consequences of his own failure to anticipate the Hells Angels' violence. She was surprised, though, by his stubborn inability to emote, to clarify his feelings about what he was seeing. Some of it was undoubtedly stereotypical British reserve, but Jagger's refusal to defend himself against the unspoken allegation contained in the footage was telling. Had band advisers told him to be careful about what he said? The relative silence seemed damaging, too, in its own way.

In a way, it also reflected the limitations of direct cinema. At no time did David, Albert, or Charlotte Zwerin ask Jagger or Watts the

most obvious question of all: how did seeing the moment of Meredith Hunter's death make them feel? Albert and David were philosophically opposed to sticking a camera in a subject's face and asking
them to share their feelings. They were observers, not interviewers,
and were ill-inclined to interfere in the natural flow of events and
ask a subject to emote. This was one of their core tenets, even as
some of the most revealing moments in their past films had come
when their subjects had chosen to address the camera as if they were
responding to an unasked question.

Here in London, too, the filmmakers had clearly manipulated
reality in the service of their story. Would Mick Jagger be present
in this editing room if they had not asked him to appear? This blatant editorial interference notwithstanding, they still felt constrained
from asking Jagger about the events he had witnessed. In respect-
ing the tenets of direct cinema, the filmmakers were also limiting
Jagger's ability to explain himself.

The London footage answered the technical challenge that had
bedeviled the film since its crucial footage had first been discovered.
How could the moment of Meredith Hunter's death be slowed down
enough to allow the audience to properly see it? The answer was Jagger and Watts. Their presence as heightened spectators within the
film's frame, bearing witness to the events that had unfolded in front
of their stage in California, was the necessary excuse for the filmmakers to repeatedly show all the other presumed spectators, outside the frame and in the movie theater, the footage that formed the
crux of the film. One set of spectators stood in for another.

David Maysles showed Jagger the arc of Passaro's knife, and
pointed out Hunter's gun, seen against the white expanse of Patti
Bredehoft's crocheted dress. We watched Jagger watching, and then
we watched him get up, stretch, and bid the filmmakers farewell:
"See you all." The moment, when placed near the close of *Gimme
Shelter*, ended with a freeze-frame of Jagger's quasi-diabolical face.

Jagger was being silently upbraided for his emotionlessness, his perverse calm in the face of death. But the stipulations of direct cinema had prevented him from having a forum in which to share his feelings.

Jagger's response to Hunter's death had undoubtedly been lacking in expressions of generosity or care, but it seemed somewhat unfair to expect him to emote on cue without even the prompt of a question or conversational gambit. Zwerin's decision to place Altamont within the frame of the Stones' watching their own catastrophe was undoubtedly proven wise, but it was a bridge too far to accuse the band of callousness when the film itself prevented them from doing much in the way of speaking. The Rolling Stones had treated their fans poorly, but the filmmakers had the perverse effect of raising sympathy for the devils themselves.

The new footage transformed their Altamont story from a document of a misbegotten day in the world of rock 'n' roll to a disquisition on death, moral responsibility, and the fate of youth culture. Jagger's risky calculation to cooperate with the film relied on the idea that even bad publicity was good publicity.

When Bank had a chance to view the footage they had shot, a week or two later, she instantly knew that Zwerin's idea had been inspired. Watching Jagger watch himself, Bank felt her heart skip a beat. This would be the glue they needed. A mass of jumbled footage had now become a film. The experience of making the film had been a formative one for Bank, who felt that she had been granted the privilege of seeing a group of filmmakers work through an immensely complex series of problems while maintaining their devotion to the ideals of direct cinema. It was, she thought, the bedrock of her understanding of how a good documentary might be made.

The film's ingenious organization allowed all the brilliant but nebulous footage that Zwerin had worried would sink the movie to silently pose the question of responsibility. Zwerin had abandoned the element of surprise by front-loading the film with hints of the killing itself, allowing its ghostly presence to hang over every moment of unknowing youthful exuberance, every chord, every smile, and every fistfight. And Jagger and Watts were threaded throughout the film, watching the footage we were watching ourselves in a form of silent commentary on the steady unraveling of Altamont. The film would never be the second coming of *Woodstock* because even its most joyous moments would be haunted by the death of Meredith Hunter.

The disparate bits of misaligned footage shot by the Maysles brothers and their crew—concert tours and press conferences and partying fans and rampaging bikers and drug burnouts and rock music, all capped by a tragic and unavoidable death—had been unified by Zwerin, who instinctively understood that the film required the presence of a spectator who might observe the wreckage of the counterculture's high hopes.

Jagger had disappeared after the concert, content to hide out from the headlines and avoid the finger-pointing from across the Atlantic. But he, too, grasped—whether instinctually, or after the prodding of his advisers—that it would be better to be seen confronting the events at Altamont than be perceived as ducking them. After months of dithering by Jagger, filmmaker Donald Cammell, who had directed him in the film *Performance*, took on the task of convincing him to overcome his fears about potential embarrassment or damage to the band's reputation. Mick Jagger, with the agreement of his bandmates, chose to do something riskier, and more interesting: he agreed to let the film be released as is.

With his appearance, Jagger metaphorically signed off on the Maysleses' film, approving their investigation into the dark heart of the culture he had done so much to build. In so doing, he also subtly aligned himself with the investigators, and not the culprits.

12. "We Blew It"

The mythos of Altamont would stipulate that it had been an immediate turning point in the decade, in the story of music, in the story of the counterculture as a whole. Everything had changed on that day. The 1960s had come to an abrupt end—or so we were later told. But the actual coverage of the concert and its aftermath was sparse, confined primarily to regional or specialty publications. And of what little there was, much of it was misguided or flagrantly incorrect, on the order of the *San Francisco Examiner*'s "300,000 SAY IT WITH MUSIC." The local television coverage was largely adulatory.

Rolling Stone, as the bible of the rock world, had devoted an entire issue to unraveling the story of Altamont, but few others had seriously explored the story of the concert, beyond bare-bones reporting about Meredith Hunter's death. It would be the Maysles brothers and Charlotte Zwerin's film, now given the title *Gimme Shelter*, after one of the Rolling Stones' most famous (and gloomiest) songs, which would open the floodgates to reconsidering Altamont.

One day after the first anniversary of Altamont, *Gimme Shelter* premiered at the Plaza Theater in New York. Initially, Universal had purchased the rights to the film, seeing a *Woodstock*-sized hit in the offing. Then a financial dispute led to Universal pulling out of the project, and the far smaller Cinema 5 Distributing, owned by Donald Rugoff, taking over. Rugoff, who liked to screen films for college students before deciding whether to purchase them, had initially turned down *Gimme Shelter*, deeming it too downbeat. Then Baby Jane Holzer, an actress affiliated with Andy Warhol's Factory, saw the film and convinced her husband Leonard Holzer to put up the money for the film. Rugoff reconsidered and agreed to distribute *Gimme Shelter*.

The critics were flummoxed about how best to analyze the film, or even how to describe it. Was this a documentary? A promotional film gone awry? Was it a fiction film, in which real-life characters were drafted against their will to play predetermined roles?

The emerging American New Wave of filmmakers was only just beginning to remake Hollywood in its image—*The Graduate* and *Bonnie and Clyde* had been released just three years earlier—but there was a growing sense that its stylistic advances were rooted in the collective desire to seek out a gritty reality that its glamorous studio forebears had ignored. As Arthur Penn and Mike Nichols renovated the feature film, documentary filmmakers like D. A. Pennebaker and Frederick Wiseman promised an unfiltered glimpse of real life in their work. Music lay at the heart of this new wave of nonfiction films, with Pennebaker's *Don't Look Back*, about Bob Dylan, and *Monterey Pop* joining the likes of *Woodstock* and *Gimme Shelter*. That so many of these documentaries featured larger-than-life celebrities, and that the stories they recorded were carefully planned routines executed by trained performers, were ironies built into the foundation of the new documentary, long before *Gimme Shelter* was ever conceived.

Gimme Shelter simultaneously continued and undid this trope. It was a concert documentary in which the music itself was essentially an afterthought, a film about musicians in which the musicians were transformed into the audience for the unplanned spectacle of a misbegotten day. Its most successful contemporary, *Woodstock*, had been a lifestyle film as much as a concert movie, forever distracted, and entertained, by its cavorting, gamboling, marijuana-smoking, acid-taking, nudist sprites. *Gimme Shelter* was equally interested in its audience, but was an anti-lifestyle film, a demonstration of all that might go wrong with the counterculture. Its musicians *and* its bright young things were both sidelined, literally shoved offstage by the callous, brutish, road-hardened bikers intent on seizing control. It was direct cinema in the truest sense, with the filmmakers surprised by the gap between what they believed their movie would be and what it actually was.

The final film, clocking in at a brisk ninety-one minutes, was a hybrid product, a zippy jaunt through the Stones' American tour interspersed with the increasingly frantic preparations for the free San Francisco show. It was a crime film initially cloaked as a behind-the-scenes celebrity profile, warning us obliquely of what might follow. "Everybody seems to be ready," a voice (later revealed as Sam Cutler) observed portentously at the very start of the film. "Are you ready?"

The London shoot overseen by Zwerin had turned the film inside out, transforming a concert movie into an extended flashback that ran the bulk of the film. Jagger and Watts were observed as they listened to the KSAN broadcast, alternately rejuvenated and deflated by the parry and jab of the arguing voices. Sam Cutler's ardent defense of the Hells Angels had Watts nodding his head and smiling, while Angel Sonny Barger's referring to the bikers as "the biggest suckers for that idiot that I ever did see" made Jagger look up in surprise and frown.

The camera was fascinated by Jagger, constantly seeking him out, letting him fill the entire screen, with his bandmates relegated to walk-on roles. But Zwerin's London shoot, and the subsequent frame it provided for the film, shrank the Rolling Stones from superstars to bystanders. Jagger smiled as he watched himself performing on-stage, leaping and shouting with abandon, but the editing machine's tiny screen, a frame within the frame, made even the biggest rock 'n' roll band in the world feel more than a bit trivial. Jagger watches himself at the press conference, opining ribaldly to a roomful of journalists about his degree of satisfaction, and cocks his head skeptically: "Rubbish." The film's title, too, appears framed in the Steenbeck screen, a subtle reminder that everything we would see here had been crafted and organized by the filmmakers. Rock 'n' roll, the Maysleses subtly hinted, was not just anarchy and joyous noise; it was a posture, an extended pretense that occasionally dismayed even its most ardent zealots.

The film appeared to take place at two distinct paces: the relaxed trot of the American-tour scenes, in which the Stones bantered with each other and dazzled a series of astounded audiences, and the disintegrating landscape of Altamont, at which disorder and calamity burst into an all-out sprint. Zwerin's editing gave Albert's camerawork the room necessary to breathe, to offer its own brand of subtle commentary. In one of the scenes filmed at Muscle Shoals, the Alabama studio where part of the Stones' new album *Sticky Fingers* was being recorded, Keith Richards, his skin blotchy from one too many hard nights, taps his alligator-skin boots and sings along with their new song "Wild Horses," transported by the music. David prodded his brother to move to a close-up of the boots, and then Albert whip-panned over to a frowning Jagger, clearly more distressed than elated by their latest single. One real-time juxtaposition spoke volumes about the relationship between the Stones' two stars, and their divergent styles.

For a movie that professed to be the definitive record of the disastrous concert at Altamont, a surprising percentage of it focused

on other matters. Half the film would pass before the cameras arrived at Altamont, and almost two-thirds before we caught our first
glimpse of a marauding Hells Angel. The London frame changed the
entire feel of the film, so that every shot of the Stones playing Madison Square Garden, or of Melvin Belli pontificating about concert
parking, was fraught with foreboding. It introduced a healthy skepticism that might otherwise have been absent from the film, posing
unspoken questions that lingered over the entirety of the Stones'
frayed celebration.

The question remained: had the Maysles brothers adequately
taken the Stones to task for their failings? The direct-cinema style
prevented them from definitively articulating how much of the
blame they believed the Rolling Stones deserved. Were they wholly
responsible? Partially responsible? Entirely blameless? Direct cinema
also prevented the introduction of that which could not be filmed,
so the question of the culpability of the Grateful Dead and their staff
went mostly undiscussed in the film.

In its final version, *Gimme Shelter* documented the fraying of the
counterculture, and of the fatal illusions of rock 'n' roll. It was not,
in the end, an unalloyed indictment of the Rolling Stones in particular, or a call to action against the killers of Meredith Hunter. It
was, instead, a hybrid, continuing the backstage eavesdropping of
the Maysleses' films on Brando and the Beatles with a critique of
the culture that had made them superstars. And Meredith Hunter
was less a real figure here than a symbol—of bad planning, of generational hubris, of the Hells Angels' viciousness. It spoke volumes
that we never heard Meredith Hunter's name in the film.

Prior to the film's release, Leonard Berry profiled the filmmakers in
a lengthy *Los Angeles Times* feature, mentioning that he himself had
left Altamont early, finding it too hard to hear the music or enjoy

himself. David Maysles agreed with Berry, obliquely referencing Joan Churchill's LSD experience in describing the challenges his crew had faced in shooting the film. He complained that "I used to go home at night during the editing of this film and say, 'How could we get such incompetent photographers?' You should see the mess of stuff we have." The presence of the Hells Angels, too, had affected the quality of the footage they assembled. Having the Angels in front of you at all times "can make for an awful shaky camera."

He went on to note that the tragic arc of Altamont had imposed itself on the shape of the film: "We wouldn't even have made the film if we didn't have something that was interesting as a film. After Altamont (had there been no murder) we might have given over the footage or gone on to make a film about a world tour or something. But something happened that was very interesting, so interesting that it made it almost an obligation to do it."

For David, the unexpected factor that transformed a concert film into a statement about an entire generation was violence. The horrors of Altamont mirrored, on a smaller scale, the bloodshed taking place in Southeast Asia and elsewhere. "It's important to tell the truth about this in the same way that it's important to tell the truth about My Lai and a lot of things that are going on," he argued.

Albert hinted to Berry about the scrutiny their work had received from the Hells Angels, and the tense interactions the filmmakers had already had with the bikers intent on seeing, and potentially suppressing, their work, while refusing to share cinematographer Baird Bryant's name with the reporter.

Albert understood, though, that contrary to the initial assumptions of all involved parties, it was increasingly possible that the Altamont footage would be exculpatory, not incriminating: "Actually, it could turn out that by giving his name the Hells Angels would just love him and send him flowers and candy because it's the footage that shows not only the knifing but also the gun. So it may end up that that material may be of some help to the guy who committed the murder." It was telling, however, that Albert still used the word "murder" to describe the interaction between Hunter and the Hells Angels. The gun might be enough to get Alan Passaro off the hook at his impending trial at the Alameda County Courthouse in Oakland, due to start four days after the film's release, but Albert still believed it to be murder nonetheless.

Perhaps unsurprisingly, Zwerin was the most thoughtful on the subject of the film's genesis, and on the ultimate structure it took. "The film to me is about looking at a thing," she told Berry. "I don't like to use the word but it's a kind of ultimate voyeur experience. I felt that the Stones—being the center of the whole event, the moving force—would be the people who could really see it by seeing it again." The film's audiences would look at the fans hoping to look at the Rolling Stones, and then look at the Stones looking back at those fans.

What was the message of *Gimme Shelter*? Even the filmmakers themselves could not agree. Albert, reading from a paper clutched in his hands, suggested that "all that was wrong in America was there that day." Charlotte demurred: "I don't believe that." And David gamely attempted to link the atmosphere of their film to that of America circa 1970: "The racial thing, violence, I think it's all there."

The release of *Gimme Shelter* was, first and foremost, a belated opportunity for its reviewers to revisit Altamont, and to take a second look at a story the media had mostly missed the first time around. There had been surprisingly little coverage of the concert in the days and weeks after Altamont, and even less criticism of the events that had transpired. *Gimme Shelter*'s arrival offered up, with the benefit of a full year's hindsight, a definitive judgment on the day's failings. "For some obscure reasons, the terror of that *Walpurgisnacht* Rolling Stones rock concert on a California auto speedway has never had as much impact on the American consciousness as it deserves," argued *Newsday* in its review of the film. *"Gimme Shelter . . .* puts the event in new perspective and suggests some sobering implications."

Something about the film encouraged dramatic readings, asked audiences to see the footage of one Saturday in Alameda County as representative of the way we lived now. Its strengths and its flaws were the country's, and its makers represented the body politic en masse. *"Gimme Shelter* is a stunning film," opined the *Hollywood Reporter*, "one of the most persuasive pictures to date to reflect a reality that unspools with the force of fiction." *Gimme Shelter* was, the *Village Voice*'s Molly Haskell believed, "a film of and by America."

If the country was, as later chroniclers of the era like Rick Perlstein would argue, experiencing a sub rosa civil war between left and right, Altamont was a full dress rehearsal, with the ultrapatriotic, quasi-fascist Angels emerging triumphant over the well-intentioned but fatally disorganized liberal hippies, whose greater numbers were not matched by an equivalent ferocity of purpose.

Political and social meanings were everywhere, waiting to be drawn out from the tale of a failed utopia consumed by violence. Even William F. Buckley Jr., doyen of the conservative elite and not a man one readily associated with the likes of Keith Richards, saw fit to weigh in on Altamont, echoing the growing consensus that it had spelled an untimely end for the counterculture. Jagger was "fascinating because one simply does not know what it is that he does that is fascinating." (Buckley also described Jagger and the Stones, hilariously enough, as "homely.") At the end of the film, after Hunter is killed, "they crowd like sardines into the helicopter, and fly out of the lonely crowd, leaving behind them the corpse of Woodstock Nation."

The film felt like a symbolic representation of the turmoil of the 1960s, at home and abroad, and thoughtful commentators stretched for suitable comparisons. *After Dark*'s Martin Last compared the marauding Angels to the American soldiers in Vietnam, and to the

Soviets who trampled the Hungarian uprising of 1956. Others, like *Newsday*'s Joseph Gelmis, saw parallels between Altamont and other killings unexpectedly recorded for posterity, comparing Hunter's death to the murder of Lee Harvey Oswald by Jack Ruby on national television.

For *Time* magazine's Jay Cocks, whose review did as much as anyone's to establish the tone of *Gimme Shelter*'s reception, the arrival of the film marked the end of an era: "The Age of Aquarius ended with the flash of a knife early last December on a tumble-down raceway near Altamont, Calif." The Hells Angels were more than just the assassins of youthful idealism; they were representatives of a terrifying nihilism, intent on tearing down in an instant what others had struggled to achieve at enormous cost. "The scene at Altamont is the Armageddon between American counter-culture and unculture," argued the *Village Voice*'s Haskell, "the apocalypse in which the four horsemen of our melting-pot unconscious—Freud, Adler, Jung, and Mammon (or Sex, Power, Religion, and Money)—are suddenly in plain but hopelessly knotted view." Altamont marked the collision of eternally opposed forces, of the battle between love and death, or between empathy and fear. The documentary doubled as a passion play, with Meredith Hunter cast against his will as the suffering Christ sacrificed for the sins of the masses.

The finished product was truth that masqueraded as fiction, a real-life story that reminded many critics of a recent fictional masterwork about a murder caught unknowingly by cameras. "For anyone who saw Antonioni's 'Blow-Up,'" Louise Sweeney wrote in the *Christian Science Monitor*, "in which a photographer discovers in the darkroom that he's unintentionally filmed a murder, it's a grim reminder that reality can be stranger than fiction." The *Village Voice*'s Haskell similarly described the film as "'Blow-up' with a real murder and real us having to sit in judgment."

The references to Antonioni were about more than just the murder-mystery framework; much of the critical response was searching for language with which to indicate that it had seen something that seemed simultaneously realistic and impossible. Reaching for a similar comparison, Michael Lydon would liken the final scene of *Gimme Shelter* to "the mad consummation of Fellini's *8 1/2*." Here, real life expanded to the carnivalesque dimensions of Fellini, or the enigmatic shrug of Antonioni. The comparisons were high praise—the Italian filmmakers were two of the acknowledged masters of 1960s cinema—and also a veiled critique. They treated the Maysleses' truth as a kind of advanced fiction, in which the unfiltered march of unscripted events could only be understood as a heightened metaphor. They betrayed a certain lack of confidence in the Maysleses' own ideals, silently expressing the belief that all this, while real, was still somehow less than genuine.

And the fact of bearing witness to murder made the audience, many critics believed, accomplices after the fact. "We are the patrons," argued Haskell, unspooling the thread that linked us to Meredith Hunter, "who buy the tickets to see the movie that paid for the concert that featured the Stones who hired the Angels who killed the black whose death is the box office attraction for us."

The *New York Times'* Vincent Canby argued that a concertgoer's description of Altamont's "ugly, beautiful mass" was equally applicable to the whole film, but then hedged his bets: "It's true, that is, if you can regard it simply as a neutral record of fact. I'm afraid I can't." The film was "touched by the epic opportunism and insensitivity with which so much of the rock phenomenon has been promoted, and written about, and with which, I suspect, the climactic concert at Altamont was conceived." Canby found the film ultimately deflating. The youth culture was broken, but not for the reasons the Maysles brothers and Zwerin enumerated. Instead, Altamont demonstrated that culture's moral failings. *Gimme Shelter*, Canby concluded, "is not a concert film, like *Woodstock*. It is more like an end-of-the-world film, and I found it very depressing."

No one was to maintain a moderate view of the Rolling Stones' front man. To some, he was the epitome of the rock star as huckster, selling death as a lifestyle to a nation of unwitting addicts. If you watched closely enough, you could see Satan's horns underneath the omnipresent Uncle Sam top hat. "When Jagger sits impassively watching the murder replay and murmurs his soft disapproval," wrote Gail Rock of *Women's Wear Daily*, "it is the pusher watching the junkie go down."

Newsday's Joseph Gelmis reached for an unlikely cinematic comparison in the hopes of defining Jagger's culpability: "Like the sorcerer's apprentice, the wizard Mick Jagger became just Mickey Mouse when he tried to control the demons whom he had summoned." One reviewer suggested that Jagger had proved himself to be nothing more than a mock revolutionary, who had called for the audience to cool off when "the real thing came." (The distinction between violence and revolution had seemingly been misplaced somewhere along the way.)

Life's Richard Schickel saw the film's release as a blatant attempt to retire the Rolling Stones' debt from Altamont, "since even philosopher-kings like Jagger don't work for nothing, whatever their faithful followers like to think." Jagger was not just crass; he was testing the fervor of his fans, Schickel believed, by rubbing their faces in his amorality: "He could, of course, have refused to permit release of the film, but before we credit him with being a champion of free filmic expression I think we must at least consider the possibility that by letting us see him in so unflattering a light, he is restating his alienation in yet another way. I think he is declaring that his hold on his cult is so powerful that it will accept anything he does or says and that the good opinion of the larger, more respectable audience is of no consequence to him. This is, of course, a heady and radical freedom for any performer to savor. And a terrible one."

Jagger was treated as the film's star, his performance reviewed and assessed as if every action, every gesture on display had been carefully choreographed. Critics made little distinction between *Gimme Shelter* and Jagger's other star turn of 1970, in Donald Cammell and Nicolas Roeg's *Performance*, in which he played a dissolute rock star who takes in a gangster on the run, and flummoxes him with his mystical/sexual charms.

Numerous critics were struck by the yawning gap between the onstage and offstage versions of Jagger. He was, *Variety* argued, "seldom less than mesmerizing" onstage, while "a withdrawn, almost catatonic individual" offstage. The *New York Times*' Canby took notice of "the camera, which cannot make up its mind whether it adores Mick Jagger or loathes him, whether it is an instrument of exploitation or a victim of it."

John Simon of the *New Leader* would gaze at the Altamont crowd with the same sense of barely restrained horror as Buckley. The concertgoers were zombies and cannibals, all at once: "They stare at the Stones with an expression that could be described as stoned, zonked, glazed, but also hungry and somehow vicious—like a rabble that has just smashed the store windows and is getting ready to loot. Greedy polyp-like arms stretch out toward Jagger and the rest; when repulsed, they tenaciously, tentacularly return to the task. You feel that this crowd is a Moloch that would as soon devour its idols as listen to them."

It came as little surprise that the perpetually ornery Simon disliked *Gimme Shelter*, but he did notice a resemblance between the counterculture it sought to depict and the mass culture it so thoroughly disdained: "From these films, and a few others we have seen lately, we get a curious insight into our youth culture. It clearly apes adult culture without realizing it. It has its aristocracy, the college students; its middle-class, the dropouts who take on various more or less flimsy jobs; its proletariat, the street people who hang around college towns to scrounge off students and their facilities; its warrior caste, the blacks and other militants; its artists and philosophers, the rock musicians and self-styled gurus; its whores and courtesans, the groupies and super-groupies; and its madness, though manifested in different ways." *Gimme Shelter* was not only a record of the counterculture's failings, but of its illusions. In attempting to create the world anew, it only succeeded in aping the broken one it sought to escape.

Sol Stern, who had attended the concert with Kate Coleman, Frank Bardacke, and the other members of Fisherman, their living collective, contributed a thoughtful essay on Altamont in *Ramparts* magazine with the provocative title of "Altamont: Pearl Harbor to the Woodstock Nation." Woodstock, Stern argued, was the comforting story preferred by both the counterculture and its chroniclers; Altamont was the distressing reality. The media had ignored the story of Altamont because it required too rapid an about-face: "The deflation of the Woodstock myth—so soon after they had helped inflate it—was apparently something the masters of the mass media were not up to." Stern alleged that Altamont had attracted a different crowd, more rural and working-class than the expected Berkeley student elite, and that this, too, had contributed to the unrest.

Stern believed the concert had been predicated on the belief, shared by the likes of Michael Lydon, that musicians like Jagger and Bob Dylan would soon provide the "programs and plans" for the forthcoming revolution. But at Altamont, "all the energy flowed from the stage," with the audience relegated to passive observers. The music would never—could never—politicize a new generation, all insistence of radicals to the contrary. Altamont was the "hopeless shipwreck" of the counterculture, the exposure of all its illusions. Stern, like one of the callers to Stefan Ponek's KSAN postmortem, compared the death of Meredith Hunter to that of Kitty Genovese, powerfully arguing that, like Genovese, Hunter had been abandoned by the counterculture who had claimed him as one of their own. The hated police, Stern observed, were the ones left to care for Hunter's dead body.

But the most prominent critique of *Gimme Shelter*, spread across numerous reviews, regarded its apportioning of blame for the chaos of Altamont. The Maysles brothers, many argued, had soft-pedaled any criticism of their stars, preferring to stay in their good graces. "The Maysles [*sic*] treat the Stones gingerly, reverentially, and with all the uncritical good faith they withheld from the Bible salesmen in the documentary 'exposé' of the subject," carped the *Village Voice*'s Haskell. The film veers so far from pointing the finger, argued *New York* magazine's Judith Crist, that it made the Rolling Stones look even worse than a more evenhanded effort might have. The film, wrote Crist, "can be faulted for its lack of polemic, for so uninvolved a viewpoint that one almost sees it as a surface exploitation of the Rolling Stones in a scene that provided them with a shocking kind of background."

Where some faulted the film for its defective evenhandedness, others saluted its immersion into the disturbing reality of Altamont. It showed us a "hate fest," in the words of the *New York Daily News*' Kathleen Carroll, where "the Angels stand by, like Neanderthal men, hungering for the kill. And we are left sickened by the total bestiality of it all." Even in life, we are constantly being reminded of death. As Crist astutely noted, much of the film's imagery was death-haunted: "The bodies of freaked-out men and women are passed overhead like corpses; the stolid faces of Angels are studied in close-up; the beautiful long-haired girls with dead eyes get their moment on camera." The critics paying tribute to the silent juxtapositions and parallels that formed the Maysleses' critique had come closer to understanding the purpose of their work. To assail a work of direct cinema for not bringing the hammer down definitively on the bad guys was to misunderstand its core values and its techniques.

Perhaps the most influential, and misguided, reading of *Gimme Shelter* came from Pauline Kael of the *New Yorker*, who compared the task at hand to reviewing the Zapruder film, or the broadcast images of Lee Harvey Oswald's murder. She opened her inquiry by questioning how one might even approach the film. "This movie," she noted, "is into complications and sleight-of-hand beyond Pirandello, since the filmed death at Altamont—although, of course, unexpected— was part of a *cinema-verite* spectacular." *Verite* was almost a dirty word for Kael here, an implication that the filmmakers had been so intent on documenting the grubby underside of humanity that they had somehow—how, Kael could not say—summoned it. Kael was skeptical of direct cinema—so much so, in fact, that the original version of her *Gimme Shelter* review would erroneously claim that the Maysleses' film *Salesman* had been cast with actors. (Kael had reversed cause and effect; Bible salesman Paul Brennan had been convinced *Salesman* was his big break, and had quit his job and moved to California to pursue a career as an actor. His bold move did not meet with success, and Brennan eventually had a breakdown. Later versions of the essay would silently retract the career-damaging claim.)

Kael drew a comparison with Leni Riefenstahl and the Nazi propaganda film *Triumph of the Will*, another document, as she saw it, of a mass spectacle whose hollowness was self-evident to anyone not already a disciple of the gods being worshipped onscreen. Kael went on to wonder: "If events are created to be photographed, is the movie that records them a documentary, or does it function in a twilight zone? Is it the cinema of fact when the facts are manufactured for the cinema?" Direct cinema, as Kael noted, prided itself on its ability to render itself invisible, but here, it was impossible to forget the cameras. "There is no reason to think the freaked-out people in *Gimme Shelter* paid much attention to the camera crews, but would the event itself have taken place without those crews?"

Kael believed the film was guilty of excluding information that might have conveyed a more truthful sense of the musicians' and filmmakers' roles in Altamont. She argued that the film and the concert were substantially more intertwined than *Gimme Shelter* allowed for, and that by letting the Rolling Stones off the hook, Albert and David were, by extension, releasing themselves of any burden of guilt for their role in Altamont. Kael singled out the Maysles brothers' having been hired by the Rolling Stones to shoot the show, and argued that the film's producer, Porter Bibb, had helped to produce the festival as well. "*Gimme Shelter* has been shaped," Kael argued, "so as to whitewash the Rolling Stones and the filmmakers for the thoughtless, careless way the concert was arranged, and especially for the cut-rate approach to keeping order."

Kael was especially turned off by the figure of Mick Jagger, who troubled her as both a performer and a representative of the breakdown of the moral order of the counterculture. Jagger, she argued, "symbolizes the rejection of the values that he then appeals to." He was a gangster in love beads, summoning the darkest impulses of what Kael saw as "the disintegrating people" at Altamont, and then cynically calling on them to maintain order, even as the Hells Angels fomented the violence.

Reading against the grain of the film, Kael argued that the Hells Angels were the "patsies" of *Gimme Shelter*, set up by the guilty parties as a means of obfuscating the truth. Jagger and his cronies appear in the film's London framing scenes, looking puzzled as to how such a calamity could have befallen their lovefest, silently deflecting blame onto the bikers they had set up to fail. "Altamont, in

Gimme Shelter," she concludes, "is like a Roman circus, with a difference: the audience and the victims are indistinguishable."

Kael seemed unsure which crime she was referencing here, or who was fundamentally to blame. If the young people summoned to Jagger and the Maysleses' coliseum had been lured to ecstatic excess through the Stones' black mass, what role had the Hells Angels played in the chaos of Altamont? Kael was intent on indicting Jagger for incitement, which required her to argue that the crowd, and not the Angels, had somehow been responsible for the worst of the day.

The Maysles brothers would respond to Kael with a letter to the magazine's editors, which would not be published for decades. (At the time, the *New Yorker* did not publish letters to the editor.) In it, the filmmakers refuted Kael's claims both small—they had played no part in organizing the show's lighting—and large: "Miss Kael calls the film a whitewash of the Stones and a cinema verite sham. If that is the case, how then can it also be a film which provides the grounds for Miss Kael's discussion of the deeply ambiguous nature of the Stones' appeal?. . . . These are the filmmakers' insights and Miss Kael serves them up as if they were her own discovery." In a *Variety* article about the fracas, Albert Maysles called Kael to task for what he saw as her outrageous accusations: "Anyone who believes those charges will never be able to look me in the eye again, or believe what they're seeing in 'Gimme Shelter' is the truth." Zwerin, too, was puzzled by Kael's critique: did she think all documentary filmmakers were merely lying in wait, cameras running, for a murder to occur?

Kael and many of the other middle-aged film critics reviewing the film wrote as outsiders to the "hyped syntax of rock criticism," as Vincent Canby described it, and to the frenzied world of the counterculture. Michael Goodwin of *Rolling Stone* wrote from within the belly of the countercultural beast, and read the film with a notably more nuanced eye, while also introducing a take on Hunter's death that was itself at odds with the newspaper's own journalism.

"If you weren't at Altamont," he told his readers by way of introduction, "you can still get the same lesson if you see *Gimme Shelter.*" In its structure, the Maysleses' work was an instantly familiar genre exercise, but not quite the one audiences might expect: "The first half of the film teases us, alternating various concert footage with dire hints of the terror to come; the second half takes us to Altamont, and from dawn to dusk—from Woodstock West to the seventh circle of our own Aquarian inferno. It's a real horror movie." Goodwin was not enamored of the London editing-room frame, or the slow introduction of the Altamont material, but admired Albert's intrepid camerawork, and the pacing of the concert sequences themselves: "Once we're at Altamont, *Gimme Shelter* moves with the force and inevitability of a Greek tragedy."

Goodwin saw *Gimme Shelter* as a critique directed at his own generation: "There's no way to escape the image on the screen, nor any way to deny its truth. We blew it at Altamont. . . . *Gimme Shelter* lets us watch ourselves blowing it, and makes us understand how and why." This was, for Goodwin, more than a metaphysical statement; it was the author's take on the violence at Altamont. The Angels' violence was met with a rhetorical shrug, while the audience's violence was decried: "There's been a lot of weight put on the Angels for the Altamont debacle, and while there's no question that the Angels were beating on people, the film clearly shows that the flower children were putting out their *own* psychic violence. Everybody, Hells Angels and hippies, were striking out that day, and nobody gets any brownie points. The Angels were more overt about it, of course, but that's the way Angels are."

Contrary to the eyewitness testimony in the *Rolling Stone* Altamont issue, Goodwin was convinced that Hunter had pointed his gun at the stage, and understood the day's events accordingly: "We'll never know for certain what was going to happen, but under the circumstances the Angels who brought him down seem rather more like heroes than villains." Even the possibility that the Hells Angels had overreacted was dismissed. Hunter had sought death by bringing out his gun, and he had found it: "If you're going to bring down a cat with a gun, you'd better do it right the first time, because if you don't you won't get a second chance. That's a hard thing to say, but it's a true thing." Even *Rolling Stone*, which had presented eyewitness testimony (soon to be contested) that Hunter had been stabbed before brandishing his weapon, was now upending the narrative and suggesting that the Angels had served as protectors of an unruly and defiant crowd.

For Goodwin, *Gimme Shelter* was a first stage in the process of accepting the traumas of the recent past, and moving past them. "No purpose will be served by pretending Altamont didn't happen—the only way to salvage it is to work it through, encompass it, and transform it. That's what *Gimme Shelter* is for, and that's why you should see it. It's not easy, but the important things never are." Goodwin understood that *Gimme Shelter*'s depiction of Altamont posed a mortal threat to the counterculture's understanding of itself, and asked its viewers—his friends and compatriots—to accept the critique, internalize it, and overcome it with love and humility.

Goodwin's endorsement of *Gimme Shelter* was simultaneously a call to contemplation and a partial defense of Meredith Hunter's killers. The fraught question of what to make of the Hells Angels—friends or foes? Killers or protectors?—would hang over the other Altamont-themed colloquium of late 1970, in which the subject of Meredith Hunter's death would at last be addressed in a court of law.

13. Spontaneous Declaration

"Don't say 'nigger' in my office." Bob Roberts, president of the San Francisco chapter of the Hells Angels, had come to visit George Walker at his office on Battery Street, only a few short blocks from the Embarcadero. The defense attorney, reclining in his black padded-leather desk chair, already quietly fumed at the unmitigated gall of his putative clients. Roberts and a handful of bikers had lumbered into his office, jostling the file boxes and leather briefcase in one corner and clumsily approaching his enormous glass-and-marble desk, kitted out with a chair large enough to accommodate his basketball-star legs. Walker, lanky and circumspect, was a former star at Cal—a key player on their 1946 Final Four team—turned successful attorney, and Roberts was here, surrounded by framed newspaper clippings of Walker's past successes and a plaque commemorating his being selected by Harvard as one of the nation's top defense lawyers, to ask him to represent the accused killer of Meredith Hunter for his forthcoming trial.

"Get out if you want to talk like that," the mixed-race Walker told the Hells Angels gathered in his office, and the bikers instantly grew polite, and almost deferential. Walker might be, by virtue of the color of his skin, a subject of scorn for the Angels, but he was also the best protection they could find to keep one of their own from the gas chamber.

The case against Walker's new client seemed relatively open-and-shut. Alan Passaro had been arrested in San Jose three days after Altamont, a bloodstained knife found in the backseat of his car. Worse yet, film footage of Hunter's death was said to show Passaro repeatedly stabbing the eighteen-year-old concertgoer. It would require some ingenuity to even mount a credible defense against such daunting accusations.

Perhaps in laying down the law with the Angels in such decisive fashion, Walker was preparing the groundwork for his case, which similarly revolved around the challenge of racial prejudice. If the case were to be summarized by a casual, modestly informed observer, it would be "Hells Angel kills black man at rock concert." The optics of the case were entirely against Passaro, which made it all the more important that Walker reorient the case in a different direction. If the jury believed that the Angels were racists, and that Hunter was killed because of the color of his skin, the prosecution would have a motive, not just a mass of disembodied evidence. The jury would have to see the case anew, to see a fresh explanation for the deadly encounter between Passaro and Hunter.

Walker was himself the product of a Norwegian mother from Minnesota and a half-Cherokee, half-African-American father. He had followed his glittering athletic career with a law degree from the Hastings College of the Law in San Francisco. Walker had cut his teeth as a civil rights lawyer, representing the likes of Fannie Lou Hamer in Mississippi. He still remembered being given the bedroom in a house on the black side of town just outside Tula, Mississippi, sharing a bed with two colleagues and darkly pondering the threats that might be lurking just beyond the door.

Work in Mississippi had been followed by a stint as a lawyer in none other than Melvin Belli's office. Belli, a fixture in the San Francisco legal world as well as a social butterfly, was known as "the king of torts," and Walker saw his boss as a great teacher, providing a daily education in what it meant to be a superlative attorney. Personal-injury work made for solid business, but Walker was assigned a one-off criminal case that came through Belli's shop, representing an accused hit-and-run driver in a criminal case. The tightrope walk of criminal defense was unexpectedly exhilarating. George Walker became a defense lawyer.

Defense attorneys did not, as a rule, have to take out advertisements in the newspaper. You built a reputation as dependable, or even better, as creative, and clients would know how to find you when they needed you. Representing clients as a defense lawyer meant putting one's faith in the system, providing all clients with the best possible defense regardless of their own moral flaws or failings.

For Walker, the Angels were more like medieval brigands than out-and-out racist zealots. They were outlaws, societal outcasts who were still capable of surprising acts of kindness. They were incorrigibly, preternaturally violent, and yet they could often be found by the side of the road, jump-starting stalled cars and rescuing stranded drivers.

Walker's client, moreover, was not an outsized presence like Roberts or Sonny Barger. Alan Passaro was unlikely to spout racial epithets in a lawyer's office, not one to assert his authority in an unfamiliar situation. Walker, some two decades his senior, saw Passaro, who had had to sell his beloved Harley-Davidson to pay Walker's attorney fees, as fundamentally a rule-follower. He was respectful, quiet. Above all, he was malleable. He had become a Hells

Angel to be part of a group, and now it would be Walker's responsibility to remake his client in the fashion necessary to elicit an
acquittal.

Walker saw that his case required that Passaro be seen as defending himself from Hunter's potentially murderous assault—or better
yet, protecting others from Hunter's gun. It was not enough to say
that Hunter had pulled a gun on Alan Passaro and the other Hells
Angels, because that would inevitably raise questions: just why had
an eighteen-year-old African-American teenager felt the need to
wield a weapon when in the presence of Altamont's security staff?
A violent showdown between the Angels and Hunter at least raised
the possibility that the bikers had done something that spooked him
enough to remove his gun from his jacket pocket.

But if Hunter were attacking someone else, the case would be
simpler. Walker could argue that Meredith Hunter was on the verge
of murder when Alan Passaro, unassuming security guard, hero-
ically intervened to save the lives of others.

Passaro's defense ultimately relied on a little-known argument
known as "self-defense of others," which had no precedent in California trial law. There had been unconfirmed reports that someone—
perhaps another Angel—had seen Hunter take out his gun and
called out "he's going to kill Jagger!" In most circumstances, such
a statement would be entirely inadmissible as hearsay. Walker dar-
ingly planned to push for its introduction in court, arguing that
it fell under the hearsay exception known as the spontaneous
declaration.

The exception applied to circumstances in which a statement that
would otherwise be classified as hearsay could safely be assumed to
be true, such as a robbery victim shouting that an assailant was
stealing his wallet, or a woman's phone call to the police after her
husband's shooting. Walker planned to argue that the spontaneous
declaration proved that Meredith Hunter had been planning to mur-

der Mick Jagger, and only Passaro's intervention had prevented the assassination of the lead singer of the Rolling Stones. Walker cast the dead Hunter as a failed aspirant to the pantheon of American assassins, alongside the likes of Lee Harvey Oswald, James Earl Ray, and Sirhan Sirhan.

Without the exclamation being submitted by the defense, there was no evidence of Hunter's desire to kill Jagger. Hunter had shown no interest in Jagger or the Rolling Stones before the concert. He had told no one of his murderous intent, nor had he exhibited any notably suspicious behavior before the encounter with Passaro, other than his having fetched his gun from his car during the chaos of the concert itself. The anonymous witness shouting that Hunter was aiming at Jagger would be the fulcrum on which the case turned.

Given that Meredith Hunter had been stabbed to death in a crowd of three hundred thousand people, surprisingly few people could be considered witnesses to the killing. Besides Hunter himself, who did not live to identify his attackers, or explain his actions, and the defendant, there was Hunter's girlfriend Patti Bredehoft and Paul Cox, along with a small handful of others who had caught a partial glimpse of the events in question. Each would be heard from over the course of the six-week trial, their recollections of those frantic minutes differing from each other in both subtle and essential ways. The prosecution and defense would each seek to stack the testimony in a fashion befitting their own theories of the case, but neither could quite corral the facts into an immediately recognizable array. Was Hunter a victim or a menace? Was Passaro a hero or a villain?

Time and again, the defense and prosecution would turn to the footage from *Gimme Shelter*, shot by cinematographer Baird Bryant, as the source of their authority, and the wellspring of their doubts. Walker knew that the prosecutor, John Burke, would be leaning heavily on Bryant's footage to prove his case. The footage, when Walker considered it closely, was damning and exculpatory, all at once. It clearly showed Passaro stabbing Hunter twice—or at least lunging at him with the knife. But it opened the door to an argument that Passaro had *only* stabbed Hunter twice, and no more.

For the prosecution, the *Gimme Shelter* footage would likely be the most powerful evidence they would wield. The defense's best protection was in turning the footage against them, finding ways to take that very same evidence and render it inoperative. If Walker could argue that Passaro had not been responsible for Hunter's four other stab wounds, and that the ones he had unquestionably caused were not life-threatening, Walker could point to the possibility that some unnamed other assailant had been responsible for Hunter's death.

Walker's trial strategy changed the significance of the film footage for Passaro and the Hells Angels, transformed from highly incriminating evidence of their culpability in the death of an African-American concertgoer to, they now hoped, proof of their innocence. The Angels' initial response to learning of the existence of the Maysleses' footage indicated, at the very least, a discomfort with the idea of a recording of their actions on the evening of December 6. Would people who saw themselves as defending others from a threatening stranger wielding a gun have been so intent on stifling footage of their handiwork from seeing the light of day?

The Hells Angels initially feared the existence of documentary proof of their interaction with Meredith Hunter. Now, though, the brief glimpse of Hunter's gun, flashing against the white crocheted dress of Patti Bredehoft, had turned the situation upside-down. The Angels could now plausibly define themselves as acting in self-defense in a volatile, potentially life-threatening situation.

The prosecution would call on a number of witnesses, including Alameda County sheriff's sergeant Robert J. Donovan, who had been among the detectives on the Hunter case, but the bulk of its case rested on Bryant's film footage, and on eyewitness testimony. Much would ride on the portrait of the fatal scuffle they would paint.

During the second week of the trial, after the jury selection and opening statements, Judge William J. Hayes and the jury, accompanied by the accused and the defense and prosecution attorneys, adjourned to the auditorium of the nearby Oakland Museum for a screening of Bryant's footage. (The judge had been unable to darken the courtroom enough to allow for proper viewing.) The museum screening was immediately followed by an encore presentation, this time in slow motion, in the grand-jury room.

Bryant's footage, which would be shown about twenty times over the course of the trial, captured a few seconds of a fluid, shifting scene, hard to see and harder to interpret. The footage thrust viewers into a wildly chaotic scene *in medias res*. It captured an event that had clearly already begun, in a manner and fashion we could not see. While careful study revealed the two weapons on display here, and even allowed for the hazarding of a guess about who was attacking and who defending here, events also took place outside of the camera's frame, both physically and temporally, that were likely decisive.

We could see Hunter and Passaro's fatal dance, but in the critical matter of who had summoned the other to the floor, the film footage remained decidedly silent. Likewise, it failed to capture the chaotic moments after those seen in the footage, in which Passaro and the Angels had, according to eyewitness testimony, stomped and beaten Hunter, hit him with a metal-rimmed garbage can lid, and stabbed him as many as four more times. The film footage was simultaneously definitive and, in its definitiveness, utterly misleading.

Walker would attempt to transform the prosecution's proof of Passaro's guilt into a demonstration of everything that the film footage did not show. Walker's son Dany, then a teenage film buff, suggested running the footage backward as well as forward, thereby allowing the jury to see the action more clearly. The flurries of activity at the very beginning of the film clip, with Hells Angels moving to the left and the crowd seeming to back up before Hunter emerged, pointed, Walker argued, to the possibility that he had already been stabbed before we first saw Passaro lunging at him. The twinned arguments—that Passaro had not been the killer, and that he had been acting in self-defense of others—were logically inconsistent but overlapping, with each stripping him of responsibility for the crime.

Having seen the footage for themselves, the jury now prepared to hear from the prosecution's key witness. Paul Cox had been closest to Hunter and Passaro during those crucial moments before the killing, and would likely be the voice the jury would trust most implicitly on the fundamental question of culpability. His testimony would serve, along with Bryant's footage, as the centerpiece of the prosecution's case. Cox had testified to the grand jury, and then disappeared from sight, fearful of the Angels' wrath, with the prosecution only able to track him down a week before the start of the trial. Cox had seen firsthand what the Hells Angels were capable of, and only agreed to testify on two conditions: that he be allowed to testify under an assumed name ("Paul Cox" was a pseudonym), and that he not be required to disclose his home address, as most witnesses at a jury trial would.

Walker moved to exclude Cox's testimony, considering it the most potentially damaging to his client's case. Before Cox took the stand, Walker argued that the Alameda County sheriffs' showing mug shots to potential witnesses violated due process. The sheriffs, Walker claimed, placed a thumb on the scales of justice by portraying Alan Passaro as a criminal before a witness had even identified him in a lineup. And who was to say that the police had not given Cox a friendly nudge before reaching Passaro's mug shot? The judge rejected

Walker's motion, ruling that there was "no impermissible emphasis" in the showing of the mug shots.

Walker also pressed the witness to give his real name and address. Cox balked, insisting that doing so would put him in danger of reprisal from the Hells Angels. Walker argued that it was prejudicial to his client to have a key prosecution witness testify under an assumed name, thereby denying Passaro the right to fully confront his accuser. Looking to drive a point home about the danger the Hells Angels represented, prosecutor John Burke asked Cox why he preferred to keep his identity secret: "Because I don't want to get killed . . . I watched someone killed."

The prosecution called a fleet of witnesses to attest to the Hells Angels' propensity for violence, and for violent retaliation against those who testified against other Angels in particular. And so the courtroom was filled with references to men named Dirty Bob, Big Tiny, and Pretty Terry, and stories told of men forced to dig their own graves before being shot and killed, and other horrors. Keeping in mind Hunter S. Thompson's warnings about the overblown law-enforcement response to the Hells Angels, the collected weight of the testimony nonetheless spoke to a certain ruthlessness and efficiency in the dispatch of violence that could not help but be reminiscent of the events at Altamont. Cox would be allowed to testify. But the wily Walker, having fought so hard to keep Cox out of the witness stand, had other plans to discredit his testimony.

The jittery Cox, wearing a blue yachting jacket and baggy off-white twill pants that were almost bell bottoms, struggled to sit still in the witness box. He was undoubtedly thinking about how exposed a courtroom could feel, open to anyone interested in a case or intent on badgering a witness. Cox had seen Meredith Hunter's death, been covered in the dying man's blood, had caught a glimpse of the Hells Angel who had been responsible, and was so intent on justice for the dead that after some trepidation he had agreed to appear in open court. But anyone in Cox's position would likely have been scanning the audience for associates of Passaro's, wondering what might happen to him when he stepped out of the witness box, what would happen in a day or a week, when another biker might recognize him on the street, or at the supermarket.

So Cox bounced his knee up and down, up and down, loosing his jitters in the rocking motion of his legs, and the tapping sound of his heels against the courtroom floor. The presence of a handful of Hells Angels in the audience, staring menacingly, must have made a frightening experience even more unsettling. The rocking and tapping only increased when Walker pressed Cox on the question of whether or not he had been shown mug shots by the police before being brought in to pick out the culprit from a lineup.

Throughout his testimony, Cox was directed by the prosecution, led by John Burke, to step to the blackboard and point to his position relative to the stage, and to Hunter. Cox testified that he and Hunter were both in the scrum of concertgoers "scrunched together" to the right of the stage. The fight, Cox argued, had begun with the Angels grabbing Hunter by the head and knocking him off the box he was standing on. Hunter fell to the ground in a sitting position. He struggled to get to his feet, reaching into his coat and removing his gun. He gripped the .22 in his left hand as he arose, and began to run.

Cox heard a young woman he later determined was Patti Bredehoft, who "shouted not to shoot." Hunter made to run off, but as he dashed away, "someone grabbed him," Cox recounted, and "a man stabbed him in the back." The man was "short and very stocky with a cut-off jacket on . . . I couldn't see the insignia." Cox spotted Passaro stabbing Hunter twice, and then Hunter fell to the ground once more: "I saw him fall down. Then still being kicked around. But this time he was underneath the scaffold."

Cox used a pointer to pick out Alan Passaro as the jacket-clad Angel who could be seen lifting his knife above his head and bringing it down in a stabbing motion into Hunter's back. Burke's line of questioning established that Passaro was indeed the biker seen in the film footage. Cox's testimony lined up with Bryant's footage, but it also picked up the story a few crucial beats earlier. It established that before pulling his gun, Meredith Hunter had already been assaulted by a Hells Angel. The initial provocation was the Angels', not Hunter's.

Walker's cross-examination sought to pull apart Cox's unequivocal testimony. He tried to get the nervous but unshakable Cox to admit that Hunter's gun had been pointed toward the stage when he arose, underscoring his assassination thesis. Cox demurred, responding that it was "not a fact." But Cox's narrative had notably shifted since his interview with *Rolling Stone*, and Walker capitalized on his inconsistencies.

Why, he wondered, had Cox told *Rolling Stone* that Hunter had been stabbed before he brandished his .22, if he was testifying to a different chronology of events under oath? Cox stated that *Rolling Stone*'s line of questioning had put words in his mouth, but his credibility as a star witness had been severely impugned. Cox had been exposed getting a crucial detail regarding Hunter's death wrong, raising doubts about the remainder of his testimony.

Walker scored another point when he referenced the *Rolling Stone* interview to highlight Cox's belief that a second attacker had also stabbed Hunter. Here was the prosecution's foremost witness, inadvertently helping to build the defense's own murky case, even as he insisted on Passaro as the culprit. The inconsistencies between Cox's two statements, the first (to *Rolling Stone*) saying that Hunter had been stabbed before he had pulled his gun, and the second saying that he had been stabbed after he pulled his gun, had been savvily wielded by Walker to undercut the impact of Cox's testimony on the jury, even as much of his testimony went unchallenged by the defense, seemingly damaging to Passaro's chances. Walker sought to impeach Cox's trustworthiness, thereby rendering all of his testimony moot.

The prosecution also called Patti Bredehoft to the stand, but her testimony was, like Cox's, cannily mined by Walker to support his client's case. She discussed Hunter's fetching his gun from the Mustang's trunk, and said she saw an "orange flash" from the gun during the fight with the Hells Angels. One of the investigating officers had already testified that ballistics testing indicated Hunter's gun had not been fired, but Walker would later argue that more sophisticated ballistics testing might demonstrate it had indeed been fired. Walker would go on to argue that an orange flash, seen in the Maysleses' film footage, was evidence of the gun being fired. The police had stated that Hunter had *not* fired his gun, but Walker's line of argument made it seem just as likely that he had.

It would now be the defense's turn to craft a counternarrative, in which Passaro was not a cold-blooded killer but rather a heroic defender of the helpless. After the court returned from its Christmas break, and 1970 turned into 1971, Walker concentrated his efforts on the placement of the knife wounds on Hunter's body. The defense brought a store mannequin into the courtroom in order to mark the location of each of the knife blows. (The prosecution generously made no effort to disallow the mannequin, even though it was female.) Walker used the incriminating footage as a fence around his client, transforming it from an acute disadvantage to a source of protection. Of all the confusing or hard-to-see actions visible in the brief film clip, perhaps the clearest was that of Passaro lifting his knife above his head before bringing it down in a stabbing motion. The arc of Passaro's knife implied an entry point on Hunter's body roughly corresponding with the two shoulder-height wounds, neither of which was, according to testimony, life-threatening.

Doubts were raised about whether Alan Passaro was the sole stabber, or whether, as Walker hoped to convince jurors, there might have been another attacker who had dealt the fatal blow to Hunter. If Walker could limit the damage to his client to agreeing that those two wounds were his responsibility, and argue that the mortal stab wounds were the work of unknown others, then the burden of the first-degree murder charge would be lifted from Passaro. (Later in the trial, Walker argued that it was even possible one of Passaro's two documented thrusts had not punctured Hunter's skin, accounting instead for the scratch on Hunter's neck.)

Walker called Dr. Robert Hiatt, the first medical professional to treat Hunter at the festival. He testified that when he examined Hunter, he was already unconscious, and "very close to death." The laceration to Hunter's left kidney alone would have likely been enough to kill him, and Hiatt believed that "major surgery" would have been necessary to save him. The chaos of the festival had also contributed to Hunter's death, with the ambulance intended to rush him to the hospital blocked by a sea of parked cars. The defense's multipronged approach simultaneously implied that Passaro had been defending himself, that he had not been responsible for ending Hunter's life, and that there would have been no way to save him, anyway.

Several defense witnesses testified that Hunter's provocative actions had prompted Passaro to act in self-defense. A security guard named Stephen Ellis, who had been standing at the back of the stage when the fatal attack took place, stated that Hunter was "moving his gun in an unsure manner," pointing it in the direction of the stage, and that the Hells Angels at the front of the stage had leapt down to the ground and surrounded him. "There was a scuffle," he told the jury, "then the person with the gun was taken out of sight."

Ellis was soon followed by twenty-eight-year-old Larry Tanna-hill, another of the Rolling Stones' biker escorts. Tannahill, who stated in his testimony that he had possibly drunk more than twenty beers over the course of the day of the concert, had seen Hunter at the center of a disturbance in the crowd just below the stage. According to Tannahill, Hunter had been yanked out of his spot by someone in the crowd—not a Hells Angel. "He fell back," he said of Hunter, "and then turned around, spun around and had a weapon in his hand . . . and he came back toward the stage with a gun in his hand . . . He stepped back on the box . . . I hit him and yelled, 'He's got a gun.'" Tannahill demonstrated the forearm shiver he delivered into Hunter's chest for the jury.

Two weeks after Paul Cox took the stand, providing the closest thing to a definitive narrative of Hunter's death, Walker summoned his client to the stand to tell his version of the story. Passaro was nearly unrecognizable now, his hair neatly trimmed and styled into a slicked-back pompadour, his upper lip no longer covered by a drooping mustache, his cheeks shorn of the messy mutton-chop sideburns that had once adorned them. In his leather jacket, neatly pressed gray pants, and black shoes, Passaro could have passed for a baby-faced colleague of Walker's, not the greasy-looking biker accused of ending a young man's life.

Walker led Passaro through the outline of his story over three days of testimony. Passaro said he was one of the Hells Angels assigned earlier that afternoon to escort the Rolling Stones from their helicopter to their dressing room, where a member of the band—Passaro did not remember that it had been Mick Jagger—was accosted by a bystander. "Was the man subdued?" Walker wondered. "Sure was," Passaro answered, a note of swagger entering his otherwise deliberately mild testimony.

Passaro had positioned himself at stage right for the Stones' set, but moved over to stage left to provide additional assistance when a gallon jug of wine thrown from the crowd toppled over one of his fellow Angels' motorcycles. According to Passaro, he had seen the jam-packed crowd open up on the right side, and noticed a scuffle taking place near the stage. He spotted Hunter taking out his gun, which was pointed in his direction, and lunged at him. "I reacted in fear," Passaro said, describing his instinctual response as "self-preservation." He had only taken out his knife after Hunter had already fired his weapon: "The flash in his gun hand I saw. I think the gun went off. I wouldn't want it to be more than that."

Passaro saw the gun pointed in his "general direction." When Hunter swiveled, his back made contact with Passaro's chest, and Passaro leapt onto Hunter's back, straining to reach for his left hand, which held the gun. "I went for my knife. I attempted to get his gun hand. I tried to shake the gun loose. I struck at him on the upper shoulder with the knife." Passaro described himself as "riding" on Hunter's back as he stabbed him twice.

Once the other Hells Angels took notice of the threat, Passaro went on, "everybody started flying all around," and he was "knocked away." He landed on the ground: "I couldn't see the guy no more." When Passaro spotted Hunter next, "they were carrying him to the hospital tent." Passaro claimed that he had had no intention of killing Hunter, wanting only to rip the pistol out of his hands, and keep him from firing again.

Walker sought to downplay the bloodiness of his client's testimony. Passaro was careful to say that, in the scrum of hand-to-hand combat, he was not even sure if he had actually stabbed Hunter. Moreover, Walker took pains to avoid using the word "stab." In the cautious language of his defense lawyer, Alan Passaro had never stabbed anyone. The defense described him as seeking to "strike" and "blow," or having "struck" or engaged in a "striking motion." "I struck at him twice," Passaro stated, deftly matching Walker's phrasing. "I didn't have no intention of killing." Even Passaro's knife, which had been tested and found to have traces of human blood on it, might have been bloodied, the defendant suggested, by his cutting his finger while eating some turkey legs for lunch on the Angels' bus.

On Passaro's final day of testimony, Walker sought to walk back some of the more damaging assertions he had made to the police during his interrogation. He had not been smoking marijuana that day; he had lied to the police out of fear when they threatened him with the gas chamber. He may have drunk some beer, but that was all. He also sought to clarify what he had done with his clothing and weapon after the incident. After stabbing Hunter, Passaro had stuck his knife into the ground next to a van belonging to one of the Angels. (How it had gotten back into his sheath, and then his car, was left unexplained.) He had also removed his windbreaker because there was blood on the collar and the right elbow, as well as across its front.

Passaro's defense was predicated on the idea of a logical and deliberate response to a potential threat, but little else from the concert indicated that the Hells Angels' collective mind-set was capable of so thoughtful and measured a series of actions. Eyewitness testimony and the footage shot by the Maysleses' crew documented a security force entirely out of control, intent on proving its own mettle through an overwhelming show of force. The violence had been doled out messily and unpredictably, its intensity only loosely linked to its supposed root cause. Given Cox's testimony, it seemed more likely that, as in so many other encounters at Altamont, the Angels had wildly overreacted to a concertgoer's efforts to defend himself, and then escalated even further after his calamitous decision to pull a gun. Nonetheless, Walker had masterfully sheared away each tent-pole of the prosecution's case, undermining their argument at every step.

In his closing statement, Walker asked the jury to acquit his client, on the grounds that he had acted in self-defense in stabbing

Meredith Hunter. Hunter, he argued, was a misguided young man with a liability for recklessness, and some combination of amphetamine haze and aggression had led him to wave his gun in front of three hundred thousand concertgoers, the Rolling Stones, and the Hells Angels.

Walker's task was to downplay the damage done by Passaro, arguing that he had not inflicted the fatal blows, while Burke's was to emphasize the tragedy of Meredith Hunter's death. But the prosecution, surprisingly, had little to say about the eighteen-year-old who had been the victim. Meredith Hunter was little more than a name in court, a specter in a lime-green suit with a girlfriend but seemingly no family, no past, and no future. In a typical murder case, witnesses would be called to speak to the victim's character, not because good character was a prerequisite for justice, but for the jury to feel the burden of the dead man's worth. The prosecution presumably chose to avoid all discussion of Hunter's past out of the fear that his juvenile record would be entered into the proceedings. Why allow the defense to tarnish the victim as a thug with a criminal record, a repeat offender who had undoubtedly graduated to attempted murder on that Saturday?

This resulted, though, in a victim whose death felt secondary to the matter being adjudicated. What was the worth of this black life? The prosecution's unwillingness to talk about Meredith Hunter as a human being who had assumed he, too, would return home to sleep in his own bed that night rendered the crime unexpectedly bloodless. Hunter's life was not valued as others' might have been. In the California of 1970 and 1971, a black teenager was promised equal treatment under the law. But its delivery was inconsistent, and the prosecution ultimately chose to treat Meredith Hunter as a name without a face—or a body—out of the fear that he would be judged more severely for his youthful missteps than the man accused of ending his life.

The trial ended January 23, the same day that Charles Manson's fate was decided for the murder of Sharon Tate. The next day, the jury asked Judge Hayes to clarify his instructions on the various charges in play, of which there were five. They also requested another showing of the Maysleses' footage.

The jury was out for twelve and a half hours before returning with a verdict. Jury foreman Charles J. Shields declared Alan Passaro not guilty of all the charges related to the death of Meredith Hunter. Passaro, freed from the straitjacket of respectability imposed by the trial, released a primal howl of relief, and his wife Celeste, sitting behind him, burst into tears. Passaro blew kisses to her and their four-year-old son Michael. Smoking a cigar that had been handed to him by a guard (had he brought one to the courtroom that day in case Passaro was acquitted?), he told a reporter, "I'm happiest for my mother." The bailiffs took Passaro back to prison, and his wife exulted: "Oh, Lord! This has renewed my faith in humanity."

Burke blamed Cox's testimony, and the diligent work Walker had done to counteract it, for sinking the prosecution's case: "He was impeached by his inconsistent statements." But much of Cox's testimony had stayed the same from the *Rolling Stone* interview to the trial. Hunter had been assaulted by Hells Angels, had been pursued by them, had fought back, had been stabbed and then beaten to death long after any potential threat was subdued. Cox had told *Rolling Stone* that Hunter had been stabbed before he pulled out his gun, and the jury that the stabbing had happened after. This undoubtedly damaged the jury's trust in Cox's testimony, but it distracted from the larger question of Passaro's culpability in the violent assault on Hunter. Walker successfully changed the conversation to one more conducive to his client.

Walker embraced Passaro, and shook hands with jury foreman Shields, an executive at a steamship company in Oakland. Walker told a reporter that the film footage had been "a key" to winning the case. Three witnesses—two for the prosecution, and one for the defense—had underscored his argument that what we saw on film was only the tail end of a fight that had begun earlier. Passaro's efforts, Walker believed, were only incidental, the true killing blows having taken place even before he had joined the ruckus. By the time Passaro grabbed for Hunter's gun, Hunter had already incurred the lower stab wounds on his left side that would ultimately kill him.

Walker had succeeded, as good defense lawyers did, by muddying the waters—by crafting alternative narratives and substitute timelines that challenged the assertions of the prosecution. There was little substantive proof that Meredith Hunter had been stabbed prior to Passaro's twin lunges, but the trial had never truly addressed the question of what had taken place *after* Baird Bryant's snippet of film concluded. The centrality of the film footage to the trial rendered Passaro's guilt primarily a matter of whether what the jury saw onscreen was justifiable as self-defense. But Walker had capably elided the issue of Hunter's four other wounds, and the question of who had caused them. If it had been acknowledged that Passaro had been responsible for all of Hunter's wounds, how might that have changed the jury's perspective?

George Walker would go on to serve as the San Francisco Hells Angels' defense counsel for five more years. The Angels would consistently rack up additional prison time for themselves by fighting with the police and leaving themselves open to charges of resisting arrest. Walker advised the Angels, forever in trouble with the authorities, to cooperate with the authorities when being brought into custody. Walker won numerous cases for the Angels, who were subject to persistent police surveillance and occasional harassment. Resisting-arrest charges were harder to contest, though, so Walker, who had beaten a murder charge by presenting Alan Passaro as a soft-spoken, well-dressed defender of the defenseless, sought to remake the Hells Angels into cooperative citizens.

The bikers didn't stop getting arrested, but did stop fighting the cops, and a few years later, grateful for his assistance, the San Francisco chapter of the Hells Angels presented a trophy to their African-American lawyer. Walker displayed it in a prominent spot in his office, in close proximity to the plaque from Harvard. On its face was an inscription: "From San Francisco Hell's Angels to George Walker, Attorney at Law, for outstanding services."

14. 8:15

Altamont created its own set of memories, not all of them trustworthy. Like any copiously documented event, it warped its own witnesses' recollections, often replacing their own memories with a set of images culled from *Gimme Shelter* and other media accounts. For many of the people who attended Altamont, their own memories began to bleed into those preserved for the benefit of posterity. Memory was fallible, deteriorated by time, weakened by alcohol and drugs, but enfeebled above all by the confusion between life and art, the personal and the collective.

The people I spoke to in researching this book would regularly ask casually if others' memories jibed with their own. This was, in part, a reflection of the passage of time. Almost half a century had elapsed since that December day. It was hard to remember, so many decades later, what had happened to you as opposed to what you had seen happen to someone else, what you had watched take place in front of you versus what you had watched take place on celluloid. Memories would have to be tested, assessed for their trustworthiness, poked and prodded to ensure their truthfulness. It could be safely agreed that Altamont was like a collective bad acid trip for the entire counterculture, but the specific details still mattered. A young man had died, and if for no other reason than to do honor to his tragically curtailed life, it was important to determine what had really taken place, both during the concert and afterward.

Six combination locks hung on the rusty white gate, with a sign lashed to its front that read PRIVATE PROPERTY: KEEP OUT. The Altamont Speedway was now closed to the public, and the view from outside its gates allowed visitors to just make out the lights overlooking the grandstand of what had once been the racetrack at the bottom of the hill.

Wind turbines scattered like bow ties towered along the hills leading to the speedway, and the twisting two-lane road that took drivers the last miles was dotted with alternating patches of gold-and-terra-cotta-colored fields. The 580 freeway was like a line of calligraphy drawn across a landscape of undulating hills, with cool air juddering down their ridges on a sunny December day.

It had been on a day like this, forty-six years prior, that three hundred thousand impassioned fans had piled into their cars or hitched rides to attend the concert of the century, and been grotesquely disappointed for their efforts. ENTRANCE CLOSED read a sign visible in the distance, beyond the gate, and it felt like the sign was here in order to communicate a message. The entrance to the past was closed, and this totem of the unwritten, unwriteable past was a reminder that the entire story of Altamont could never be told. But the grass underfoot felt spongy, and prickly to the touch. I stood there, denied access to what remained of Altamont, and thought about how uncomfortable it likely must have been to sit on such grass. These were the fleeting impressions that slipped through the cracks of time.

. . .

The Rolling Stones would endure the backlash from the *Rolling Stone* exposé, and then again, with renewed vigor, after the release of *Gimme Shelter*, but kept away from the United States, ill-inclined to answer for their actions. Altamont was yesterday's news, a set of bad headlines that would soon be buried by other scandals, other crises. Reporters caught Keith Richards at Heathrow Airport, where he offered a blasé assessment of the carnage in the Bay Area. Altamont, he argued, had been "basically well organized, but people were tired and tempers got frayed."

Mick Jagger also returned to London, dogged by persistent rumors that his longtime girlfriend Marianne Faithfull had taken up with Italian artist Mario Schifano. He won her back temporarily, but worse news lay on the horizon. After parting ways with the band's manager, Allen Klein, Jagger hired a new financial adviser, Prince Rupert zu Loewenstein. Loewenstein discovered that Klein had structured the band's finances in such haphazard fashion that the Stones would owe the entirety of their earnings from the 1969 U.S. tour to the Inland Revenue to pay off their hefty British tax bill. Not only had Klein negligently advised the band, their morally dubious manager had absconded with the copyrights to all their songs from 1965 onward. The Rolling Stones no longer owned the rights to "Satisfaction," "You Can't Always Get What You Want," and many of their other classic songs.

In order to protect their income, the Rolling Stones would have to live overseas. The onetime paragons of hippie idealism moved to the French Riviera in order to protect their earnings from the tax man. Could anything have been less true to the spirit of hippie idealism than becoming a tax exile in the hopes of salvaging a heftier percentage of your income? Did anyone still believe Mick Jagger portended a revolution to come?

And yet the Stones, like their doppelgängers the Hells Angels, were inclined to surprise, disappointing their loyalists and astonishing their detractors. The album they would record during their Riviera expatriation would be their greatest work yet, and one of the very best records in rock 'n' roll history: 1972's *Exile on Main Street*. The glamorous beach of Villefranche-sur-Mer, foreign soil for these London boys, freed them to repatriate, in their imaginations, to their true home: America. Jagger sang like a Southern good ol' boy describing his fictional hometown of dirty roads, dirty sex, and dirty secrets.

The lyrics were mostly impenetrable, and the sound was muddy and grungy, a mash-up of proto-punk rhythm, soul-music horns, and Richards's magnificent guitar riffs. They were, at long last, the blues masters they had dreamt of as teenage boys with Muddy Waters records clutched under their arms. The album's penultimate song, "Shine a Light," offered a blessing, too, directed to all the lost American souls in search of a good song and a touch of evening sun. Were Jagger and Richards thinking of those fans, in search of their favorite tune, who had been left with tears in their eyes in the evening sun of Altamont?

The Rolling Stones were still in their most fertile period as musicians, but Altamont, and the Inland Revenue, had scared them away from politics. Henceforth, they would reinvent themselves as gilded hedonists, jaded sensualists with little interest in the world beyond their immediate ken. Jagger's wife Bianca, whom he married in 1971, would become a star in her own right on the dance floors of Studio 54. Within a decade, the lead singer of the Rolling Stones would be paramour to a disco queen famous for having been photographed on the back of a white stallion.

They were still a great band, still recording classic anthems like "Midnight Mile," "Tumbling Dice," and "Miss You," but they had pulled away from their audience. They were now rock gods, visiting occasionally from their restricted-access Mount Olympus with the gift of music for the masses. The former promise of ecstatic union with their fans had been abruptly scuttled, never to be revisited. There would be no more intimations of evil, no more Prince of Darkness. Jagger now had, as Stanley Booth put it, "more darkness than he ever wanted." And for years to come, when each tour was being planned and set lists were being hashed out, one song was silently excluded from consideration: "Sympathy for the Devil."

The Grateful Dead had been crucial to the early planning for the free show, but in Altamont's disastrous aftermath, only the Rolling Stones were tarred with its brush. The Dead rendered themselves invisible as the media and counterculture storm raged.

Jerry Garcia had cowered in his trailer while Hells Angels rampaged through the Altamont crowd, beating and assaulting innocent bystanders with impunity. His ability to go on associating with the Hells Angels on friendly terms, and even consorting with them professionally, betrayed a lack of empathy for the very audiences who had come out to see Garcia's band perform. The Grateful Dead would play a benefit show for the New York City branch of the Hells Angels less than a year later, and would lend the Angels the money to make their film *Hells Angels Forever*. Garcia would later argue that hanging around with the Hells Angels made him less of a jerk. "I ought to take you everywhere with me," he later told Angel George Christie, "because I don't act like an asshole around you." The Dead's calculation was wise; the band sidestepped the avalanche of criticism the Stones received, and would continue to receive for decades to come, over Altamont. Their reputation was secure.

There was not much that music itself could say about the events that transpired at Altamont. The Dead paid elliptical homage to the concert with their song "New Speedway Boogie," on their 1970 album *Workingman's Dead*. The song philosophically shrugged in the face of the death of a concertgoer. But perhaps it would be better to listen to "New Speedway Boogie" as an acknowledgment of the band's limitations, and those of the culture from which they had sprung. The Dead had been guided by everything they had ever said or done or thought to Altamont, and even after arriving at a dead end, they knew of nowhere else to go. It was a reflection of their helplessness that they understood so little, and knew they had so little wisdom to share.

Greil Marcus was not the only one who believed that no one had described Altamont better than Don McLean, who alluded to it in his 1971 hit "American Pie." McLean depicts Hunter's death as a ritual sacrifice, a placatory offering to the gods of rock overseen by Satan. The image indicates that McLean had at least a passing familiarity with the argument put forward in the *Berkeley Barb* in the weeks after Altamont, and juddering through the counterculture in the months that followed, in which a concertgoer claimed that the concert was a musical Black Mass overseen by the Stones, with Hunter the sacrificial offering. McLean was toying with the notion of Jagger as a Satanist, summoning dark forces with his music.

McLean was composing an elegy to rock 'n' roll in crude verse, its lyrics a tribute to the celebrated dead of its mythological past. Altamont was the fifth and final of McLean's representative days in rock history, and the only one in which the musicians were required to share the stage with the fans. Hunter's death was the final indignity suffered by the music, but once again, and unsurprisingly, the dead man was nowhere, not even summoned as a symbolic figure in the tragedy of rock. He was merely the faceless victim, the helpless plaything of the Rolling Stones' sacrificial performance.

Sam Cutler wound up hiding out at Grateful Dead drummer Mickey Hart's Marin County ranch. Cutler felt lost, abandoned by the Rolling Stones in their haste to flee the country, and singled out as the designated whipping boy for Altamont. Cutler had undoubtedly failed to plan adequately for the show, and had not covered himself in glory with his seeming lack of concern for fans during the show itself, but he had been a paid employee of the band that had not seen fit to apologize, or even comment on, the failures of Altamont.

Invited to stay in Hart's barn, and then Jerry Garcia's house, Cutler fell in with the band and found himself attracted to their shambling surrogate family. Cutler wound up working for the Dead for a number of years as their tour manager. They occasionally discussed Altamont, and Garcia always made sure to mention that Cutler had not been responsible for the failure of the concert.

Being acquitted of first-degree murder did not set Alan Passaro free. After his yowl of victory in the Oakland courtroom, he returned to his jail cell, there to serve out his sentence on the San Jose grand-theft charge. Passaro was in and out of prison for the rest of his life, never able to break out of the hold that Angel life had on him. In 1985, Passaro's body was discovered in Anderson Reservoir in Santa Clara County. There was a bag with thousands of dollars in cash slung over his shoulder, and his black Mercedes was left parked by the lake, with the keys inside. The parties responsible for his death were never found.

Passaro had been acquitted, but the Hells Angels had already begun to transform from a motorcycle club into a criminal enterprise. After Altamont, the Angels searched for new friends because the majority of their old compatriots had grown disillusioned with them. Jefferson Airplane, horrified by the Hells Angels' behavior, cut all ties with the club. The Angels went so far as to reach out to the band, hoping to patch things up with their longtime friends. Grace Slick, having none of it, told the Angels that she was quite content with their current relationship—which was no relationship at all.

Bill Graham, who would later work with Angel George Christie, jointly promoting some concerts together, warned the club that the music scene was leery of associating with them altogether. They were too volatile, he argued. How could anyone hire them, or even invite them to attend a show, and be confident that chaos would not ensue once more?

Around this time, organized crime discovered the Angels as trusted accomplices. The mob sought to distribute drugs nationwide, and were looking for networks living beyond the reach of the law to serve as middlemen. The Angels, with their ethic of loyalty and obedience, were ideal candidates, and the Harley-Davidsons crisscrossing America's highways were now often loaded down with heroin and cocaine. Altamont demonstrated that the Hells Angels were unbreakable. No amount of pressure levied by the government could get them to turn on each other.

Sonny Barger described himself as having been high on cocaine for the entirety of the 1970s, and many of his compatriots were similarly addled. "The seventies were a gangster era for us," he would later write. "I sold drugs and got into a lot of shit. Other clubs tried to take our rep from us. The blacks and the Latinos didn't like us; white people were scared of us; hippies no longer dug us; rednecks couldn't stand us either. Everybody hated us. We became isolated." Barger was arrested, charged with selling heroin and kidnapping, and would eventually serve a number of years in prison. Time was, the local cops would panic when the Hells Angels blew into town, engines roaring. Now, the federal government, employing the RICO Act, originally drafted to counteract the Mafia, was mobilizing to face off with the Angels.

Barger got out of prison and became an unlikely celebrity, another grizzled 1960s burnout whose very existence testified to the deleterious effects of drugs and the unlikely survival of some of the hardest-living members of their generational cohort. Barger would help transform the Hells Angels into an omnipresent brand, the once-feared death's-head now imprinted on everything from leather jackets to T-shirts. SUPPORT YOUR LOCAL HELLS ANGEL read the popular T-shirts, selling a counterculture worship of the antihero already well over a decade past its sell-by date.

Barger made himself a wealthy man monetizing the Hells Angels brand, and in so doing, infuriated many of his fellow Angels. Bob Roberts complained that Barger had enriched himself at the expense of his brothers. Where were their health insurance policies? Where were their benefits? It was almost as if the Hells Angels had doubled back on itself, part criminal enterprise, part pension scheme for aging bikers.

The Hells Angels blamed the Rolling Stones for the disaster of Altamont. The Angels had been left pissing in the wind, facing the unbridled wrath of the authorities and the general public—so this line of thinking went—while the Stones partied in the French Riviera. More than that, the club had to pay Passaro's hefty legal expenses without the band contributing what the Angels believed was their fair share. The Hells Angels demanded $50,000 for Passaro's defense fund, which the band flat-out refused to pay.

The Rolling Stones would eventually send a representative out to see the Angels in New York, informing them that they would not be paying the $50,000, now or ever, and threatening the bikers with a glimpse of the firearm in his waistband. The Angels, twice burned, fixated on Mick Jagger as the source of their difficulties. They had run into Keith Richards a number of times over the years, and found him affable and without a trace of condescension. Richards was not responsible for the Altamont snafu, they decided; it was Jagger who haughtily insisted on cutting the Angels dead. The Hells

Angels had always worked on a handshake, and they believed that by hiring them as security at Altamont, the Rolling Stones had also agreed to stand by them in case of trouble. The club was appalled by what they perceived as Jagger's duplicity, and by the drawn-out war of words over the money they viewed as rightly theirs.

Hells Angels meetings of the early 1970s regularly took up the issue of how to resolve the dispute with the Rolling Stones. The New York branch of the club ultimately decided on an audacious revenge plot: they would assassinate Mick Jagger as comeuppance for his failure to support the men he had hired as Altamont security. (There was a dark irony somewhere in here; the men who claimed to have protected Jagger from an assassin would then assassinate him in a fit of pique over not being properly compensated for their work as bodyguards.) Sometime in the mid-1970s, a New York Angel carrying a gun with a silencer staked out a hidden spot outside a Manhattan hotel where they believed Jagger would be staying, primed to pull the trigger. Jagger never showed, and the plan was aborted.

The Hells Angels regrouped, and in 1979, they made a second attempt on Jagger's life. They took out a raft and planned a seaborne assault on Jagger's home in the Hamptons. The Angels would dock near his house and enter his property through the back garden, bypassing the security that ringed the front of Jagger's home. They would then plant explosives underneath the house, seeking to blow up Jagger's mansion with the star inside it. On their way to commit murder, the Angels' boat was hit by a storm and capsized. All the Angels were thrown overboard. No one was injured, but much of the explosive material was lost.

These two opera buffa murder plots were indicative of the mixture of brutality and incompetence that marked the Hells Angels, or at least their New York wing, but even if the execution was often ludicrous, the repeated attempts underscored the seriousness with which the bikers took the perceived affront of Altamont.

The Rolling Stones had either remained ignorant of the Angels' attempts to harm Jagger, or deliberately chose to ignore them. But in 1983, a Hells Angel turncoat from the Cleveland chapter identified only as "Butch" appeared at a Senate hearing on organized crime and testified to the two attempts on Jagger's life. According to a former member of the Hells Angels, the Stones belatedly agreed to pay the $50,000 to guarantee no further assaults on Jagger. Half the money stayed with the New York branch, and the other half went to the treasury of Barger's Oakland Angels.

Hawkeye met a woman, fell in love, and sold his motorcycle. They had three children, but Hawkeye always missed it: the camaraderie, the raucous good times, the drugs, the feel of a good bike as it revved into a higher gear. He would sit at home silently chewing over the past, craving the feeling that came with being a one-percenter, a Son of Hawaii. He'd occasionally chuckle to himself, and when his kids asked him what he was laughing about, he'd try his best to explain it to them. Lots of bikers were in prison now, he'd think: in prison or in love. Either way, the good times were gone.

Michael Lydon stopped believing in the artists he had once worshipped. The Stones had no answers to his questions. They were just young men like him—more famous, more beloved, but unquestionably no wiser. Lydon had been a true believer in the power of mass gatherings like Altamont, but no longer. He was not interested in being part of the crowd anymore. He would find meaning by tending to his own garden.

To be a journalist, Lydon thought, was to be a bystander to the work of creation. It was time for him to make something of his own. He met a woman named Ellen who played the piano, and on a whim, he picked up an old guitar. Michael Lydon was now a musician. He might never be Mick Jagger—not that he wanted to be!—but he would find a way to express himself through music now.

For a year after Altamont, Greil Marcus couldn't listen to rock 'n' roll. Marcus was an editor at *Rolling Stone*, his career unfolding at the white-hot center of rock journalism, but the experience of being present as the music's grandiose promises of transformation were proven hollow was terribly deflating. How could Marcus summon the enthusiasm for the new Rolling Stones album, or the debut from Led Zeppelin, when the stipulated purpose of the music—creating a kinder, richer, more humane society—seemed to be little more than a fleeting fantasy?

Whenever Marcus approached his turntable, he found himself reaching for one of his country blues records—Son House, Blind Lemon Jefferson, Big Bill Broonzy. The sound was raw, unpolished, as if the reverberations of the guitar were scraping out his insides. The songs were about death and degradation and anguish, inscribed with the daily heartbreak of American racism. They were the only soundtrack Marcus could stand, feeling the sting and shame of having been a cheerleader and house intellectual for a culture that had stood by, helpless, as Meredith Hunter had been killed.

Perhaps in those desolate days Marcus first began to hear the threads that linked the past and the present of American musical culture, that conjoined Robert Johnson to Randy Newman, Elvis Presley to Sly and the Family Stone. The mythology of the music was powerful, capable of speaking to the undercurrents of dread and joy that animated American life.

A few years later, Marcus would publish his book *Mystery Train: Images of America in Rock 'n' Roll Music*, considered by many the finest book ever written on rock, then or now. Altamont was never mentioned in its pages, but reading closely, one could feel the doomed concert's presence everywhere. The book tunneled into popular culture and emerged with a story of evil and chaos and heartache, salvaged on occasion by moments of grace. It was about the traces of—as another, later Marcus book would have it—"the old, weird America" of fire and brimstone, sin and salvation, terror and bliss. Music had mostly lost the vocabulary for such elemental human experiences, and Marcus—who had watched the Hells Angels mercilessly beat his fellow rock fans, able to do nothing but watch—was prodded into rediscovering it.

Marcus was not the only denizen of the counterculture nation who went into self-declared exile after Altamont. His boss Jann Wenner, who lost none of his enthusiasm for the daily hustle of covering rock, nonetheless blamed himself, tongue partially planted in cheek, for the end of the 1960s. Peace and love had been the order of the day, the symbols of youthful enthusiasm for a better world. Woodstock had been three days of peace, love, and harmony, and even the Stones' free show at Hyde Park had sought to lovingly eulogize their lost bandmate Brian Jones. On that gray December day, Wenner thought, the decade had been turned on its head, midwifed by the Hells Angels.

The concert, and its coverage, had also changed Wenner's relationship with the Rolling Stones. He still has in his possession a cable sent to him by Jagger some months after the concert, as *Rolling Stone* was following up on the Altamont story. Jagger had written to turn down an interview request, arguing that the band had been persistently misquoted and misrepresented in its pages. For now, they were not comfortable talking to *Rolling Stone*. Eventually, the Stones and Wenner reached a truce, and the newspaper (soon to become a magazine) continued its mutually profitable love affair with the band. Wenner had gambled and won, preserving a treasured relationship while also demonstrating fearlessness in the pursuit of good journalism. *Rolling Stone* would win a National Magazine Award in 1971 for the Altamont-themed "Let It Bleed" issue. Wenner did not feel vindicated so much as heard over the cacophony of misinformation available elsewhere. The truth, once reported, was self-evident.

Perhaps the spirit of the 1960s might have lived on, Wenner would often wonder, if only *Rolling Stone* had not had the temerity to cover Altamont with such diligence. If the concert had remained a bright, sunny day in the life of the counterculture, maybe the 1960s would never have ended. Even Wenner knew this was an unlikely bet, but it said something about Altamont's place in the mental landscape of the decade that such a proposition could even be made. Altamont appeared like a boulder in a river, damming the flow of water that had heretofore been unimpeded. If only it could have been removed, the stream might have carried on forever.

For all the light and heat generated by the concert, the 1960s did not come to an end at Altamont in any fashion other than the strictly chronological. To declare Altamont the end of the 1960s was tidily convenient when describing a disastrous concert that had taken place in December 1969, but it ignored the uneven rollout of what was conveniently summarized as "the Sixties." Morris Dickstein, in his book *Gates of Eden: American Culture in the Sixties*, defined the spirit of the decade as a new Great Awakening, a quest in search of utopia: "In the 1960s, this kind of spiritual fervor linked the church-sponsored civil rights marchers to the young people who congregated at rock festivals or 'Human Be-Ins,' as well as to the antiwar protesters who recoiled in horror from what America's firepower was doing to Vietnam. This fervor also animated some of those who sought nirvana through sex, drugs, and rock 'n' roll, along with many others who simply looked for some new sense of purpose in their lives. The same utopian quest pushed others to leave a competitive society behind to go 'back to nature' or raise children in communes."

"The Sixties" were a collective search for transcendence, and no single gathering, however misbegotten or tragic, could be enough to derail the train so long in motion. 1960s youth culture remained convinced that it would transform society, and in many ways it was successful: the civil rights movement, the sexual revolution, the rise of feminism, and the gay rights movement. The sixties would go on well into the 1970s, borne aloft on a wave of enthusiasm and idealism and a deep-seated desire for meaningful change.

Altamont, though, had been a version of the story of 1960s politics in miniature, in which the well-meaning, if oft-blinkered, left was met and overmatched by the ferocious counterassault of the revanchist right. Along with the movement's successes would come the humbling realities of a country profoundly unchanged: still fighting a disastrous war in Vietnam, still locked in combat between left and right, increasingly enamored of the Cold War realpolitik and law-and-order rhetoric of President Richard Nixon. The 1960s were not over—not quite yet—but a compelling argument was beginning to form that when it did, the liberal utopians who had set the decade's progress in motion had lost the battle of ideas. Nixon was no Hells Angel, nor were his voters, but they shared a deep-seated antipathy to the New Left and the counterculture, and a desire to strike back in the name of the patriotic center. Altamont was far from the end, but it was a harbinger of further defeats to come. The hippies may have won the social and cultural battles, but the conservatives won all the elections. Republicans would hold the White House for nineteen of the next twenty-three years.

Mick Jagger and his band would expertly pivot from rock to

disco, from politics to debauchery, but his fans were slower to adjust. Music would save no one, but the counterculture was to be admired for its willingness to dream. Altamont could not definitively be said to have ended anything, but it did mark a moment at which the idealistic belief in the political potential of music was shattered, at least for a time.

What Altamont did (mostly) spell an end for was the era of the mass gathering. After Altamont, the dream of the multi-performer outdoor idyll on the model of Woodstock was rendered defunct. The Who's disastrous 1979 concert in Cincinnati, in which eleven fans were crushed to death, further underscored the fear of the hastily planned, ill-conceived rock concert. There would be no new successors to Woodstock for another generation. It would not be until the early 1990s, and the rise of the Lollapalooza festival, that the massive outdoor concert would return to favor. Woodstock, an evergreen brand, would return with twenty-fifth and thirtieth anniversary concerts, each one marred by poor planning and egregious misbehavior on the part of its crowds—mud-flinging and fire-starting. They may have been branded as successors to Woodstock, but something in their elemental DNA summoned the ghost of Altamont, as well.

In all the years that followed, the Rolling Stones almost entirely avoided the subject of Altamont. Keith Richards's much-lauded memoir *Life*, clocking in at almost six hundred pages, devotes all of three pages to the subject.

The band had been dangerously irresponsible to hire the Hells Angels to provide the security for their biggest-ever American show, and doubly so to pay them in alcohol that they would be given to drink at the concert itself. There was a galling lack of prudence in making such arrangements, and in entrusting the well-being of so many fans to such people. The Stones' audience had trusted them to provide a safe and comfortable environment, and were sorely disappointed to find themselves at the mercy of a rogue force.

The Stones' culpability was tempered to some extent by the failings of the Grateful Dead and their advisers, who pushed the Angels on the Stones, failed to anticipate the chaos that would be unleashed, and did not do more to guide a British band that had not visited the United States in three years through the particulars of planning a Bay Area concert.

More troubling, none of the band's members ever took any initiative to acknowledge Meredith Hunter's death, or to express their dismay over the events at Altamont. While nothing that Mick Jagger or Keith Richards might have said would have been enough to bring him back, Meredith Hunter's family sat alone in their too-quiet house in the days and weeks and months after his death, and never heard from any representative of the Stones other than Chip Monck, who had merely designed the stage for the show.

What would have prevented the Rolling Stones from expressing their condolences to Hunter's family, or apologizing for their role in his death? If the issue were merely financial, the Stones could easily have afforded any additional costs they might have incurred as a result. They wound up paying Hunter's family $10,000, hardly worthy of mention given the seven-figure haul for their 1969 U.S. tour—or the $50,000 they ultimately paid to Hunter's killers.

Moreover, why hadn't the Stones ever apologized to all the fans at Altamont? Meredith Hunter suffered the worst fate, but the security staff hired by the Rolling Stones beat or abused dozens of other fans. Where was the Stones' sense of shame over the horrific treatment of their own crowd? The Dead had abandoned the ship, and the Stones were to be credited for facing the chaos head-on and attempting to salvage the show. But none of the Stones ever acknowledged that they had committed a ghastly error in failing to adequately plan for Altamont, and that their failures had real consequences for everyone from the dozens of bloodied and beaten fans to Michael Lydon to Denise Jewkes to Meredith Hunter.

Many of Patti Bredehoft's friends—the ones who had hung out with her and Meredith in the park outside Berkeley High—wound up strung out on heroin, wasting away. Ronnie Brown, who had accompanied Patti and Meredith to Altamont, died of an overdose. Patti met another man and gave birth to his child. He was never violent, but he was domineering and jealous. He forced Bredehoft to tear up all her photographs from high school, including the snapshots she had of herself and Hunter. He, too, would become addicted to heroin.

As a child, Patti wanted to be a teacher, but now she could not motivate herself to attend college. She had believed she had the ability to accomplish bigger things, notable things, but she now lacked the self-confidence to demand the world's attention. She would find a comfortable job and stay there, planted in place, for as long as she could. Bredehoft wound up working for a number of small companies before taking a job at a Bay Area naval base. She stayed for sixteen years, until the base closed down, and then spent another four years working for Bank of America. Her mother was elderly by then, and she made caring for her a full-time job. Her life was scarred by what had happened before she had ever had a chance to become herself. Who might she have been if she had not had to witness her boyfriend's brutal death?

In the mid-1970s, Porter Bibb developed a film project about the glamorous Bouvier family, and hired the only directors he believed capable of doing justice to the material: Albert and David Maysles. They were to be entrusted with the job of telling the story of the childhood of Jackie Kennedy Onassis and her sister Lee Radziwill, beginning with a brief shoot with two obscure Bouvier relatives living in squalor in the Hamptons. The two women were fascinating, and a morning shoot stretched to fill one full day, and then another. After three days, with an increasingly panicked Radziwill demanding action, Bibb ordered Albert and David to continue with the shooting schedule, or he would be left with no choice but to fire them. Albert and David went back to Grey Gardens.

The private travails of two distant relatives of Jackie Kennedy could hardly be more different from a rock 'n' roll documentary like *Gimme Shelter*, and yet there was a notable overlap between these two projects. In both, the filmmakers were interested in people irreversibly imprinted by the proximity of celebrity. Big Edie and Little Edie had survived their brush with fame, unlike Meredith Hunter, but the Maysleses' two films betrayed a persistent interest in the toxic underbelly of celebrity, and the psychic impact of trauma. If *Gimme Shelter* had ultimately chased an emotional response from the Rolling Stones that had never come, 1975's *Grey Gardens* had been a patient study of two women whose entire lives were silent demonstrations of the corrosive effects of lives left unlived. The Beales were as unlike Meredith Hunter and his family as just about anyone in the United States, and yet, when studied in the right light, their story was like the untold half of *Gimme Shelter*, about people left behind by time and circumstance to ache with old wounds that had never healed.

In 2009, the Alameda County Sheriff's Office dropped a bombshell when it announced that its cold-case unit would reopen the Meredith Hunter case. The new investigation's remit was limited. It wanted to determine whether there had indeed been, as Alan Passaro's defense attorney George Walker had repeatedly argued during the original trial, a second stabber responsible for Hunter's death. The investigation, led by Sergeant Scott Dudek, looked through the old case files and studied the film footage shot by the Maysleses' crews. Passaro had already been tried and acquitted, so double jeopardy made the question of his culpability irrelevant to the investigation, but Dudek came to believe, as he told a reporter, that Hunter was "a contributing factor to his own death." Furthermore, Dudek believed that Hunter might have actually fired his gun, even though tests done at the time of Passaro's trial indicated that he had not. The investigation ultimately determined that only Passaro had stabbed Hunter.

Altha Anderson spent weeks in Herrick Hospital in Berkeley after learning of her son Meredith's death. She underwent repeated rounds of electroshock therapy and came home, ashen and partially absent, as if a part of her had been excised. There were still schizophrenic episodes, but they were not quite as volatile as they had been. But if Anderson was more lucid now, that only opened her once more to the pain of her son's sudden death. Why had Meredith been taken from her? Who could assuage her loss? She was drawn back to the Holiness congregation, which gave her the direction she needed. Religion offered answers where nothing else could, a sense of a world in balance, of wrongs being righted and the divine order being restored, in the next world, if not this one.

Anderson appeared at a meeting of the Alameda County Planning Association in early January. She was present to request that the Altamont Speedway, site of her son's death, become a public park. "My son's blood is on the land," she said, "and I would like to see the land serve a useful purpose for the youth of southern Alameda

County. I cannot bring my son back, but by your action you may prevent any more wrongful deaths at Altamont." The speedway, ignoring her wishes, remained open for business, but further musical events were barred from Altamont. There could be no more than three thousand people present at any future gathering. But there would be no tribute to Meredith Hunter's life at the speedway, no marker of his death. No one would come to Altamont to reflect and remember.

What did it mean to be a family in the aftermath of so harrowing a loss? Meredith's brother Donald would sit out in the front yard, day after day, staring out into nothingness. It was as if he were waiting for Meredith to return, loping along the street, adjusting his hat to the proper tilt, crammed full of stories of his time away. After all, he had been gone so many times before. Why couldn't this be another extended absence? Donald, plagued by his own demons, never articulated these thoughts, but his sister Dixie felt his anguish as he sat there, hoping for a ghost to make him whole again, make his family whole again.

Schizophrenia was the family's scourge, striking where least expected, decimating one generation after another. Both Donald and Gwen would develop schizophrenia like their mother had. Whether the tragedy of Meredith's loss had affected their brain chemistry was debatable, but Dixie had the sense that her brother's death was an earthquake, and the ripples of its aftershocks had taken down the remainder of her siblings, too.

Dixie kept her head down. She went back to school, studied fashion arts, got her teaching certificate. She had so much experience raising children, she figured she might as well make a career of it. Dixie studied the Montessori method, which sought to let students explore and learn in their own time, on their own terms. She treated the children she cared for like her own, like the siblings she had raised. She helped the kids who needed help, and bathed them all in love every hour of the day they spent with her. Dixie wanted all the children to know that they were provided for, that someone was there to dry their tears, that someone would listen to them. Who knew what they might encounter when they walked out her door?

She had not been much interested in the Passaro trial. The case would bring her no closure, and it certainly would not bring Meredith back. The verdict, too, was no surprise. Dixie firmly believed that a white man would never be convicted of killing a black man in America, and the trial did nothing to disabuse her of the notion.

It had been her mother who had been convinced by an opportunistic lawyer to sue the Rolling Stones. Anderson, hardly in a position to oversee any lawsuit herself, was won over with vague promises of riches from a fabulously wealthy British rock band. The Rolling Stones' lawyers attempted to have the wrongful-death suit tossed out on a technicality, claiming that papers had never been served to Mick Jagger. The lawyer negotiated with the Stones on Anderson's behalf, and eventually made off with a good chunk of the $10,000 she had wound up receiving.

Dixie was more struck by the response, or lack thereof, of the Rolling Stones and the other parties involved with the concert. No one had come to apologize, no one had offered their condolences, no one had even acknowledged the extent of her family's loss. What could $10,000 do when Meredith was, now and forever, absent? Dixie would never get to banter with him again. Life would go on, and he would be absent. There would be an empty space in the family where Meredith had once gone, and where Dixie could imagine, in her more desperate or wistful moments, what might have been. What would it have cost Mick Jagger or Keith Richards to merely acknowledge her grief? She never watched *Gimme Shelter*, either. She did not want to see her brother in his terrified last moments, did not want to remember him that way.

Dixie's mother was sick, the same terrible disease plagued her siblings, and Meredith was gone. Her husband was dead, and Dixie was raising her children alone. Four years after the loss of her husband and brother, she met DeWitt Ward. It was not love, not like it had been with Jesse, but he had no children of his own, and he would give her children what they needed. DeWitt was stoic, and often hard to read, but Taammi and her siblings got along well with him.

Dixie and DeWitt got married, and they bought a house on a quiet street in Oakland. This was where Tim and Tanya and Taammi grew up, where they became a family. Dixie was there during the days, too, caring for her kids. It didn't matter who they belonged to, they were all her kids. Dixie kept her head down because there were no opportunities to lift it up. Every time she thought she might, another catastrophe or crisis intervened.

There was no one for Dixie to talk to about all she had endured. Her siblings were stricken now, too, her mother was absent, and her children had to be protected from knowing how unbearably cruel the world could be. It was too painful to remember, too painful to be reminded of those moments listening to the radio, hearing the reports of the Hells Angels subduing a maniac with a gun, and not realizing yet that that "maniac" was her Meredith. It was too painful to think about that solitary trip to pick up Meredith's car, too painful to think about all the things he would miss. He would never see Tim and Tanya and Taammi grow up, would never have children of his own. He would never be able to console Dixie again, never be able to share in her joy. He would be forever absent.

Dixie didn't talk about Meredith with her family because she didn't want to remember the nightmare of his death. She didn't visit his grave, a short drive away. She wanted to remember him quietly, with joy. She would not give herself over to her feelings because then she would have to acknowledge the enormity of what she had lost: her brother, her husband, her mother and siblings mostly lost to illness. It was too much for a single human being to bear. But each year, when early December came around, and she spotted the Christmas trees beginning to sprout in living room windows around the neighborhood, she remembered the tree that had been in her mother's living room that day. Christmas was a time of painful remembrance, bringing up all the memories she tried so hard to stifle. The tree was supposed to represent life, and it hadn't. The tree was supposed to spread and grow, and it hadn't. Neither Dixie nor her mother ever had a Christmas tree in their homes again.

Dixie would tell her son Tim, time and again, to come home before dark, to avoid standing on corners. She could walk to her corner and see young white men and women standing outside bars and restaurants, smoking and talking and laughing. They could do it, but her children could not. It simply wasn't safe. If a group of white boys were standing on a corner, they were enjoying themselves. If a group of black boys did it, they were a gang, and the police would be summoned. And violence could strike without warning, from any direction, at any time.

In the mid-2000s, a filmmaker named Sam Green was surprised at how little he knew about Meredith Hunter. He had made a film on the violent leftist radical group the Weathermen and had come across Hunter's name a number of times when researching the era. He was taken aback by how little information was available about Hunter's life, and decided to pay a pilgrimage to Hunter's gravesite. The grave was unmarked, and a cemetery employee named Mr. Wilks offered to escort him there.

Green was charmed by Mr. Wilks, and by his musings on the meanings ascribed to cemeteries, and kept thinking about Meredith

Meredith Hunter's headstone. (Courtesy of Saul Austerlitz)

Hunter, forever young, lying for eternity in an anonymous grave. He decided to come back to Skyview and re-create his experience of walking and talking with Wilks, and turned it into a film he named after the location of Hunter's grave: *Lot 63, Grave C.*

The resulting effort was not really about Meredith Hunter so much as it was about all that Hunter symbolized about the 1960s, and about the passage of time, but the film's numerous admirers were troubled by that unmarked cemetery plot. Without being asked to, strangers began sending donations, in small amounts and large, in the hopes that a gravestone could be placed to remember the life of Meredith Hunter. Today, Meredith Hunter's grave is no longer unmarked. Visitors to Skyview can make their own way over to Lot 63, Grave C, and find his final resting place, which reads: IN LOVING MEMORY—MEREDITH CURLY HUNTER JR.—OCT. 24, 1951—DEC. 6, 1969.

. . .

Taammi Parker had never seen her uncle's gravestone. She had been two years old when he was killed, and while her mother Dixie Ward occasionally spoke of her brilliant, funny, protective younger brother, she knew there were certain questions she was not supposed to ask. Her uncle's death hurt Dixie so much. From as early as she could remember, Taammi knew that, more than anything, she wanted to protect her mother from further pain. That was, she believed, what she had been put on this earth to do.

It was a mostly happy childhood, she thought. She had vague memories of a less happy time, a period of emotional collapse, but most of her youth was shaped by her mother's determination to give the children what she had never had: stability, comfort, a rooted love. The children had come first, always. One summer, Dixie had taken Taammi and her siblings on a tour of nearby amusement parks, one after the other. The kids had shrieked on the roller coasters and gorged on the snacks and been transported to a rung just below heaven, and Taammi only realized after the trip was over that her mother absolutely hated amusement parks.

Dixie took the children everywhere. Anything she had not been able to do as a child, she strove to do for them, from swim lessons to trips to Carmel. But there were other times, too: times when the phone would ring, and their mother would tell them, "I have to go." They would never have any idea where she'd gone, or what she had to do, but Taammi suspected it had something to do with how, every time anyone mentioned their uncles Meredith or Donald, a wave of pain would cascade across Dixie's face. Even on their roller coaster tour, there were places Dixie would not stop, fearful of what might happen to the children at the wrong gas station, the wrong restaurant. Taammi remembered having to pee in a jar on occasion.

She knew that her uncle had been killed, but the details eluded her. Whenever the Hells Angels appeared in the news or on TV, she could feel her mother stiffen. Neither she nor her siblings ever asked her about it, because they could see how much it hurt, and they didn't want to make her relive the pain on their account. Their mother's philosophy seemed to be to take the things that weighed you down—grief, anger, the horrors of the past—and prick it silently with little holes until you felt slightly more buoyant. There were hints, though, of the absent members of the family, and the pain Dixie silently carried. When Taammi's aunt Gwen, stricken with schizophrenia, died in 2008, the same year that her grandmother Altha died at the age of eighty-three, her mother said, "She never had a chance either." The family's history was a palimpsest, with traces of the past now rendered illegible, but still visible under the surface.

Parker was in her early thirties, and already a successful internet entrepreneur, before she discovered the truth about her uncle's death. Her mother's silence on the subject had left her unaware of how he had died or the larger significance of his death.

She was watching a VH1 program called *The 100 Most Shocking Moments in Rock & Roll* when she heard the name "Meredith Hunter" mentioned, and saw the now ubiquitous footage from *Gimme Shelter*. Parker was flabbergasted. Shock forced a laugh out of her chest, then she went quiet. She turned off the television, turned off the lights. She lay down and cried, letting the tears roll down her face. She didn't bother to wipe them away. There was no point.

Knowing what had happened to her uncle rendered her momentarily catatonic. Her brain still worked, but her limbs had stopped functioning. It was too much for her to take in, to know that her uncle's last moments had been spent fleeing from a man who was intent on piercing his body, over and over, until he could not lift himself up anymore. She was sad and grateful for her mother's forbearance, her stubborn resolve to feign normalcy for her children, even as the story of her brother's life and death likely played in an endless closed loop in the theater of her mind. The strength to be that determined was beyond her imagining. Only then did Parker begin to understand the enormity of what her family had endured, and the weight of what her mother had silently carried for her entire life.

Dixie had spent thirty-seven years caring for other people's children. She had been a fixture in the community for so long that she looked after some of her children's children. She helped the children who needed help, and ministered to them all. It was essential that no one be forgotten, no one slip through the cracks. But now she was tired. She did not have the energy anymore. DeWitt was sick, and after caring for him on her own for years, Dixie had to move him to a facility. After seventy years of life, Dixie had some time to think, and the traumas of the past were catching up with her. She felt the ghosts creeping at the door once more.

Dixie found it too painful to honor Meredith's memory, but Taammi crafted her own ritual for the uncle she had never really known. Every night at 8:15, a reminder on her phone beeped. It was time for her to honor her ancestors. She would mention them each by name, her uncle Meredith's prominent among them, and let their presences slip past like images on a screen. In this way, she paid tribute to the lost members of her family, and to her mother, who bore it alone for so long.

Now, any mention of Altamont took Taammi's breath away. Each allusion was like a renewed death, a reminder that, in all the hoopla about the death of the 1960s, the teenage boy who had actually died that day had been forgotten. Her family had been forgotten, too, a footnote to a footnote. It was terribly painful that something so enormous in their lives could feel so unacknowledged.

Parker belatedly came to understand that her mother had loved her own siblings as if she had been a mother to them, too, and that their absence was the central fact of her life. The family's stories were silenced, because the women who remembered them found them too painful to recount. The past was a vast unknown country. When there was so much to bear, all you could do was push forward. And later, when it might have been a better time to reflect, or mourn, the protective gambit had become a habit, and you kept doing it, even though it did not necessarily serve your interests anymore.

The state of race relations in the United States had improved on its façade since 1969, but Parker worried that there had not been enough changes made to the foundation to effect any serious transformation. She took to volunteering with organizations seeking to improve the lot of African-American men and women. The deaths of young black men, particularly those in encounters with armed representatives of state force, affected her deeply. When a New York police officer choked Eric Garner to death in 2014, she called her mother to vent her grief and anger, and her fear that nothing would ever change. "No," Dixie told her. "This time everybody can see." But everyone had seen Meredith Hunter's encounter with the Hells Angels, too, and had still condemned the victim for his own death.

Taammi Parker believed the reason she had been born was to be solid for her mother. She was determined to remember what her mother simply could not, to contemplate her mother's difficult life, and the unbearable times she had endured, and in so remembering, to honor what her family had experienced. This was the story of black people in the United States, she thought, but her family had been served an even more distilled potion of bitterness to choke down. Meredith Hunter was not just a name, not just a dead man at a rock concert. He was her uncle, and he was loved. Each night at 8:15, she remembered.

Acknowledgments

Writing about this disastrous day in the life of the 1960s was frequently a somber exercise, but conducting more than eighty original interviews also offered me the opportunity to learn about the lives of a wildly disparate array of people who happened to be at Altamont, or who know people who were. The most interesting stories were often the ones that had nothing at all to do with my subject. One day, someone should write an entire book about Adele Kubein, who dropped out of grade school, hung out with the Hells Angels as a teenager, lost a daughter in Iraq, became a prominent antiwar protester, went back to school, got her bachelor's, master's, and a doctorate, and became an esteemed professor while fighting cancer.

My deepest thanks to all the people who answered my questions, and to those who fielded my innumerable follow-up queries. I would particularly like to offer my thanks to John Burks, George Christie, Evelyn and George Walker, Adele Kubein, Randy McBee, Jay Siegel, Denise Kaufman, Sam Cutler, Ronnie Schneider, Louie Kalaveras, Dorothy Kalaveras, Judy Maysles, Johanna Demetrakas, Peter Smokler, Nelson Stoll, Stephen Lighthill, Chip Monck, Joanne

Burke, Michael Lang, Todd Gitlin, Langdon Winner, the late John Morthland, Sol Stern, Joan Churchill, Mirra Bank, Sergeant Ken Gemmell of the Alameda County Sheriff's Office, Insha Rahman, and Greil Marcus. Any mistakes that remain are, of course, my own.

Dixie Ward and Taammi Parker graciously invited me into their homes and agreed to speak to me about some of the hardest and saddest moments in their lives, and their candor and emotional forthrightness were absolutely essential to my understanding of what this story was about. David James Smith of the *Times* of London and Kevin Fagan of the *San Francisco Chronicle* were kind enough to share some of their research materials, and their insights into the story of Altamont, with me.

Much of this book was written in the Kensington branch of the Brooklyn Public Library. My thanks to all the staff and patrons there.

My deepest thanks go to the friends and family who supported me through this project: Carla Silber, Dan Silber, Abby Silber, Jason Seiden, Zack Seiden, Josh Olken, EB Kelly, Mark Fenig, Dan Smokler, Erin Leib Smokler, Eli Segal, Shana Segal, Choomy Castle, Ari Holtzblatt, Marina Hirsch, Olia Toporovsky, Jeremy Blank, Menachem Tannen, Jeff Abergel and Brooklyn ReSisters, Jennifer Keishin Armstrong, Sarah Rose, Aaron Zamost, Zev Wexler, Adi Weinberg, Jesse Kellerman, Ari Vanderwalde, Joanne Gentile, Helane Naiman, and Daniel Mizrahi. Reuben Silberman and Ali Austerlitz read draft versions of some of the chapters of this book, and their insights were invaluable. My agent, Laurie Abkemeier, believed in this project from the very outset, and her guidance and perceptiveness made all the difference. I would also like to thank the remarkable team at Thomas Dunne, including Stephen Power, Samantha Zukergood, Bill Warhop, Gabrielle Gantz, Jason Prince, and Ryan Jenkins.

My parents bought me a Discman for my bar mitzvah, perhaps inadvertently kicking off a life obsessed with music. They have always been my fiercest supporters, and I owe them everything. My children, Nate and Gabriel, are not yet old enough to read this book (nor, regrettably, is it about fire trucks or dinosaurs), but this is for them anyway. And none of this could ever have happened without the love and support of my wife, Becky. She is my most trusted editor, my voice of reason, my compatriot, my love.

Index